This book is a **biovel**, a novelized biographic story which narrates the author's visit to Colorado USA in the nineteen eighties and his investigations of the forces that shape, move and control American society.

Arriving from India where he had spent eight years, the writer uncovered little known or hidden facets of America's history and political system. He evokes the Eastern influences that have played a role, from the nation's genesis within the British Empire to the vedantic inspiration of the New England Transcendentalists, from the theosophical and occultist connections of free masonic sects to the 'Indic' references in the writings of Herman Melville and other novelists.

Those connections help explain the fascination of some leading scientists, statesmen and military commanders for Hindu and Buddhism mysticism and metaphysics, often related to the spreading use of psychotropic drugs and the rise of the New Age Movement, but the Conservative Puritanical reaction and the ruthless power of a mighty Deep State bore the seeds of events which shook America in this century, from the 911 terrorist attacks to the ensuing invasions and continuing wars in the Middle East and the election of Donald Trump.

The book reveals that America's long standing high level interest in esotericism came of age when some of its ruling elites came into contact with what they could only regard as the Supernatural. That is perhaps the greatest secret that has been kept until today and it may account in part for the current state of the USA.

By the same author
From India to Infinity
Memories of a Hundred and One Moons: An Indian Odyssey

A Shining City on a Hill

N.O.S. (Novus Ordo Seclorum)

Côme Carpentier de Gourdon

Letter to Steven Greer MD
International Director, The Disclosure Project, April 21st, 1994

From what I know your assessment is correct about the group which is controlling the issue we discussed. I suspect they have very good reasons not to inform the public and therefore I am highly sceptical about your chances of success.

Hans Adam II
Sovereign Prince of
the State of Liechtenstein

HAR-ANAND
PUBLICATIONS PVT LTD

To
Whitley Strieber, Richard Dolan Michael Salla, Linda Moulton Howe, Paola Harris, Rebecca Hardcastle, Steven Greer, Stephen Bassett, Neil Gould, Scott Jones, Stan Ho, Denis Roger Denocla and other fellow travellers on the quest for the Great Beyond.

Copyright © Côme Carpentier de Gourdon, 2018

All rights reserved. No part of this publication may be reproduced in any form without the prior written permission of the author and the Publisher.

Views and facts presented in the book are those of the author and the publishers are not responsible for the same.

Published by Ashok Gosain and Ashish Gosain for:
HAR-ANAND PUBLICATIONS PVT LTD
E-49/3, Okhla Industrial Area, Phase-II, New Delhi-110020
Tel: 41603490
E-mail: info@haranandbooks.com/haranand@rediffmail.com
Shop online at: www.haranandbooks.com
Like us on www.facebook.com/haranandbooks

Printed in India at Vinayak Offset.

Preface

I have meant to write this book for a long time but I knew it would not be easy to do justice to events and meetings that took place during more than seven years. I decided to start by recalling the first months of my life in the United States back in 1983 when I moved to Aspen from India and began a personal investigation into certain aspects of contemporary American and global reality which I wanted to understand, if possible by uncovering some of the less known factors at work behind them. During the last three decades I have had the occasion to think a lot about the things I saw and heard, in the light of what I have learnt since then. I was able as a result to put many more pieces of the puzzle together. One often does not comprehend what he perceives on the spot but only gradually in later years as he processes, compares and confirms the information in the context of other experiences and discoveries.

Readers will see why, although I call many of the people I met and sometimes got to know well by their real names, I have preserved the anonymity of others whose statements may be too controversial or compromising, especially as I have to rely on memory to give the gist of what they told me and am compelled by the format and style of the book to modify, summarize or expand on their words. I am not in a position to ask them to verify and approve of my account of their ideas and opinions, either because they are no more or because I have lost touch with and track of them. What they said was often confidential and not for publication. The only proper way to quote them was therefore to change their names. Jack the East Coast billionaire, Joy and

Elizabeth the 'New Agers', Lowell the Texan oilman, Ingrid J. the healer, Robert Desbois the French scientist, Laura Glenn Hollyfield the journalist, Bruce Adams the frontier researcher, Mary Jean Dartmoor, Jerry the Army veteran, Generals O'Kennan and Caswell are all pseudonyms whereas the other figures in the book appear under their real identities which are often easy to verify through a google search.

This can be called a "factional" writing, a literary text in which real characters and events are described in a way which presents, highlights and enlivens them. I have created a neologism for this book which I call a *biovel*, meaning a biographical story that reads as a novel. It is often easier to report matters that stretch credibility and lie far out from daily experiences and conventional accounts of reality in such a format, instead of laying out a cumbersome array of references and proofs that rob the narration of its attractiveness without necessarily convincing a reader bridled by common beliefs and prejudices. Proofs are indeed available aplenty in innumerable technical, historical and journalistic articles and books, to many of which I refer incidentally in these pages but I feel that the style and format I have elected are more accessible and entertaining for the general public.

The United States has been for most of the last hundred years the dominant power in the world and it naturally elicits universal attention since the country's circumstances and deeds affect, in one way or another all other nations, whether politically, economically, socially or culturally. Even though decline has clearly set in, it will probably take many more years to result in the lasting reduction of the country to second class status. The Roman and other empires disintegrated over long periods of time, sometimes for centuries and the American Empire is perhaps the first to be truly global, even larger than its British predecessor which never had overwhelming military superiority on other large

European states and relied mainly on a large fleet and colonial resources to maintain its preponderance over its few rivals. Until recently the USA scientifically, technically, militarily and financially dwarfed all would-be challengers and it is only since the beginning of this century that newly rich China and a potentially united but fissiparous and strategically dependent Europe can dream of matching America's strength.

The circumstances and ingredients that combined to make the USA what is has become, for better and for worse, are innumerable but some are far more important than others and yet they are either little known, utterly disregarded or held to lie beyond the pale of admissible discourse, because they are too strange to be believable or too inconvenient for the powers-that-be to be discussed. With the advent of the Internet and the infinite proliferation of social media, many topics which were traditionally restricted to confidential discussions are now spilling into the public domains through thousands if not millions of websites, blogs and news channels, often called 'fake', rightly or wrongly by the mainstream opinion-makers.

This book reflects some of the things I heard and read from credible, high level sources at a time when those media did not exist, at least in an electronic, easily available format. The information was of course much less abundant then for most of us but it was also more likely to be authentic and reliable. Quantity does not always destroy quality but it makes it harder to find and identify. As such this work may be seen as a modest but collective contribution to the history of the world's present superpower in some of its bizarre and dark chapters and especially with regard to what is probably the greatest and most significant issue in the history of our species. Indeed the momentous importance of the subject matter is the reason why it has remained a secret to the overwhelming majority of people, even to those in very high positions. Whether this has been a factor behind the worrying or even frightening state of affairs in that country and in the world at large is a matter of discussion and readers will have to form their own opinion but it surely influences emerging developments and forebodes the shape of things to come.

I would like to conclude this foreword with thoughts for those whose lives ended tragically, long after the period to which the following events belong. Nancy Pfister and her friend, the famous Gonzo journalist met violent ends. Jerry was killed in a shootout involving members of the organization he said he had joined when I met him. John Denver's plane crashed at sea in 1997 off the coast of Southern California and a few of the other famous or less famous people depicted here have left this world as well in diverse circumstances. I wish to pay homage to or at least pray for them in gratefulness to those who extended to me their friendship and in recognition of the trust others showed by opening up about grave and disturbing subjects during casual or deep conversations.

CÔME CARPENTIER DE GOURDON

Contents

I	Rocky Mountain High	11
II	Design for the Future	21
III	New Age, Dark Present and Ancient Aeons	43
IV	Eastward in the West	57
V	Entering the Maze	71
VI	A Supper at Higman's	87
VII	Over the Mountains	105
VIII	Pieces of a Puzzle	123
IX	Some Veils are Lifted	144
X	From Mysteries into the Mystic	161
XI	Death Has Raised Itself a Throne	181
XII	A House Divided	203
XIII	The Belly of the Beast	217
XIV	Secrets from Outer Space	234
XV	A Vault Opens	253
	Epilogue	270

I
Rocky Mountain High

He climbed cathedral mountains, he saw silver clouds below
He saw everything as far as you can see
And they say that he got crazy once and he tried to touch the sun
And the Colorado Rocky Mountain high
I've seen it raining fire in the sky.

John Denver, Rocky Mountain High

SHANGRI LA IN THE AMERICAN WEST

The small twin-engine purring liner of Aspen Airways hugged for almost an hour the snow peaked, conifer draped sierra spread beneath my eyes. The sky shone around us like a slab of cobalt. Gradually, after heaving itself above one last range the plane began to descend, touched ground in the high valley and motored down the single runway. The passengers alighted on the sunny tarmac. Waving at me in front of the small brand new airfield building was Nancy, wearing a broad rancher hat, large sunshades, a buckskin jacket, levis and cowboy boots. She was picture perfect for the location, a movie cowgirl in the heart of the American West. I congratulated her on the attire and she smiled with a hint of the faint sadness that never seemed to leave her.

Nancy was lean, honey-blond with blue grey searching and smiling eyes, an infectiously friendly manner and the uninhibited sensuality of a woman sure of her status if not of herself. We had known each other in India where she had gone to promote permaculture, play elephant polo and hobnob with fellow millionaires and Nepalese royals. Our fling was casual like all she did but before leaving Delhi she had invited me to visit her in her twin homes, in Colorado and in the Hawaiian island of Molokai. And that is how I had come all the way to Aspen.

Although Nancy was in her early thirties, she had a glamorous romantic past and had almost married Michael Douglas a few years before. Many leading politicians and Hollywood stars skied every winter at her family-owned resort. She was spoiled, willful and rather unpredictable, which heightened the spell she cast on men. Her sharp intuition in the course of a few conversations had rapidly told her what I would do in the United States although she could not know everything.

"Aspen is the playground of America's rich" she told me "but it's also one of the key chakras of the country's psychic grid." Her choice of words evinced that she was a child of the New Age "Dharma bum" generation.

She drove us in a rustic four-wheel drive up the slope of Buttermilk mountain which was part of her parents' T-Lazy 7 ranch. We parked in front of a simple wooden house that would be home for a few days. Vast vistas of snow dappled crests and dark-green fir forests basked in the late June Sun. Further below in the Maroon Creek valley the pale green, heart shaped leaves of the aspens that gave the town its name shivered rhythmically in the morning breeze.

Before I walked into the pine-scented, tawny wood-paneled living room I noticed the little ruby-red Pontiac parked on the side. "The housekeeper is cleaning up" Nancy remarked. Coming from India as I did, the notion of a maid driving what might qualify for many as a sports car, albeit an inexpensive one, triggered a brief philosophical distraction interrupted by my hostess: "Get comfortable and relax" she said "you must be tired after the long flight. I have invited a few friends for dinner and my parents will come too although they don't fit in that well with my crowd. Tomorrow the conference begins but today if you feel upto it you can go down to the town and take a stroll. See ya...." A kiss and she was gone, leaving me to contemplate the majestic scenery.

I was tired, from sleeplessness and perhaps also by the altitude almost two miles above sea level but my head was throbbing and I felt a bit dazed. I made some coffee and sat outside on the porch on one of the sturdy wooden chairs to acclimatize myself and take in the rugged landscape.

This was the summer of 1983 and I had come to the United States to try to pierce some of the heaviest secrets of that most powerful nation. The words of one of Balzac's youthful characters: "*A nous deux Paris*" was on my lips but the French capital was replaced in the challenge by the country where I just arrived. I would need a lot of help from many people on this task but I had time and some leads.

Ronald Reagan had come to power three years earlier and his administration was committed to reversing the decline that had set in since the Vietnam War and to expand the country's global empire while rebuilding the economy on the basis of liberal capitalism and the most modern technologies. Allied with Thatcher's Britain, the US Government wanted to bring the world under its hegemony and was on its way to achieving that goal. The USSR, the old adversary was in full decline and China had become in effect an ally, depending on American investments and technology transfers for its economic development. Japan, South Korea, The Arab world, Africa, Latin America and South East Asia, with few minor exceptions were in thrall to Washington and the Western Europeans were loyal, if occasionally touchy confederates. Although it had only a handful of formal colonies the American empire was even bigger and vastly richer than its British predecessor had been in its heyday a century earlier. The White House made no mystery of its intentions to bring the Soviet Union to heel while forcing into submission the remaining reluctant outliers such as India and rebels like Iran. After the fumbling Ford and Carter years, the USA was on the offensive all over the globe economically, culturally and militarily. I had come to find out what that might mean for the future and if there was more to the American powerhouse than met most eyes. There were many stories to be unfolded.

By then, with the suddenness of alpine weather, the Sun had been snuffed out behind a flock of heavy leaden clouds and a drizzle quickly turned to snow. Soon, a thin blanket of fluffy flakes carpeted the slopes and shone in the glow of the momentarily eclipsed summer.

I felt I had been given a glimpse of the fleeting moods of the country and its people. Impressions and reactions were instantaneous and short-lived. Minds and bodies ran at the speed of the ever more present electronic media. Feelings were as unpredictably fickle as the warm light and snowfall of that late Colorado spring. The motto was not the *Carpe Diem* of the ancient Romans but rather "enjoy the minute" for it was always almost over.

I took advantage of the clear afternoon to go to town, still glazed in a thin gauze of flakes. Aspen was, as I more or less expected, a quaint Victorian village, partly authentic but spruced up and partly recreated as a ginger bread fantasy for multimillionaires. One could have expected to meet Ansel and Gretel in cowboy hats and the parade of sunshaded fashionistas matched the storefronts sporting the luxury brands of Fifth Avenue and Rodeo Drive. Silver mining had built the original settlement and brought wealth until a crash emptied it but soon after the second World War the long deserted village had been resurrected by a few ambitious tycoons who wanted to make it a Mecca of the arts, culture and of the high life. The air itself, spare in oxygen, crisp and scented by the nearby forests and meadows seemed perfumed by jet set glamour. I began to sing low the tune of John Denver's melodious *Rocky Mountain High*. Women I crossed in the streets were usually beautiful, in the statuesque and sporting style of the American elite and had an easy smile. It was impossible not to love the place, despite the visible veneer of good natured make-believe, the fantasy that great wealth creates around itself.

Dinner at Nancy's

I returned to the house on Buttermilk in time for the typically early dinner. The housekeeper had almost finished cooking. Soon Nancy sashayed in with the beaming appearance which is almost a rule among privileged Americans. The guests began to arrive, first Art and Betty, Nancy's parents. Her father was tall, laconic and commanding as could be expected of a descendent of Swiss gold prospectors who had made a fortune in ranching before becoming one of the kings of winter sports; Betty was petite but tough despite her graceful physique. She had become a legend during the second World War as a rescue pilot in a helicopter called Tinker Bell. They were both members of the generation that had brought America to the top of the world pyramid and visibly knew it. I felt right away the silent discomfort that flowed as an invisible rivulet between their daughter and them.

The guests picked by Nancy were of a different breed; Tom Crum was a seasoned environmentalist and mountaineer who had set up with John Denver the Windstar Foundation on a thousand acres of virgin land in nearby Snowmass; two others were officers of the Aspen Institute, Jerome Canty, a lanky angular man was a veteran teacher of macrobiotics, the Sino-japanese school of health and nutrition brought to America by Michio Kushi in Boston and he had come with a quiet, handsome youth called Curt; there were two single women who owned houses nearby and a forty year old self-described importer of health foods from Japan.

Both the conservative and the New Age Beat Generation facets of American society were represented at the table where the food however was a creative interpretation of Japanese and Mediterranean cuisine, with the predictable tofu, hummus, sushi, seaweed, stir fried vegetables, whole wheat bread, Peruvian quinoa, buckwheat and brown rice. I felt that Art Pfister missed a steak or a hamburger but he was clearly used to his daughter's culinary choices and did not complain. His wife braved her daughter's sarcastic disapproval to smoke a cigarette with her pre-dinner Scotch.

The conversation soon came to the Aspen Institute and to its genesis in the aftermath of the second World War when German American millionaire Walter Paepcke and his wife Elizabeth discovered the abandoned mining town of Aspen and decided to rebuild it as haven for the financial and political elite.

"He decided that he owed it to his ancestors to revive the prestige German civilization had before the Nazi era in the minds of his fellow Americans" one of the men from the Aspen Institute told us. "He picked Goethe as the symbol of what was best in that then most unpopular nation and held a first conference about the great man here for his birth bicentennial in 1949. You must realize that at least one in every two Americans has German blood so Paepcke felt it was important to restore the old connections with Europe's defeated but formerly most powerful country."

"Then came Robert O Anderson, the chairman of Atlantic Richfield, another millionaire educated at Chicago University who was told about Aspen by the Paepckes and also fell in love with the spot" said his colleague. "Anderson was a fan of the Bauhaus school and he knew Herbert Bayer, the leader of the movement who designed a house for him here. By 1950 the Aspen Institute started under the intellectual guidance of Mortimer Adler, Paepcke's mentor and it has grown ever since."

I had heard earlier most of what the two men had just explained. I also knew that the leading foundations in the country, Carnegie, Ford and the Rockefeller Brothers Fund had been involved in building up Aspen as a retreat centre for their patrons and members. Anderson with their help had launched the Aspen Center for Physics, the Strategy Group, a thriving international music festival and finally the Design Conference which was just about to start for the thirty third time. Everything had been done to attract the brightest and the most powerful.

"I know that Albert Schweitzer, Ortega y Gasset and Thornton Wilder were among your many famous guests" I noted "but I must tell you that I am no great admirer of Professor Adler, an inveterate cultural chauvinist who barely acknowledged non-western civilizations in his work. His selection of world literature in the 'Great Books' collection is highly subjective and leaves little room for masterworks not written in English or German."

Most of the guests nodded or smiled.

"People here were ingenuous some decades back" the Director

commented apologetically. "Americans knew little outside of the Anglo-Saxon sphere and I am not sure there was much need for a list of 'Great Books' but Butcher, the president of the University of Chicago where Adler taught felt that average citizens needed some reference point for literature as most of them had barely ever read and did not even know where to get quality material. We have progressed though and this year we are holding the first East-West Conference in Aspen."

"That is why we needed the Beatniks, the flower kids" Nancy chimed in, "we were stuck in a stodgy provincial English culture until those guys opened the rest of the world for us...."

I looked at her as she spoke with a flash in her blue eyes, visibly pleased to provoke once again her parents who kept impassive faces. Though a daughter of privilege she was also a child of the Hippie revolution with its taste for oriental mysticism, free love and drugs. America's puritanical society had been soaked for twenty years by waves of dissent and transgression. Reagan's government wished to put the genie back in the bottle of old-fashioned protestant capitalism but that seemed to me a vain pursuit.

"In this country we need "How To" manuals for everything," one of the ladies commented, shaking her head…"Even to make friends, conversation or love. No wonder grown up people want some professor to tell them what books they should read and what they should think about them."

She was a beautiful blonde woman in her early forties and I instantly liked her contagious smile and spontaneous manner.

Jerome Canty told me about his teaching and healing experience. He said he had written a book inspired his encounters with luminous flying saucers whose propulsion system was based on the harmonics of Beethoven's Fifth Symphony.

"I got in touch with them in meditation as part of my Zen and macrobiotics practice" he added as if he had said a very natural thing.

I was only a little surprised, and mainly by the connection with Beethoven's music. Diverse worlds were quietly colliding around Nancy's dinner table. Some guests discussed paragliding in Nepal and river rafting in Ecuador while others argued about Aspen's municipal issues.

"This is a socialist republic mostly for millionaires" the blond woman whose name was Camilla quipped for my information.

"It is probably the only way that socialism could really function" I retorted. "Once everyone has more than enough it is easier to share since there is no need to."

"Let us be fair" Betty Pfister retorted, "we have all sorts of people, including many who live paycheck to paycheck working in bars or shoveling snow but they all feel equal in some way. Most of them ski on the same slopes and call one another by their first names."

"Except that those who are not rich have to look farther and farther away from the town to find affordable rents" the other woman said "and they commute for a hour to come to work. It was not like that ten years ago."

"What can you do?" Art Pfister pointed out, "when there is money the cost of living increases. It's a mathematical law, unless you really go communist and then all the wealthy people leave or are no longer rich so that the dream is over. That will also happen in Aspen if they raise the land and other local taxes too much."

An instant of silence followed this remark which made me think of the effect of a red rag on a bull. "If you question the economic system or even think differently you will be suspected of being a commie" Jerome Canty told me in an undertone "and yet many of our best intellectuals were and are close to communism. That says something about our society."

"Dad, Aspen is socially egalitarian, that is the surface and utterly capitalistic in reality" proffered Nancy. "For a poor person I guess it must be nice to have very rich people pat you on the back and crack jokes with you as long as you can pay the rent."

"You'll see how open and international Aspen is when you attend the Design Conference" the man who was a part of its executive committee said to bring the conversation back to a more consensual topic. "We have outgrown the anglo-germanic moorings of the country. You may know that for more than a century we were divided between the Wasps who hark back to their British ancestors and the newer immigrants mostly from Central Europe and German speaking, many of whom did not even learn English in the first and second generation. Now we are becoming a real global salad bowl with a lot of input from Asia, Africa and Latin America. This year's conference is titled 'The Future isn't what it used to be.' That says something."

"I think that Thomas Jefferson wanted Greek to be the official language, just to make us more democratic in the ancient sense and to distance ourselves from the old country" Camilla reminisced. "I wonder what America would be like if that had happened."

"That was rather unrealistic" the Aspen Institute man opined with a shrug. "No wonder many of his colleagues including the very Anglophile Alexander Hamilton opposed the proposal. Neither Washington nor the other founding fathers wished to go back to school to be able to speak with each other, not to mention the average citizen who was barely literate."

"This is in my view the great quandary of the USA" I pointed out; "trying to make a rural colony steeped in rather rigid Christian beliefs into a classical utopia for what was already envisioned as the New Age … Mingling Solon, Montesquieu, Rousseau and now Cesar to either replace or blend with Calvinist Puritanism is no easy task."

I noticed that my reflection had aroused mixed feelings. There is an innate almost atavistic suspicion of the humanities in the United States, originally because they were pagan and later because they are elitist and austere. Americans may readily accept the inequality and even the inequity associated with wealth and birth but they are uncomfortable with the privilege conferred by intellectual status. I knew that Ronald Reagan personified, after other likeminded presidents and public figures the distrust of eggheads widespread among his countrymen.

"Don't mind Côme" Nancy quipped smilingly, "he is from France and India where people are used to arguing about philosophy and history all the time. We are too busy with our day-to-day chores here."

"Yet," I noted consolingly "Aspen is an athenaeum for thinking and debate, despite its glamorous reputation. The patrons of the city were children of university professors and remain academically inclined, even though they are tycoons. That is a rare and enviable blend."

After the guests had left, Nancy and I ended the evening on sofas around the low table of the living room with cups of Celestial Seasonings teas.

"I'll take you to see one my friends near here in a couple of days' she announced. "He has become a national celebrity as the one and only 'Gonzo journalist'. I think you and I will agree on many things."

So ended my first day in Aspen in the heart of the Rockies and of that massive continent so far from the others in more than one way.

II
Design for the Future

... But in your perishing you will shine brightly, fired by the strength of the God who brought you this land and for some special purpose gave you dominion over it and over the red man. That destiny is a mystery to us... The end of living and the beginning of survival.

**Purported letter of Chief Seattle to the
President of the United States (1852)**

FAB CONFAB AND THE RISE OF STEVE JOBS

The next day was mostly spent at the Design Conference amidst a diverse and colourful array of local denizens and visitors from various parts of the country and the world gathered in and around the famous tent designed by Paavo Saarinen. People could be placed by their appearance on a gamut covering many ideological nuances, from the ecologically unkempt to the fashionably informal. The average reflected the understated but opulent hipness that characterizes Aspen culture. Among the many talks by noted designers such as Milton Glaser, Henry Wolf and John Whitney, introduced as the creator of computer special effects for the movie and video industry, one struck me; a lean, black haired thinly bearded young man with almond-shaped eyes and a self-confident grin talked about his company's projects for the future. He was heard with rapt attention as he had made a fortune before twenty eight and was regarded as a rising star in the field of electronics and computers.

The speaker reminded his audience that the first personal computer had gone on the market in 1976, only seven years earlier and predicted that by 1987 more such machines than automobiles would be sold in the country. He emphasized his resolve to lend aesthetics and functionality to those hitherto cumbersome electronic boxes, thus addressing the primary interest of his audience. He talked about the vast amounts of money that would be spent promoting and advertising the new products and explained in an informal style, as if he were giving a fireside chat, the basic technology at stake which, he noted, was very simple but puzzling because it manipulated invisible electrons.

He further pointed out that computers were not only changing the context of communication between people but also the way in which they would exchange information, no longer by speaking on the phone but by sending written messages from one screen to another at the speed of light, anywhere in the world and he predicted a transformation in the methods of education as a result of the instant visual, auditory and graphic interaction made possible by the merger of the television set with the telephone set, the fax machine and the cassette recorder and player. He confidently announced that in about five years all offices could be connected with all others via personal computers and within ten years individual homes would all have access to the same network.

For the first time, I heard him say "and one last thing," a rhetorical ploy which was to become his trademark over the years and he proceeded to explain the potential of connecting video games to the phone lines and of purchasing musical scores at a distance instantly by paying with a credit card from computer to computer.

"Now Apple's strategy is really simple" he intoned with a hint of oratorical emphasis...." What we want is to put an incredibly great computer in a book that you can carry around with you, that you can learn how to use in twenty minutes. We want to do it this decade.... And we really want to do it with a radio link in it so that you don't have to look upto anything to be in communication with all these larger databases and other computers."

He went on with his vision, aware that he had conquered that technology oriented and optimistic audience. His talk was followed by various questions which included an inquiry into the possibility of a computer translating spoken language into a text and he responded that voice recognition was a difficult achievement for a machine.

I asked Nancy whether she thought that the young man could produce the futuristic instrument he had outlined so rapidly.

"Steve Jobs is really a genius and he has already created some neat machines," she pointed out, "and here we believe that if we set an unrealistic timeframe for a project we are more likely to achieve it, on target or later.... Remember the favourite American saying: 'I need it yesterday'."

Some other people talked about the revolutionary computer being designed by Apple which was expected to hit the market in the following year. It would be known as McIntosh I.

I had the feeling, after listening to Jobs that he had been exposed to some of the futuristic technologies he had described with communicative enthusiasm. He had mentioned MIT to indicate that some of his visions had already already translated into reality and that inkling confirmed my intuition about how scientific breakthroughs were constantly seeding industrial innovations entrusted to young and ambitious entrepreneurs.

"Steve is one of us," Nancy added with a wink. "He went to India in 1974 on the Hippie trail and that is where he got a lot of his ideas about the world. He is a Zen Buddhist and he dated Joan Baez." I had gone to India with my father in that same year and on the same road and I recognized the spiritual background for the sharp featured young man's emphasis on "underlying processes of our experience" rather than on the experience itself. That was a result of Buddhist mind training.

I could feel the electricity in the air that emanates from a cluster of wealthy and ambitious individuals, even far from boardrooms in that lofty alpine meadow cradled by gurgling torrents and fir-clad slopes. Time was indeed money for them when either was spent for recreation or socializing and there was a lot of the latter after the events of the day. That evening we went to a party in one of the large chalets that dotted the hillsides around the town and I noticed the mix of old "oil and real estate money," East Coast financiers, Californian media and high tech entrepreneurs and eager pretty girls that one meets in most privileged circles the world over.

I was introduced to Barbara Marx Hubbard, the philosopher and psychologist who had been listed as a possible Democratic candidate for the vice-presidency of the United States. She announced the dawn of a new era characterized by the fusion of the sciences of the mind cultivated by oriental civilizations with the emerging technologies. She had founded the Institute for Conscious Evolution to promote her vision. Born in a privileged family and educated at Bryn Mawr and the Sorbonne, Barbara gave the impression of being a blend of feminine softness and intellectual sophistication, with her satiny complexion, silvery bob of hair and confident composure. She explained to me in slow but grammatically correct French that she advocated a strategy of human "co-creation" of a future civilization according to the laws of nature.

I recognized the balding, sharp featured Gerald Edelman, a 1972 Medicine Nobel Laureate who had spoken in the morning about his work on the physiology of the brain. He was the author of a book called *The Mindful Brain* which sought to explain mental processes on the basis of evolutionary cell biology which he called biotopology. He rejected theories predicating the non-physical nature of consciousness but his own hypothesis was far from proven. The bearded and cordial Jivan Tabibian, a member of the Institute's planning staff introduced me to the chairman Joe Slater and to the veteran *New Yorker* contributor and architectural critic Brendan Gill. I also noticed the Australian writer Robert Hughes who was mainly known at that time for his articles in *Time* Magazine and his book *Heaven and Hell in Western Art*.

One eccentric-looking long haired man was known as Razame de la Crackers. He was an offbeat film actor and director whose odd stage name was an ironic homage to his family which owned the NABISCO biscuit brand. Another noted Aspen resident was more down-to-earth. André Ulrych was a Polish Prussian immigrant who owned the most popular restaurant and night club in the town and happened to practice the macrobiotic diet. A veteran mountaineer, he had climbed some of the highest Himalayan peaks and I found him and his wife to be friendly, sincere and well read. I told the short, thin and silver-haired André that he was indeed a *Junker*, which made him beam with good natured pride. I knew I had made friends.

AT THE HEART OF POWER

Another evening we went to Elizabeth Paepcke's house where the octogenarian hostess greeted us with the genteel and reserved manners associated with the nation's blue blood even though she was known as 'Pussy', a nickname which did not arouse any visible sniggers. Mrs. Paepcke, widow of the late Walter, was a sister of Paul Nitze, a leading figure of US foreign policy since the second world war and the White House's chief negotiator for the Intermediate Range Nuclear Forces Treaty. She was the grande dame of Aspen where she owned a lot of prime property.

I was keen to engage her in conversation on many topics that she and her brother would have known about but I had to be careful not to step into restricted territory. She quickly brought up memories from Europe when, as a child of twelve she had travelled in Germany with her family on the days when the First World War had erupted.

"I remember Munich in early August 1914," she reminisced. "The patriotic enthusiasm of the crowds was unbelievable. It really felt as if a huge party was about to start."

I knew that the Nitzes had kept a natural attachment to their Germanic roots. Paul Nitze had been the first American to meet Albert Speer, Hitler's Leonardo, after his surrender to the Allies. He had also been an architect of the Marshall Plan whereby Germany had been rehabilitated while he was known for his staunch anti-Sovietism. As such this former assistant of James Forrestal had been instrumental in hiking up the Cold War against the USSR while supporting the immigration and assimilation of former Reich officials and scientists into the US academic establishment. Blood is thicker than water and much of the American business elite, tied to major German companies by industrial and financial links, had followed similar policies. That had led to Operation Paperclip and various others, sponsored by the ruling circles of the United States.

Robert "Bob" Anderson with his broad Nordic face, imposing presence and sporting look was in tune with the local Zeitgeist which he had helped create. The son of a banker of Swedish descent, then in his mid-sixties he had led Atlantic Richfield to the seventh position among America's oil companies and had discovered a few years earlier the Prudhoe Bay offshore field in Alaska, the biggest ever found in North America. A close friend of the Rockefellers, avid modern art collector, expert skier and voracious reader he was an embodiment of American success and power, resting on a tripod of money, high level connections and philanthropic activism.

A tall, rather athletic bald man in his fifties who turned out to be a friend of his struck a conversation: "So you are French" he said smiling expansively. "Do you know George Berthoin?"

I acknowledged being aware of his name and position. I remembered that he was the European head of the Trilateral Commission but I did not mention that.

"We must continue to talk on another occasion, the man suggested, you can call me Jack. Pussy will connect us" and he ploughed into the crowd of guests.

I felt there was more to this short casual conversation than it seemed. It was an opportunity to step forward in the course I had set for myself.

The Gonzo Journalist

However before seeing him again I wished to gather more background information and I was happy that Nancy drove me two days later, on a gloriously sunny afternoon to the rustic Owl Ranch in Woody Creek amidst the tenderly green aspen groves where her friend, the Gonzo journalist had lived since the early sixties.

We reached that rather ramshackle house which marked a departure from the rarefied atmosphere of understated luxury of the town. I was fleetingly reminded of America's perfunctory banality outside its manicured and glossy enclaves of privilege. There was no deep rooted tradition of aesthetics outside the circle of those who lived in style. The purpose of the people was money and if there wasn't enough no traditional culture was available to make up for the lack of resources. Vulgarity tends to assert itself wherever beauty is disdained. What could be expected of a civilization that describes houses, cars, art works and people by quoting their market worth?

The lanky bespectacled man who greeted us, with his dolichocephalic bald head and rather small features and high cheekbones looked strangely boyish for someone so well known for heavy drinking, drug abuse and for his wild and dangerous profile. He struck me as a naturally thoughtful and sensitive individual who had, since his troubled childhood strived to build a legend of recklessness around him. It was a common tendency in that culture where being macho to excess was a highly praised characteristic and the author of *Fear and Loathing in Las Vegas* and *Where The Buffalo Roam* could be expected to aim for ideals of the pervasive Middle Class in which he was born.

There was a big poster of Che Guevara on the wall. Thompson offered us bourbon which we declined, settling for Coors beer instead. He was loquacious and vehement as I expected from his writings. I sensed that, like many Americans who had never travelled outside their continent, he was a bit intimidated by a European but tried to hide that beneath a banter that easily turned to swagger although he was also self-deprecating.

He quickly came to his favorite topic, the depressing state of his country of which he was a powerful and bitter critic.

"We are a land of savages that have quickly become degenerates although as a nation we are barely two hundred years old" he said with a smirk.

I resisted the temptation to quote Clemenceau, a French Prime Minister in the early part of the century who had made a similar assessment of the United States.

I knew that Thompson's father had died when he was still a child, leaving his widow and their three boys in poverty and that Hunter's mother had taken to drinking. His difficult early years surely influenced his assessment of what others worldwide saw as a land of milk and honey.

"We have been taken over by a gang of robber barons who have made America their hunting ground and their property" he said "and they have convinced the average citizen that he is free and sovereign ... Bullshit!."

He was clearly voicing his views, with which Nancy was familiar, for my benefit. If he expected to unsettle me he must have been surprised by my easy and unreserved approval but he did not show it. He was used to generating opposition and anger and took it in stride. In fact he was one of those people who enjoyed it. He had what Baudelaire called "the aristocratic pride of being unpleasant."

"Don't you think though" I said "that Aspen enjoys an unusually high level of intellectual freedom and activity because of the wealthy but gifted people who rebuilt this town as we see it?"

"You mean the richie rich Paeckpes and Andersons, Rockefellers and associates," he shrugged. "Pirates also like to have fun and when they have gone to school they find thinking cool and useful. Anderson is one of the guys who runs our nation. He has his fingers in every big pie and his land holdings are bigger than Luxembourg or Rhode Island. He was behind the building of the Alaska pipeline which has ruined so much pristine land and yet he sponsors many of the environmental organizations. You are looking at real oligarchy. The government belongs to those guys as much as if they were feudal lords in the Middle Ages."

"You are seen by many as a Communist," I remarked. "Do you really advocate a Marxist economic system?"

"You know" he said, "we Americans are not naturally armchair thinkers. We are not good at building philosophical theories. Not too long ago we were all shopkeepers, ranchers, cattle pokes and horse thieves. We used to love our freedom although I don't think that is true anymore. Many of us still want to be left alone to run our lives. The trouble is that the smart ones who come along with a lot of money or know how to make it hijack the wagons. They have turned the place into their casino where everyone has to gamble but they alone can win in the end. So yeah, I think you need at least some socialism, some welfare system to keep greed in check and prevent cheating. This being said I am an average yank, I love my guns. I am a member of the NRA by the way and I don't want the government to control me so I am also a libertarian of sorts. If someone breaks into my property, whether he is a robber or a cop, I shoot."

I thought that his bragadoccio reflected the stereotypical American attitude and its inconsistency. Most people do not want the financial elites to have all the power and pay low or no taxes but they also believe that the right to own firearms, bizarrely guaranteed by the Constitution assures their protection against the Government's intrusions. Not many have realized that the United States has come a long way from its agrarian beginnings as a federation of small towns and isolated farms intent on defending their land claims and possessions from the indigenous inhabitants and from all intruders. I pointed this to the journalist and he did not disagree.

"In the end we love fights and death" he affirmed somberly. "Our founding fathers were puritanical losers awaiting the End of Days with fire and brimstone and you can't kick the Bible freak out of us. That is why we fell in love with the atom bomb and could not wait to use it on the Japs. Racism comes naturally. We slaughtered the local Indians and imported masses of African slaves. Talk about a bad beginning despite all the sanctimonious claptrap of our founding fathers. Some of them were more fit to be called fuddy duddies."

This was typical Hunter Thompson provocation and Nancy vicariously enjoyed it more than I did, but there was a sad element of truth in his tirade. I was reminded of what he had written about "the dark, venal and incurably violent side of the American character." It echoed a similar assessment made by D H Lawrence in his day.

"Many great people in this country agree with me," Thompson added, as if to shake the aura of isolation that clung to him. "Take my friends Jack Nicholson or Bill Murray and I could quote many others. They know how bad the system is but, what the heck you have to survive and Aspen is probably still one of the best places if you can afford it, in spite of Anderson and all his billionaire friends."

I knew he viscerally loathed the Republican Party and it did not take much to arouse his verve against Nixon, the President he had most harshly attacked in his day: "I don't admire our Democrats, he warned. Carter is a nice guy personally but his presidency was overall a disappointment. He was unable to control, much less change the system which is really geared to serve the GOP ... Or rather the Republicans are its best operators. Our Vice President George Bush is cut from the Nixon cloth. He is an SOB, bred and brought up in the CIA and he has been involved in most dirty tricks carried out by our secret government since the Kennedy assassination, if not before."

I had heard about the deep Intelligence affiliations of George H W Bush who had campaigned for the Presidency against Ronald Reagan before joining his team as Vice-President.

"Do you think he is the real power now?" I asked.

"For sure" came the reply. "Reagan is an old B-grade actor who embodies the middle class dreams of a patriarchal movie star-like president. A tall, pontificating figure like Washington and Lincoln, at least physically. Bush is the insider who knows the ropes and the hidden files. He has the goods on everyone. You know that he and his buddies held up a deal with Iran to release the US embassy hostages until after the election, don't you? The point was to make sure that Carter was defeated for failing to secure the diplomats's freedom. The moment the new regime came to power, hey presto! on cue the Ayatollahs let the prisoners go. That is US politics for you. Our Intelligence boys have many contacts in the Iranian government since they helped them fight Iraq, which we also supported of course. Let the two sides pummel and decimate each other as long as possible and make money from the killing."

As we left his house I wondered about the tone of quiet if ironic despair that pervaded his words and also about the incoherence of much of his writing and of his life itself which had made him nationally famous as an anti-Establishment iconoclastic counter-cultural model. Yet his books, as his own person seemed not to follow any purposeful, meaningful course and quickly drifted into ranting portrayals of hallucinatory states, like Beat generation poetry.

Perhaps that man reflected in his articles the derelict state of the American mentality and that may have been the secret of his success. He was the flip side of the 'Drugs Sex and Rock & Roll' personified at one time by the photogenic and eloquent Timothy Leary who had promised happiness and freedom in artificial paradises. Instead, the 'Gonzo' reporter described rambling and self-destructive forays into a psychedelic limbo from which one came back broken and hopeless. The meaninglessness of his lifestyle was suggested by the habitual sobriquet which had no clear interpretation although it might be traced back to French argot and was usually understood as denoting craziness or irrationality in the vein of one of Glenn Larson's *The Far Side* cartoons that one saw in almost any daily newspaper.

The "Doctor" as he liked to be called since he had assumed that fictitious title, just as the founder of KFC had declared himself a colonel, embodied America's troubled state and the inchoate instinctive revolt of much of its people.

Andre's Crowd

A day or so later I went to the downtown Natural Food store to buy a few edibles and found myself next to John Denver who was its frequent visitor and whose broad, high cheekboned, bespectacled visage and straight linseed-coloured mane I instantly recognized. I introduced myself and told him in a few words about some of my interests. He reacted with his usual calm and good natured spontaneity and suggested that we meet again. He scribbled a contact number on a slip of paper and told me he wanted to get me together with Ron Lemire, a Canadian healer and nutritionist who was his house guest.

That evening I went to Andre's bar and restaurant on Galena Street with my new friend Scott Halazon, the macrobiotic food importer, Camilla whom I had met at Nancy's dinner and her friend a beautiful Egyptian archeologist descended from the khalifs of Baghdad who was spending the summer at the legendary and faintly musty Jerome hotel. Our quartet soon merged into the crowd of patrons that gave André's its festive, glamorous and yet cozy atmosphere. I spotted in a group the blonde Linda Evans, one of the stars of the immensely successful *Dynasty* Television series and, at another table, Robert Wagner and the stunning redhead Jill St John who had recently become his companion following her third divorce. I still remembered her as Tiffany Case in *Diamonds Are Forever* and also for her performance in *Tender is the Night* as Rosemary Hoyt. The couple was surrounded by a hallo of glamour and by the whisper of rumours about Natalie Wood's mysterious death by drowning off Wagner's yacht two years earlier. All those stars were friends of the place's owner André who, with his wife greeted us with the relaxed cordiality that made them so likable. The top floor had a retractable roof so that one might dance under the stars on balmy summer nights and even, was I told, on some cold and crisp winter evenings.

A young woman with short auburn hair sitting at the bar swiveled on her stool to tell me: "Hi, I am Joy, I saw you talking to John this morning at the Nature Food Store. Are you an artist?"

Realising the hamlet-like ambience of Aspen I concluded that everything became known to residents very quickly and told her in few words what I did.

"I want you to meet my friend Elizabeth" she said instantly. "She has a lot to share with you and there are some things you may also tell us that we are trying to find out." We exchanged cards and I saw that she was a psychic and astrologer who resided on at Snowmass village, close by. Paranormal themes and skills very much in demand in that hotspot of New Age enlightenment.

Before the end of the evening which by then had become an early morning, Jyoti and André invited me to dinner the next day at their home.

I duly arrived at dusk with flowers and a bottle of wine to an unusually shaped multi-level stone and timber chalet which I found out later was called the Mushroom House because of its outer appearance. André had designed it together with his architect and it was roomy and comfortable with its vast living room-cum-dining area and kitchen so that the host might cook while remaining among his guests. I saw some acquaintances, including Jerome Canty, always gaunt and brooding and Scott Halazon who had kept from his Central European ancestors an unmistakably Viennese nonchalance.

After the duly macrobiotic dinner with its miso soup, sushi, sashimi, brown rice, vegetable nitukes and steamed fish, André reverentially produced a thick, richly bound volume and leafed through it to show us the complex and lavish engravings that adorned almost every page. "P Manly Hall's *The Secret Teachings of All Ages* in the golden anniversary edition of 1975" he said in a hushed tone of voice. "Can you believe that he published this for the first time in 1925 when he was only twenty three years old? He was a young Canadian raised by his mother and his grandmother in Santa Monica and did not know his own father. That he acquired that amazing knowledge so early is just incredible. He must have been inspired by some superhuman entities from above."

I had heard of Manley Hall long before knew that he was still active at the helm of the Philosophical Research Society but had not seen his magnum opus which was one of the first among his many books.

"I met him once in his building at Griffin Park in L.A.," André continued. "What an impressive figure! Six feet five tall and the face of a magus. He mesmerized me."

"Is he not a 33rd degree Mason in the Scottish Rite?" Scott asked.

"Yeah but that came as a ceremonial honour late in life" André said. "I am told he did not undergo any formal Masonic training and is mostly self-taught. That explains why he knows so much. Most masons I met don't go very deep into the occult stuff."

"That he was raised in Los Angeles is in itself a symbol" Jerome pointed out. "California is our promised land; first the Eldorado of gold miners and then the cradle of the film industry which has taken over the world and of the computer revolution in the Silicon Valley now conquering the planet. No wonder that America's greatest occultist is based there."

"He had a big influence on Ronald Reagan or so I heard" opined Bill Stirling, a tall handsome silver-haired man with a trimmed goatee who was the Mayor of Aspen.

"On Elvis Presley too, Scott added. "I heard the 'King' was an avid follower of his teachings. So here you have two of the biggest icons of the country, the founder of American Rock and the Gipper."

"Manley Hall says that America has been given a mission by the forces that rule history and guide humanity" André explained. "According to him the Declaration of Independence was inspired by a divine messenger who came into the Philadelphia State House, even though the door was locked, and gave a speech which electrified the delegates gathered there."

"Old American popular books are full of these smoke and mirrors stories about the founding fathers" Scott grinned with gentle sarcasm. "I guess we are such a young country that we need to create a national mythology to catch up with more ancient cultures, We need our own patriarchs and wizards outside of the KKK and Manley Hall is one of them."

André produced from a bookshelf a slim well worn volume and handed it to me. It was entitled *The Secret Destiny of America* by P Manley Hall. I looked at the date of publication. It was 1944.

"That is based on the speech he gave at Carnegie Hall during the war" the owner explained. "I am told this brochure inspired President Reagan to enter politics and even though he is not a big reader he kept it close to himself for years and often drew from it to make his speeches. He is a believer in the supernatural."

"Who isn't?" Jerome concluded laconically.

André insisted that I take the book home and I promised to return it soon, knowing that it was hard to find.

Annuit Coeptis—He Blesses Our Undertaking

About that time, an article about my father and me with a big photograph had come out in the Aspen Times under the signature of its editor, Mary Eshbaugh Hayes who was a household figure in Aspen. It had been arranged by Florian Scott Halazon who knew everybody. Shortly afterwards I got a call from the man I had met at Mrs Paepcke's party inviting me for a drink on the next day. He gave me directions to his ranch and warned me that it would take me about half an hour to reach there.

I drove out of town into the rolling forested countryside punctuated by chalets and wooden cabins half hidden amidst the conifers and deciduous groves. There were few cars on Highway 82 snaking along the Roaring Fork valley. The weather was cloudy but warm. After about thirty minutes, I noticed an unimpressive wooden gate with no name on it but that was what I had been told to look out for. The gate was open and I drove right through it. There was no interphone or visible security system. The metalled driveway stretched under the firs and aspen as far as the eye could see. Tall dark hills rose on both sides and a foaming creek rushed at the bottom of a ravine that hugged the path on the right. Eventually a low stone and timber, slate roofed house appeared on the other side of a small wooden bridge, covered in the fashion of New England ones. The car crossed it and I alighted in the front yard. I could see a large swimming pool in the middle of a lawn on my right in the distance. A thick door opened and a Mexican butler, clad in a white jacket with silver buttons bade me come in. I followed him past an atrium-like hall decorated with Native Indian art and lit by Tiffany-style stained glass windows. The pale tiled floor was partly covered in colourful Navajo rugs and russet cowhides. A corridor lined with paintings from the Old West and some valuable cubist and impressionist oils led us into a living room whose bay windows looked out on a panorama of green-carpeted hillsides surpassed by the iconic Mount Sopris in the distance. On the other side a large photo of a forest landscape in the fall by Ansel Adams lit the adobe wall with vermillion and gold.

Before I could sit on one of the plush taupe leather sofas the master of the house walked in with a mug in his hand and greeted me. He looked different in a checkered cowboy shirt and jeans which seemed a little out of character with his urban corporate personality.

"Welcome to my home" he said in a cultured voice where one could detect the East Coast twang. "I am glad you made it in time and did not get lost. This area is so sparsely populated that you could go on for miles before finding a house."

While we settled down, I glanced at the framed photos that camped on a corner table near me. There were pictures of children and a rather attractive blonde who must have been my host's wife and then there were signed photos of him with various famous figures, as one could expect in an elite American home. Ronald Reagan, Vice-President George Bush smiling alongside the bald and pale Walter Annenberg, probably at the latter's Rancho Mirage; Secretary of State James Baker and veteran Arizona senator Barry Goldwater; David Rockefeller as he had looked some years earlier and a young Middle Eastern looking man with an impish smile and a close cropped beard and moustache. I recognized Prince Bandar bin Sultan, the son of the Crown Prince of Saudi Arabia and the King's personal envoy to Washington. There was also an elderly commanding and bespectacled figure who looked familiar and it only took me a minute to identify him.

"I see you know the Reverend Herbert Armstrong" I noted after the first few sentences of polite conversation.

The lord of that Mansion nodded with a faint smile. "How come you heard of him?" he inquired "but let me first offer you a drink. I was having some herb tea" he added without waiting for my answer. He asked the butler for Scotch and I settled for iced tea.

"I know about Armstrong and his Worldwide Church of God through his publications, especially *The United States and Britain in Prophecy*" I explained. "Do you believe in his doctrine of Neo-Israelism which describes Britons and Americans as descendants respectively of Ephraim and Manasseh, the two sons of Joseph, son of Jacob?"

My host shook his head evasively. "I have known Herbert for years, mostly for his philanthropic work," he clarified. "Of course like many Americans I believe that our country has a special calling from God if you will and that is why we have become such an exceptional nation. See how much power we have. It does feel like the fulfillment of a biblical promise and we are indeed closely allied with Israel and the Jewish people who have prospered here like never before. England has a long tradition of calling herself the New Israel and her kings claim descent from David and, as you know, are crowned on his throne, the Stone of Scone at Westminster. It may be a legend but it carries a lot of weight. You see when you are familiar with the importance of advertising as anyone in business should be, you can't ignore the power of images and symbols."

"I gather that your president is quite convinced of that national divine mission" I said.

"Almost all our presidents have been" he stressed, "but some like Carter relied too much on moral convictions without enough strength to back them up. Reagan is an idealist but he is restoring the military strength and the economic dynamism of the country. He has revived our alliance with Britain which under Margaret Thatcher is also resuming her historic role as a global beacon for democracy and economic freedom. The time is now. Socialism is fading everywhere and the Soviet Union is on the backfoot while China is taking its cue from us."

"Are you so sure Marxism is on its way out?" I inquired. "I know that Communist parties in Europe and in many other places are giving up orthodox Marxism and that France has reversed most of its socialist policies but is it not too early to cry victory? After all your country has not been in the best of economic health since Nixon pulled out the gold standard and there is a crisis even now…"

"We are emerging from it" was the confident response "and we are going back to America's original philosophy: privatise, deregulate, trust the entrepreneurs, get the state out of the economy as far as possible and unleash competition. There is more than enough here for all to get a good deal if the best are as successful as they are capable."

He noticed that I did not look fully convinced by that assurance. He leaned forward slightly and looked straight into my eyes. "America's time has not passed. It has come" he emphasized. "We have access to much information that is not always in the public. The Soviets made a fateful mistake by sending the Red Army into Afghanistan. It is turning out to be their Vietnam. We will escalate the support to the resistance and it will bleed the Russians for years to come. The regime in Moscow is a gerontocracy. Brezhnev is ailing and most of the top leaders around him are not much younger. The country is exhausted and the Union is weak. Soviet Muslim states in Asia are undermined by separatist movements and so are the Baltic Republics. It won't be too many years before they fall like ripe fruit. The United States will continue to wear the mantle of leadership when the whole world becomes the free world!."

I guessed why he was taking pains to convince me. He soon confirmed my impression by coming to the point.

"I know that you are interested into what goes on behind our political and economic scene" he stated. "You, like many think that we have secrets but in fact our ways of working are not really hidden. Of course there are closed door meetings and private unpublicized gatherings as everywhere else in the world. The Trilateral Commission is quite well known as an international equivalent of our Council on Foreign Relations and so is the Bilderberg Group and a lot of their literature is readily available even though for influential people to speak candidly, they must be assured of discretion. There is no cloak and dagger, only natural confidentiality. For global leadership a nation needs to rise above internal divisions. That has been the role of our elites which look beyond the Democrat-Republican disagreements."

He smiled briefly and I made no comment. I expected that disclaimer and knew that by "elites" he implied the oligarchic network whose uncrowned kings were the Rockefellers and their stable of experts which included financial tsars in charge of the Fed, diplomatic sherpas and wonks such as Kissinger, Nitze and Bzrezinski and a panoply of unelected officials and business tycoons. That was the real permanent government of which my host was visibly a member.

"Let us get back to the economics" I said. "This Republican administration says it is reviving growth by bending labour laws, breaking unions and slashing taxes while boosting the military budget. Are you not providing ammunition to the Leftists at home and abroad by openly championing the cause of the rich against the poor?"

He took a sip of whiskey and stared through the window. I caught a glimpse of a deer ambling through the parkland bathed in the honey glow of the late afternoon.

"We are at the beginning of a new cycle" he explained. "The last thirty years, what you call "the thirty *glorieuses*" in French, are over. We have reached the limits of the high tax, high inflation, high spending system and we must now expand production and consumption by reducing the fiscal burden. Our country is full of whiz kids like the ones you have seen at the Design Conference here and their inventions and energy are already bringing about the next technological revolution. The new companies will replace our dinosaur quasi-monopolies like GM, AT&T, IBM and the rust belt industries. We are giving them a free rein and they'll change the world within a few years. Just watch!."

"I notice that you are not simply cutting down on government investments" I said. "Rather you are redirecting it into the defence and space budget."

"Right" he conceded. "We are pushing national strategic programs. If you come to Washington you should meet General Abrahamson. He is in charge of the Missile Defence Initiative, the SDI that people have nicknamed Star Wars. It is boosting R&D in cutting edge sectors where the financial needs are too big for most entrepreneurs but which provide employment opportunities to lots of engineers. Having mastered the sea and the air we will control space. The Soviets will try to compete but they can't afford it and they'll have to accept our primacy."

"Many predict that you are deliberately increasing economic inequality and giving a raw deal to the middle class" I objected.

"Again it is a matter of circumstances" he said with a shrug. "The previous economic model has run out of breath and old Keynes is no longer relevant now that the welfare state is overextended. Way too much money has accumulated in banks, inflation and unemployment surged so that consumption went down. We need some fresh air from Chicago and Milton Friedman is pointing the way: time to expand, invest and let people spend, instead of the government."

That assertion also came as no surprise. It was well known that the Reagan White House, under the guidance of Martin Feldman subscribed to the neo-liberal theories of that economist who had hitherto been seen as unrealistically extreme in his recipes.

"Are you not relying a lot on debt, public and private to achieve this expansion?" I inquired.

"Debt is not a problem if we mostly owe to ourselves as Americans" was the prompt response. "Remember that the greenback is the world's reserve currency and since it is no longer tied to gold, the Fed can print it at its discretion and I trust Paul Volcker, its chairman, to be discreet."

"You asked me from the start whether I knew the representative of the Trilateral Commission in Paris," I reminded him "so you must have been aware of my interest in that and other organizations. How do you react to the widespread view in your country and abroad that America is ruled by a permanent bi-partisan league of financiers, industrialists, generals and men of influence behind the façade of democracy?"

He did not flinch and was clearly not caught off guard.

"Reality imposes its own rules" he said thoughtfully. "Democracy is an ideal which we strive to attain but then the respect of liberty implies that people are free to use their talents and pursue their ambitions unhindered. Those who are wealthier and more influential will naturally play leading roles in shaping society and as long as their interests are congruent with the general welfare, nothing should be done to change that. There is only a slip between freedom and socialism or tyranny and in America since Jefferson and Hamilton we chose to put individual autonomy above the wish to enforce equality. We are all children of the English liberals, especially Locke and Adam Smith here."

He went on to argue that the country and the world benefited from the existence of an overarching structure of people who placed economic and geostrategic stability above partisan goals, pointing out that only such a consensus could prevent serious strife between the many contending ideologies. "Between the white supremacist right wingers in Dixieland, the liberal internationalist WASPS in New England, the Zionists, the Mormons, the Born-Again Evangelists and the former hippie New Agers of the West Coast and Aspen" he rattled off with a hint of sarcasm. "Mind you, many people keep moving and shifting between those various affiliations" he added.

Dusk would soon seep up from the western range and I took my leave. The amphitryon walked me to the door. I had noticed in him from the first the typical American desire to explain and justify oneself which was both curious and commendable given its apparent unnecessariness. Did that stem from the inferiority complex of a young and awkward giant nation eager to dispel negative impressions in ancestral Europe or was it due to a lingering puritanical sense of guilt?

During the drive back to Aspen I thought about the words of my hosts and remembered the photographs in the living room. They attested to the convergence of interests that had led to the coalition of powerful people who ruled the country. Reagan, the conservative anti-Communist from California, surrounded by Nelson and David Rockefeller's men, had come to power with the support of tycoons such as Walter Annenberg, Nixon's former Ambassador to London, son of an Ashkenazi boss of the Chicago mafia, linked by marriage with mighty banking dynasties of New York . Reagan had taken as Vice-President George Bush, the former Director of the CIA who owed his fortune to investment banking on the East Coast and oil drilling in Texas. He also had the blessing of the millionaire pastor Herbert Armstrong who saw the USA and Britain together ruling the world with the scepter of Judah and David and paving the way for the Second Coming.

American nationalism and Zionism were hand in hand with the Royal Family of Saudi Arabia whose bottomless coffers also funded political and business careers for its US partners. That grand alliance was cemented by money and by the resolve to maintain a global empire. It crossed party lines. On the democratic aisle John Kennedy had been elected with the support of the Mafia's Chicago Outfit thanks to his bootlegging father's connections and Lyndon Johnson also had well known Underworld moorings at the King Ranch and through his "fixer" and patron Abe Fortas. The web of influence and wealth was tight and widespread and isolated, idyllic Aspen was one of its many knots.

III

New Age, Dark Present and Ancient Aeons

"Since I entered politics, I have chiefly had men's views confided to me privately. Some of the biggest men in the United States, in the field of commerce and manufacture, are afraid of something. They know that there is a power somewhere so organized, so subtle, so watchful, so interlocked, so complete, so pervasive, that they better not speak above their breath when they speak in condemnation of it."

President Woodrow Wilson (1913)

DRINKS AT LITTLE NELLS

Shortly after I moved from Nancy's guest house to an apartment I rented at the swiss-chalet style Fasching House, at the upper end of Galena Street and at the foot of the Aspen Mountain where I would stay for more than a year. I needed to be independent and the Pfister family hosted an uninterrupted series of out-of-town guests for whom they needed the space at their ranch. The summer music festival was ongoing at the quaint Wheeler Opera House and beneath the grand tent designed by Herbert Bayer for Robert Anderson. Life felt enchanted in that environment which evoked Gstaad and Saint Moritz in the western hemisphere.

At one concert I came across Joy, the girl first met at Andre's. She was with an older woman whose white-blond mane of hair and pale blue eyes made a strong impression. She introduced us and I was told that Elizabeth, whom she had mentioned in our first brief encounter was also a practitioner of what we call the esoteric arts. We agreed to meet on the following afternoon at Little Nells, a fashionable watering hole for "après ski" in the winter, located at the foot of one of the Silver Queen gondolas, on East Hallam, very near my new residence.

I got there punctually and settled at a table in a corner. Less than ten minutes later the two women arrived and apologized for being late. We ordered soft drinks and began with small talk.

"We saw the article about you in the paper," Joy said "and I understand why you and John Denver have things to discuss. He is like both of us into the Native American culture and he is aware of many issues this country is confronted with."

While she talked Elizabeth watched me closely and I also studied her sharply featured, slightly lined face. She was in her early, healthy and suntanned sixties and when she spoke I recognized a Southern California accent.

"I am from Tucson, Arizona, she explained in response to my inquiry but I lived many years in LA where I met Joy and we moved here a few years ago to escape the Valley madness." That remark was punctuated by a faint smile.

"I receive psychic messages from the spirits of shamans of the Ute tribe that lived in this area" she pursued "so I get a lot of secret knowledge about what is happening to America at the spiritual level and that is how I help people."

I felt a bit disappointed by that prologue. Channelings of vanished peoples, celestial beings and extraterrestrials were very popular by then in the USA but most sounded to me fanciful and softheaded. As for everything else in the country, many made a business of it, whether they received genuine messages from somewhere else or were merely making them up by spinning out supermarket psychology.

Elizabeth must have read my thoughts because she addressed them right away.

"I know it sounds corny and hairy fairy" she said "but I am not naïve and I can tell the grain from the chaff. The Utes are related to the Mexican Aztecs and their original home is in the Four Corners Area between New Mexico and Colorado. Like the better known Hopis, they have a great wisdom inherited from the vanished Anasazis."

"Elizabeth is very well informed" Joy assured me. "We have been living and working together for years. We are not Lesbians but we complement each other spiritually and in our work. I am a follower of the RA material which you may have heard about."

"We are not only into mystical trips," Elizabeth assured me, sensing my lingering skepticism. "In Arizona and California I have known a lot of powerful people and see what has been done to this nation in the name of democracy. In fact we are ruled by organized crime syndicates. They began to assert themselves soon after the Civil War and took over the economy when the Federal Reserve Act was passed in 1913 by a coalition of the Rockefellers and the Rothschilds. Then came prohibition which created huge fortunes from bootlegging and the great depression and America is now split into territories ruled by mob families. They control the electoral system, gambling, the drugs industry, the media and Hollywood because they know that to rule people's lives you must manage the information and sell them dreams and pleasure. That is why they call the American Dream now. The real money and influence are secured by those who supply women, alcohol and entertainment. The capital of this country is not Washington DC, it is Las Vegas where all the underworld syndicates come together as in a federal territory where anything goes."

I was both impressed and slightly disturbed by that peroration. The basic assertions carried the seal of truth, allowing for some exaggeration but I wondered if Elizabeth saw one single grand conspiracy at the heart of the American state. Was she dismissing the formidable ingredient of scientific research and advanced technology in the American power cocktail? Was that too in the hands of criminal syndicates?

Again she seemed to sense my unspoken objection.

"We are a big country full of talented people," she went on "but the system is under the control of those who hold the money pumps.

Nothing can be done in business without the banks and they own the basic good and services, directly and indirectly which means that they own the politicians, the workers and the entrepreneurs as well."

"Do you think that the Reagan Administration is under Ayn Rand's ideological influence?" I asked. "That should certainly be of concern because Rand's so-called objective philosophy or rational egoism, aside from its inconsistencies can be quite damaging to any society that takes its cue from it."

"I went to one of Rand's lectures" Elizabeth said with a dismissive gesture. "Pure materialism and yet promoting romanticism. She wanted people to get what they wanted at all costs but claimed she was against violence. She called for total individual freedom but made fun of anarchists. She was against the Vietnam war but despised spiritual pacifists. She struck me as an odd mixture of a love-starved Russian little girl and of a cold-blooded narcissist who badly wanted to be recognized as one of the great thinkers of all times. When she died two years ago the garland on her grave was shaped like a dollar sign. A fitting tribute!"

"You know" I pointed out "much of her fame and success came from her confessional or ethnic community. Even though she claimed to be above race and rejected any religion, she still stuck to her Jewish roots and enthusiastically supported Israel in its wars against the Arabs, claiming that only the Jews were civilized in the savage Middle East. Her prejudices against non-western society were strong and deeply misguided. In the end her bunch looks like a secular *yeshiva* of Rand worshipers."

"It is a familiar story in the US" Elizabeth commented half-smilingly. "Power flows from one central spring. FDR owed his presidency to the Lehmans and Henry Morgenthau, Lyndon Johnson to Arthur Krim, the chairman of United Artists and to the Kleberg King Ranch Caucus which helped him enter Congress with trumped up ballots. Nixon was largely funded by Mickey Cohen, the Las Vegas Mob boss and Arizona, the state of my birth is held by senator Barry Goldwater and his family which controls both the Republican and the Democrat parties with the former bootlegger and beer bottler

Hensley. They and head gangster Moe Dalitz built up Ronald Reagan as a political leader after he served the syndicate's interest by sabotaging the Screen Actors Guild in the name of fighting communism. Reagan owed his career, despite his mediocre talent to his social and oratorical skills and to the patronage of Jules Stein and Lew Wasserman, the bosses of MCA. You may not know that the bulk of the money for the Las Vegas casinos and Hollywood films was channeled from unions like the Mafia-controlled Teamsters led by Jimmy Hoffa for years."

Much of that information was not new but the way she made the connections was thought-provoking and yet not quite convincing. Was it not too neatly put together?

"You remember Jill St John at Andre's the other evening" Joy said. "Elizabeth met her when she was a struggling young actress still known to her friends by her real name as Arlyn Oppenheim. She got a big break when she was picked as a Bond girl by Cubby Broccoli on the request of Sidney Korshak, the king maker in Hollywood, Las Vegas and many other places. Incidentally Robert Wagner had Broccoli as his agent and that is how he and Jill first met. Guess where the huge promotion and success of the James Bond series came from? It is all in the same hands. They make and break careers and fortunes, and not only in the movies."

"I do agree that Reagan's political connections are heavily tainted by the underworld and its money," I objected "but not all politicians are so suspect. Jimmy Carter for one came up on a wave of decency, or so it seemed."

"Carter was also manipulated by the usual ruling interests" Elizabeth retorted pitilessly. "The Rockefellers surrounded him with their men and made sure he did not break their rules. They needed a clean, provincial reassuring guy after the shady, discredited Nixon-Ford era and Carter lasted only one term. The conservatives sank his foreign relations and economic policies. He lost Iran and Afghanistan and presided over stagflation. He was seen as the head of nation in decline."

"No one can rise to a certain level in our society without submitting to the protocols" added Joy. "Either you come from one of the insider families, or you are picked up early in life by one of the elite secret societies such as Skulls & Bones at Yale or some other masonry or lobby. The top of the pyramid is made to look clean to outsiders. It is occupied by investment bankers, big lawyers, oil men and Fortune 500 executives but if you look below deck you find the mechanics and the cooks who really run the ship and their business is not to be exposed. That is where you have the arms and drug tycoons, the gambling kings and the stock market speculators."

"This government is all about giving more power to the super-rich by removing the regulations that hobble them" Elizabeth segued. "They are massively increasing the national debt to make up for lost tax income and pushing even the mom-and-pop Savings and Loans to invest pensioners' kitties in high risk financial instruments and bad loans. This will lead to a crash in the next few years. Now people are getting easy money, especially those who don't need it but the bill will have to be paid by the average citizens. The beneficiaries are protected by their offshore holdings and trusts."

I could see in the picture these women were laying out the reverse of the optimistic predictions made by Anderson's friend at his ranch. They were all right in their assessments but they looked at the facts from very different viewpoints.

THE GEORGIA COMMANDMENTS

"Tell me" I asked "what do you think will happen if the system brings about the crisis you predict. Will people revolt?"

"Americans are too divided to rally around any common goal" was Elizabeth's pessimistic response. "Ayn Rand's supermarket philosophy resonates in people's minds because she glorifies the individual and says everyone should only be concerned with personal business. That strikes a chord with people obsessed with asserting their rights, not as a class or a nation but as isolated agents. Yet in practice that suits only the multimillionaires who are not really isolated because of their power and because they support each against the little guys other even while they compete.

New Age, Dark Present and Ancient Aeons

We have two contradictory currents in America as the RA messages tell us, the positive force that leads us upwards towards service to others, since the days of Ben Franklin and the Transcendentalists and the contracting pull of selfishness voiced by Ayn Rand and economists like Milton Friedman. Native American wisdom says the same thing and the ancient native Shamans warned that the white people would bring misery to the land and to themselves by their greed and violence. No wonder we are obsessed with vampires and horror movies. They symbolize our inner world since the days of witch hunts, slavery, lynching and Indian massacres leading to the KKK. Have you heard of the Georgia Commandments?"

"Do you mean the huge granite edifice of granite slabs on a hill top near Elberton? That is all related to Albert Pike's masonic teachings, is it not?"

"That's right" Joy confirmed. "It is all very mysterious but apparently a secret group paid a lot of money to have those statements carved on giant slabs of rock as if a new Bible were being presented to America."

Elizabeth reminded me of the message carried by that colossal monument which was commissioned in 1979 by an enigmatic "Christian" who never identified himself further nor revealed his connections and affiliation. She thought it was linked to a faction of the hidden power that dominated the country and to which various presidents, including Woodrow Wilson and Franklin Roosevelt had alluded to in private conversations or even in speeches.

"R C Christian sounds like a pseudonym linked to the Rosicrucians and the cardinal statement is written in four ancient languages if I remember right: Hebrew, Sanskrit, Babylonian Cuneiform and Egyptian Hieroglyphic, which is indicative of an esoteric cult" I pointed out "but the American Headquarters for the Rose Cross are located in San Jose, California so that one wonders why this stranger came to a small town in devout Georgia to plant this monument which is inspired by a philosophy reminiscent of New Age ideals quite alarming for conservative Christians...."

"It is about the supremacy of reason, a quest for harmony with Nature and the Cosmos and world unity in language, laws and government" Joy noted "but the first commandment is to keep the human population at about five hundred million, even though when the monument was built we were already five billion. The second advises eugenics. How do the people behind this project, whoever they are, plan to reduce our numbers by 90%? Otherwise the instructions given are quite sensible; they suggest a balance of rights and duties."

"There is an occult reason tied to geomagnetism why that spot was chosen" Elizabeth said cryptically. "It is part of a larger design. Our country is full of secret societies and those which are not at the top of the power pyramid vie for influence. Those who put up the Georgia guidestones did not wish to be identified. Some believe that they are the secret government which has built those clandestine underground facilities to hide itself and the detention camps in which it plans to lock up all those who resist its takeover when it will impose martial law but that is not correct. The planners of the Georgia monument want to give us a warning and show us an alternative to a global dictatorship of the Illuminati."

That was the first time I was hearing that ominous word since I had come to the country. I had one more proof that I was conversing with genuine conspiracy theorists and I was skeptical about the prediction of military coups and mass detentions but Elizabeth had firm convictions and was not intimidated by my visible disbelief.

"There are secure facilities spread throughout this land that can hold millions of people if and when that is seen as necessary by our rulers" she said slowly. "We could show you some from outside, should you wish to. The official explanation is that they plan for natural disasters or nuclear wars but there could be other reasons to resort to such measures. Keep in mind that the powers-that-be will do anything to keep their hold on the country."

Not sure of what to say about that, I went back to the Georgia Stones.

"Do you think, like some do, that the builders were members of Alice Bailey's Lucis Trust in New York?" I inquired.

"The Lucis Trust carries the message relayed by the Tibetan Master Djwhal Kul to Bailey," Elizabeth responded "and there is no direct reference to it in the monument but then it may be out of precaution since Lucis is hated in Christian America as it is in fact named after Lucifer who in theosophy is the Angel of Light and not the Devil."

"It seems to me that even before independence the American colonies were split between various Biblical confessions and Masonic lodges, some of which were deistic or even aggressively anti-Christian or Luciferian in the tradition of the Bavarian Illuminati as one can see in many statements by Thomas Paine, Ben Franklin, Thomas Jefferson and John Adams" I reflected. "Both those legacies are still very present and locked in conflict even though they sometimes cooperate. The Scottish Rite Grand-master and Confederate General Albert Pike tried to bring them together although he was a student of Sanskrit, an admirer of the Vedas and a self-proclaimed polytheist, whether out of poetic license or religious conviction."

The two women nodded. "America is both," Joy said. "That is why it is so troubled and misleading. It is perceived by many people abroad as satanic because it tends to use the language and invoke the name of Jesus and then speaks and acts in the opposite way, it is both Dr Jekyll and Hyde. To begin with Ben Franklin was a member of the Hell's Fire Club of England, a notorious Satanic coven."

That account sounded like an echo of the Gonzo journalist's verdict although he had not mentioned the positive side of the US coin.

HIDDEN HANDS FROM ABOVE?

I found that this was the right moment to bring out a subject from the back of my mind.

"Ladies" I said "hearing you both talk I assume you have an interest in UFOs and some knowledge in that field since you Elizabeth are a student of the RA material, allegedly dictated by a highly evolved being on behalf of a confederation of star peoples. What say you?"

Instant smiles appeared on their lips and there was a glint in Elizabeth's ice blue eyes.

"The visitors are involved in so many things, especially in the spiritual world" she acknowledged "but I'd rather have you meet an expert in the nuts and bolts aspect of it who is in touch with scientists and military officers. He is rather conservative in his political views but then we two are space cadets as you have probably concluded and he inspires more confidence on that subject since he keeps his feet on the ground and has proof for what he says. Have you heard of Richard Sigismond down in Boulder?"

I had not. They told me he was a colleague of Professor J Allen Hynek and Dr Jacques Vallee who were famous for their pioneering work in the field of "ufology."

Elizabeth promised to call Richard and I said that I would go to Boulder to meet him at the earliest mutual convenience. We felt well attuned in our views and agreed that we should meet again soon.

On my short walk home I thought of the Georgia Guidestones and remembered that in the year of their inauguration in 1980 a message had been published worldwide as a full page advertisement in major newspaper claiming that "The Messiah is now here." The author of that enigmatic statement was a hitherto little known English artist and occultist called Benjamin Crème who had started an apparently well-funded organization called SHARE International. He seemed to have attracted some support in high places even though he had said little about the world Saviour whom he called Maitreya in line with Buddhist prophecies and heralded so publicly, except to reveal that he had come to London from Pakistan after descending from the Himalayas in July of 1977. There was a resurgence of the theosophical prophecy in Crème's announcement and coincidentally, in 1980 as well the esoteric writer and diplomat from Chile Miguel Serrano had published his *Book of Resurrection* to predict the advent of Lucifer whom he also identified as Maitreya and Wotan, the Norse sky god. Was the relative synchronicity of those three messages fortuitous or was something deeper at work?

We always have trouble seeing our own times in perspective and tend to think that we live unique events unlike anything that occurred before but probably in each year of history many powerful and symbolic signs and changes take place, mostly outside our knowledge. We only discover them later if ever. Yet, I was struck by the growing awareness of a looming global transformation and by the increasing quest for an eschatological figure destined to provide solace and a sense of purpose and meaning to all.

John Denver's Country Road

Soon after I went to dinner at John Denver's house in the elite Starwood area inhabited by many of the rich and famous of the continent. He had invited André and Jyoti Ulrych and a couple of other friends of his. The living walls were studded with the many gold and platinum record trophies of the master of the house who had already exceeded twenty five million LPs in sales and was one of the most beloved musicians in America and a frequent guest on some of the popular entertainment shows on television. He also hosted the Grammy Award session and was even better liked for launching the Hunger Project with his friends Robert Fuller and the popular psychology guru Werner Erhard.

A good friend and supporter of the former President Jimmy Carter, Denver was not much in favour with the Reagan administration which he often criticized; he had a long and cordial acquaintance with Captain Jacques Cousteau and he told me that it had made him like France even more, although he was not familiar with it.

Denver was in some ways a typical middle class "country boy" as he liked to define himself although he had a multitude of gifts and a constantly active and inquisitive mind. Like many of his compatriots he had had a difficult childhood, mainly because of the cold and stern personality of his father and the early intrusion of alcohol and drugs into his life. His marriage to long-time sweetheart Annie had ended bitterly in the previous year and he had behaved violently when she had announced her decision to leave him. I found that he had the strength and toughness of his German ancestral side as well as the wild and poetic penchant of his mother's Irish forebears.

"It was not easy in post-War small town America to have Deutschendorf as a surname and look so Germanic" he commented ruefully. I assumed that was the reason why he had changed his name so young, as soon as he began a singing career. I did not say that it was strange, given the heavy Germanic ingredient in the American population, to hear of such prejudices but Denver hinted at the reason of his experience: "I was called a Nazi more than once in Hollywood" he volunteered "and not only by Jerry."

I knew he was referring to Jerry Weintraub, his producer for many years who had been his Pygmalion but with whom he had parted litigiously. I understood the context of his quip since a Goy could quickly be labeled a Nazi by the mighty bosses of the Music and Film industry if he fell out of favor.

"Music saved me from becoming a drifter" he confessed simply. "We Americans waver from rigid conformism to anarchical revolt. We can't break rules gently like the Latins because we are eaten by moral guilt. I revolted against my father's military upbringing. He was an Air Force officer and we kept moving with him all over the country, from Base to Base. Do you know that I was born in Roswell, New Mexico, where Bob Goddard laid the ground for our space programme?"

I was struck by that fact. "Were you there in 1947?" I immediately asked him.

"I was born in 1943" he said, showing he understood the context of my question "and we were outta there when the famous UFO crash took place. Anyway I was four then so I would probably not have known a thing but the NASA astronaut Dr Edgar Mitchell who is older than me is also from Roswell and he has a lot more to say about it although I have read quite a few things on that story."

I suddenly understood why he had such a keen interest in space exploration and had even been made a member of the National Space Society in recognition of his personal support.

I felt that the other guests were if, not well informed at least open-minded about the UFO issue and the host visibly was not at all perturbed by it.

"I am sure we are being visited by beings from various other worlds" he volunteered quietly "I wish I could see one craft, like John Lennon did in New York but I believe many of the testimonies I have heard and read and I was shown quite a few interesting photos and films. I am sure one day or another we will be told officially that we are not alone and that others are far above us in every way."

"Hopefully not only in science and technology but also in wisdom" André added with a concerned frown.

"There must every type and class of beings as we see on earth" John Denver mused "How can we expect the aliens to be all alike and like-minded?"

We went back to speaking about America and its troubles. Jyoti brought up the irony of the fact that John Denver who was an icon of wholesome clean living and music also carried the reputation of promoting the consumption of drugs and was a suspect in the eyes of many conservative citizens.

"Drugs and alcohol are part of our country's makeup," John pointed out "but then the State keeps acting as a nanny and a church at the same time and trying to ban things. You know that pot was a popular remedy until it was associated with Mexican revolutionaries and became a symbol of leftist subversion and decadence...."

"Cannabis sounded medical and European," André quipped, "while Marijuana evoked like sombreros and Pancho Villa, not Kosher."

"Two old yankee phobias in one" I interjected "Roman Catholicism and native American ethnic culture...No wonder they hated it."

"Then Uncle Sam cracked down even though the CIA was busy experimenting with more powerful, lab-produced substances on our young people as part of the MK ULTRA and other programs" Denver concluded philosophically.

"That is the trouble with our nation" another guest commented "everything becomes a business and even repression is a money making venture so that many people have an interest in carrying it out forever precisely because it is not working."

"Is it true that the CIA is really behind a lot of the drug trade?" I asked innocently.

Knowing nods greeted my query. André voiced what they all thought: "It is a huge source of income and a political weapon against dissidents" he said in his peculiar, slightly quivering voice. "It brings in money that does not have to be accounted for."

I was to learn later that he was just beginning to be affected by Parkinson's disease.

The conversation brought up Buckminster Fuller, the visionary globetrotting scientist and inventor who was a friend of John's. I had heard and read a lot about Fuller during my stay in India where he was well known.

"Thank God there are people like him and Amory Lovins in our country" Denver said pensively. "Bucky is swimming against the tide. America has turned into a huge undertaking to mechanise and homogenize people. Agriculture, education, shopping, religion, entertainment, sport, everything has to be run like an assembly line, identical from one end of the country to the other and we are doing the same all over the world by imposing our views, our language and our way of life. I wonder how long it will take for people like Buckminster Fuller to be acknowledged as the thought leaders of society, not just as eccentric geniuses. At present our politicians praise him at best but don't take up his proposals."

Upon hearing the name of Amory Lovins, a famous environmental engineer and futurist I made a mental note to call on him in the following days when I would be back from Boulder. The evening ended soon after. Our host had shown some of his deeper concerns, evincing the ecological awareness that inspired much of his musical vein and that had made the conversation valuable and enlightening.

On the next day which was the 2nd of July, we learnt that Buckminster Fuller had passed away, aged eighty seven while holding the hand of his comatose wife in a Los Angeles hospital.

IV

Eastward in the West

Apart from considerations of military security, the only reason to suppress a piece of news is that it is unbelievable

Memo from the U.S. Office of Strategic Services (OSS)

A Drive Across the Rockies

A couple of days later I went to Boulder with Scott Halazon who had some business there and offered me a passage in his BMW. I had set up a meeting with Richard Sigismond who had been informed about me by Elizabeth and I wished to discover both the cities of Boulder and Denver which play a particular role in the politics and culture of the United States for reasons I wanted to understand better.

The drive along Interstate 70 was visually spectacular and intellectually stimulating. Scott was a partly autodidactic man (aren't we all?) and he had an original mind and a quirky temperament which made his viewpoints on many topics interesting. He knew a lot about the past of Colorado of which he was a proud native. "I would not call it history as yet" he said with his habitual dry humor "as it is too new. It sounds more like a series of anecdotes and scandals but is that not the American legend?"

I retorted that all histories are made up of individual and group stories that are eventually glorified and canonized when they are preserved long enough and suitably embellished or dramatized.

"I guess so," he replied "but we are too young and too practical to build real epics. We are always half-way between a shootout and a court case and we think that makes up for comedy."

As we spoke we crossed a pass through the Mosquito Range and entered the San Isabel National Forest. To the South West we could see the towering snow-glazed peaks of Mount Elbert and Mount Massive, the loftiest mountains in the continental United States. The road climbed smoothly towards Leadville, the highest municipality in North America which we reached in less than two hours. Along Main Street filed past a picture postcard of the sleepy little western town popularized in so many cowboy films. "It is a real Wild West relic" Halazon said "At one time it was, before 1900 the wealthiest place between the Mississipi and California... The typical US get-rich-quick success story, violent, vulgar and lawless."

"Today we say, drugs, guns and Rock n Rolls, right?" I quipped.

"It is Girls, drugs and Rock n Roll," he corrected with a grin "and there were lots of girls. It was famed for prostitutes, saloons of course and also cockfights, dog fights, boxing and shootings. The only sheriff who could restore order was a trigger happy Irish alcoholic called Martin Duggan and he was eventually shot dead himself. In Europe that would sound like a medieval story but it actually happened less than a hundred years ago. The town was minting money from the gold, silver, lead and copper mines but the repeal of the Sherman Silver purchase Act in 1893 triggered a panic which ruined a lot of people and it never quite recovered although the mining picked up again. Until three years back the Climax Mine which is the largest underground one on earth supplied three quarters of the world's molybdenum but now it is closed and most miners left."

"As a child I read the life story of Baby Doe and I believe she died of cold right here in 1935 in her cabin near the Matchless Mine."

"Good memory" Scott confirmed. "She was 84 at the time and after being married to Horace Tabor, then the richest man in Colorado, she and her husband lost everything in the crash and she became a pauper after he died but she kept believing that the closed Matchless mine still held a bonanza and would reopen and make her wealthy again some day. She had been a millionaire three times before in her life and was sure it would happen for the fourth time."

"Were her daughters not named Silver Dollar and Lily?"

"Yep, that reveals a lot about us Americans. We call people after things or goods we want to have or like."

We paused at one of the few rustic establishments for coffee and chatted about the nearby Camp Hale of the US army which had had many functions until its closure in the mid-sixties.

Scott told me that it had hosted four hundred German POWs from the Afrika Korps during the last War. I was not aware of that fact but knew that the CIA and the US Special Forces Command had used Camp Hale to secretly train Tibetan guerrillas to fight the Chinese even before the 1959 flight of the Dalai Lama. The Americans had also raised a company of Muslims from China's Hui ethnic minority to wage unconventional warfare against the People's Liberation Army but those schemes had not yielded many results and had been wound up in 1965 by Lyndon Johnson who had decided there was no realistic hope of defeating the Chinese in Tibet.

"That was a project from the days of Eisenhower" Scott pointed out. "The Democratic administrations had little enthusiasm for those Republican Cold War plots. Our history is littered with failed wars and aborted military schemes. As MacArthur said, our governments like to fight wars but don't know how or don't wish to win them."

That brought back to my mind the controversial figure of Anthony Poshepny better known as Tony Poe, a Marine officer and CIA operative who had trained many of those Tibetans at Camp Hale after playing shadowy roles in the Vietnam war where he had become notorious for collecting the ears of dead Communist enemies and throwing their severed heads into the camps of the VietCong in an apparently futile attempt to intimidate them.

Although his ways may be regarded as an aberration, in fact those grisly methods were often used during the second World War against the Japanese by the GIs and even earlier against the Native Americans. After all, collecting scalp was a common practice in some units of the US army operating in the "Wild West" which they had made wilder by their presence.

"After Nehru's death the successive Indian governments scaled down their cooperation with the US against China under Soviet influence" I said "and so Washington lost confidence in India as a potential ally."

We were soon out of Leadville. On the way, I caught a glimpse of the locally famous Tabor Opera named after its sponsor, Baby Doe's last husband Horace Tabor who built it at the height of his fortune in 1880. I recalled that Oscar Wilde had lectured there during his American tour of 1883 and had attracted much derision for his foppish and effeminate ways in that rough-and-tumble environment. He had been quite amused to read in one of the saloons a sign above the piano that read "Please don't shoot the pianist, he is doing his best." Scott did not know that story but he was well informed about a notorious resident, the outlaw "Doc" Halliday who had repaired to Leadville shortly after the famous "shootout at OK Corral," adding to the mixture of gold-diggers, swindlers, gunmen and preachers that composed the local population as it did much of the American West at the time.

While evoking these picturesque vignettes which are now part of popular culture everywhere, thanks to Hollywood and the television industry we started the climb across the Wasatch Chain and later duly stopped to admire the barren and austere scenery of Independence Pass which marks the divide between the headwaters of the land. The Arkansas river and all others east of that line flow towards the Mississipi and the Gulf of Mexico while to the West all streams join the Colorado and go to the Pacific.

YANKEE MYSTICS AND THE AMERICAN DA VINCI

As we began the slow descent towards the Denver plateau we talked about the predominant schools of thought that influence America since the colonial days and how they have evolved and periodically transformed. The United States had acquired a distinct collective identity when it consisted mostly of a string of puritanical settlements before gaining independence under the primary influence of deistic enlightenment professed by Free Masons. John Locke, Newton's friend was a source of inspiration of the founding fathers and pragmatism, whether Christian or free-thinking, the guiding philosophy but in the early nineteenth century a new, more metaphysical and romantic tradition had taken root with Ralph Waldo Emerson and his fellow transcendentalists and led to the emergence of what was known as New Thought.

My travelling companion revealed that he was an admirer of the great artist and metaphysical philosopher Walter Russell whose writings he avidly read.

I knew little of that brilliant polymath who well deserved the surname of "American Da Vinci" that he was frequently given. That symbolic association with Renaissance Italy had been reinforced when late in life he had, with his new British wife Lao acquired and settled in a Medicean villa called Swannanoa in a rural district of Virginia. Although Russell had died in 1963, at ninety two, his widow, thirty five younger than him, was still carrying on there with the activities of the University of Science and Philosophy.

"Walter Russell seems to be the most gifted representative of perennial philosophy in the New World" I said. "He translated in the arts but also in cosmology and physics the philosophical intuitions of Emerson although, unlike the latter who had been deeply marked by Hindu philosophy, he does not evince any specifically oriental inspiration. He is a masterful heir of western esoteric gnosis as it came through Venice and Florence."

Scott thought for a moment before replying. "You know" he argued, "the American mind was somewhat liberated from the narrow religion of the first settlers by people like Ben Franklin and David Jefferson who were interested in faith mainly from a moral standpoint but applied the spirit of free inquiry. Franklin believed in the possibility of reincarnation and in the future ability of science to bring the dead back to life. He did not really accept that Jesus was God but did not wish to raise unnecessary controversies. Jefferson was practically a neo-pagan. So the founding fathers left the door open for the mystical insights of transcendentalism and New Thought. The fusion of Christianity with pragmatic eclecticism has given rise to many religious denominations like the Unitarian churches and the Moral Philosophy School to which Russell belonged."

"How is it that this great current of metaphysical philosophy has left so few traces in the fabric of the country?" I asked.

"Because we are a land of settlers who came here to find a better life; that means for us making money and most people who deviated from that single-minded pursuit were left more or less preaching in the desert unless they could offer tangible benefits to potential followers. When a country does not have enough of a thinking elite dedicated to speculative ideas, it can't generate a strong spiritual focus. We are left holding on to John Locke and his definition of a capitalist social contract. We took to Freud because he proposed an apparent remedy for psychological problems and hangups. Outside political formalities we don't care about social equality or even equity because they interfere with everyone's desire to make a bundle even if it hurts others."

"I suspect that nations which begin with vast amounts of land and natural wealth for a small scattered population fall for the many material temptations" I added. "When there are numerous mouths to feed and little room many people may turn to otherworldly pursuits when they realize how hard it is to remain in the acquisitive rat-race."

"The American system does not leave you in peace" Scott replied, shaking his head. "You are constantly under pressure to earn in order to pay your bills and also to prove yourself. Some decades ago here you still had to watch your step because you could be shot for very little reason. It is not so different even today with all the overarmed and short-tempered citizens one is surrounded by."

"Yet" I pointed out "there are periodic revivals of the American quest for a universal spirituality compatible with scientific knowledge. Marilyn Ferguson is one of the latest avatars with her book *The Aquarian Conspiracy* which came out a couple years ago."

"That is a facet of the New Age movement. It involves scientists like Pribram and Bohm and philosophers who seek to make sense of science in a mystical perspective such as Fritjof Capra and José Arguelles, In a way you are right, this current derives from our nineteenth century thinkers, Edgar Poe, Walt Whitman and John Muir."

Welcome to Boulder

While talking, we passed Central City and, driving along Clear Creek crossed Georgetown, another quaint red brick and clapboard relic of the Silver Boom among many Leadville-like small towns, mainly famous for miners and gangsters, in that country which seems too recent to have real villages. Soon we reached Boulder whose quiet, tree lined streets and comfortable middle class houses made a favourable impression. We were no longer in Aspen's fairyland for millionaires but Boulder had the appearance of a haven for an understated quality-conscious upper class. The University of Colorado made its presence felt throughout the town in so many ways and several buildings sported the symbols of the fraternities, sororities and other academic societies which frame student life in America and reflect its class hierarchy.

While Scott was to stay with old friends of his it had been arranged by common acquaintances that I would be hosted by Professor Howard Higman, a veteran figure of the academic establishment who was the originator and the chief organizer of the annual World Affairs Conference at the university. We briefly stopped at his large and rambling house, where the stocky and mercurial, ruddy faced sociologist welcomed me with his fabled Pickwickian joviality and took me to one of the several rooms he kept for habitual and occasional guests. He had to go to a dinner and told me to make myself comfortable. "We'll meet tomorrow in the evening at supper" he said with finality. "You must have heard of my cooking and I will feed you in my style."

His love for cuisine was indeed well known although his drinking capacity was even more famous. A local miner's son who hardly left the university where he had studied, he was a power to reckon with and a staunch supporter of liberal causes which in his country are seen as verging on Marxism.

We had an appointment in the evening at the house of Elizabeth's friends, a young couple with two children who had invited a few like-minded local residents to dinner in the potluck tradition. They lived in a typical two storied villa with a front porch and a slanted roof located on a quiet street near the Chautauqua Park, not far from Higman's abode. The main guest was the man I had been told about, Richard Sigismond, a gentle, slight bald man with a long white beard and thick glasses. He had a vaguely leonardian air about him and, sure enough, confided that his family had come from Florence and was originally called Sismondi which had led him to suspect that he might be related to Michelangelo, a fellow Tuscan genius.

Before dinner, I was asked to say a few words about what had brought me to America and what I was working on. I tried to be informative while remaining concise and eschewing controversial statements but I saw that the audience was prepared and shared an awareness of the sensitive subjects I evoked. Our hostess put it simply but clearly: "We all know our country lives in make-believe. The government treat us like children in really important matters and hides what it believes could shock us out of our immediate pursuits."

Sigismond, who had remained quiet until then cleared his throat and said in a soft voice: "There are indeed things that most people are not able to accept out-of-hand so that there is always a potential for major social trouble if you change the paradigm too abruptly and challenge the public's general convictions on which they depend for their comfort level. I understand the reluctance of the politicians and the military leaders to share all the information with the masses but I don't agree that a few powerful people should hold a monopoly on vitally important discoveries and use them for their own ends."

"For a former Beatnik, Richard you have become very conservative" the mistress of the house told him in a gently reproving tone.

"I am a patriotic American" Sigismond retorted quietly "and after dealing for years with the military, I know that many of the officers are well intentioned and conscientious. The more you learn, the more bound you feel to use the information responsibly and prudently."

STARGATES OPEN

The conversation floodgates had opened and while we ate, many stories from the extensive folklore of the para-normal came out. At least two people in the group had seen UFOs and others had heard or read first hand reports from friends and trusted professionals, policemen, army men, physicians, engineers, amateur pilots and so on. Famous cases in America such as those involving people and places like Kenneth Arnold, Roswell, Socorro, George Adamski, Howard Menger, Van Tassel, Kecksburg, San Agustin and Mantell were only alluded to in passing as most of us were familiar with them. They had inspired innumerable books, films, TV series and magazine articles, documentary and fictional and had for long been part of the country's popular culture. There was less knowledge about the innumerable similar incidents recorded in Western Europe, Russia and Asia and about older reports of "out of this world" sightings, some of which went back to the 19th century and earlier. Richard stated that both the German and Italian governments had retrieved alien vehicles on their respective territories during the nineteen thirties but he conceded that the apparent multiplication of alleged crashes of sophisticated aircraft of unknown origin stretched belief.

We were on surer ground with the long record of interventions by scientists and states at the United Nations. I had read the correspondence between Professor James E MacDonald, a reputed physicist from the University of Arizona and the Secretary General of the UN, U Thant between 1967 and 68 and I knew that even earlier, on June 30th 1965, Colonel von Kevitzky had presented the evidence collected by him and others before the world assembly. At about the same time various testimonies had been gathered by relevant committees of the US Congress with no publicly known effect because the American government was effectively under a "gag order" since the CIA's 1953 Robertson Panel had recommended, in its so-called Durant Report denying the reality of the phenomenon and discrediting witnesses and investigators.

James MacDonald mysteriously committed suicide in 1971 and his influential voice fell silent. Even the powerful message to the UN by NASA astronaut Gordon Cooper in March 1978 was almost ignored although, at the request of the Government of Grenada and with the support of Secretary General Kurt Waldheim the general assembly finally adopted Decision 33/426 on 19 December 1978 calling on all member states to research and exchange information on the matter of UFOs.

"I followed the UN process closely" Sigismond said with a twinge of emotion in his voice. "I have been friends for many years, as Elizabeth may have told you, with Jacques Vallée, your countryman, and with J Allen Hynek from Northwestern University who were both in touch with Grenada's Prime Minister, Sir Eric Gairy while he lobbied for international recognition of the reality of UFOs. On 14 July 1978, he gathered a few experts in Miami around Kurt Waldheim and himself to prepare a dossier for the General Assembly. Hynek, Vallée, another Frenchman, Dr Claude Poher, Kevitzky, Cooper and David Saunders participated in the roundtable which resulted in addresses by Gairy and Hynek to the UN in November of that year. Then the decision was adopted but the Security Council clearly decided to ignore it because that was the wont of the Permanent Five. We were told that the US would veto any proposal that came up in relation to that theme. On 13 March 1979 while Gairy was in New York, still pursuing his campaign, a coup overthrew him and his old rival, left-wing union leader Maurice Bishop took power. Despite appearances Bishop enjoyed the covert support of the USA or at least of the CIA and I am still convinced that the main reason for removing Gairy was what some American journalists called sarcastically his 'obsession' with UFOs.

In 1981 Kurt Waldheim's mandate ended too when China, allegedly in agreement with the US, blocked his reelection and supported a 'Third World' candidate as his successor."

"These are typical methods used to get rid of inconvenient people" a guest pointed out; "our government in particular prefers to promote individuals with a tainted past to high positions so as to blackmail them if needed or use the goods to get rid of them when desired."

"Yes" was Sigismond's answer. "Waldheim may have lost his Teflon suit when he ventured into the parallel reality, on the other side of the mirror so to speak. His predecessor U Thant also seems to have fallen from grace when he made strong statements on the issue of flying saucers and had to issue a denial when he was ridiculed in a section of the media and publicly derided by some US officials."

We went on to discuss the reasons for the obstinate and systematic attitude of denial maintained by the American and several other governments. We all thought that the ruling elite's overriding interests combined with their religious convictions, sincere or statutory, to prevent the acceptance of facts that dramatically challenged the status quo and potentially threatened the established order.

"A socio-political system and hierarchy always rest on an intellectual paradigm, that is on a set of beliefs" I remarked "and the collapse of the latter is usually followed by the destruction of the former."

Sigismond caressed his white beard thoughtfully for an instant.

"If you look at the people who have shaped the State during and since the second world war, the men around Truman, Ike Eisenhower and Nelson Rockefeller, you see how tough and self-righteous most of them were. They staunchly upheld their respective religious confessions and regarded all Non-Christians as lost souls or even agents of the Devil. On that chapter they were quite indifferent to scientific insights. Further, their nationalism was suspicious of any and all foreign influences, outside the Anglo-Saxon world. I am thinking of James Forrestal, Stuart Symington, Nathan Twining, Teller, Leslie Groves, Hoyt Vandenberg and the Dulles brothers. Those among them who deviated from that common line were removed, sometimes ruthlessly. I only have to remind you of Forrestal, Bissell, Wisner or Hillenkoetter for instance. Today we are ruled by a similar cast of warriors. Look at Caspar Weinberger, our secretary of Defense or at Bill Casey, the head of the CIA or even at General Alexander Haig, the Secretary of State and there are many others like them in the team. They view everything in strategic military terms, like Kissinger and their main purpose is to maintain and increase American dominance worldwide. Naturally any factor that eludes identification and control is regarded by them as a threat and anything that shows potential for technological advancement becomes a matter of national security, hence to be hidden and kept out of the reach of the public. Knowledge is power but much more so when it is not shared with others, especially with your rivals and enemies."

I wanted to go deeper into this issue but the conversation was too broad and the group too large to allow that. We agreed that I would meet Richard at his residence on the next day to go into further details because I guessed that he was privy to much reserved information.

The debate continued on matters of theology and science. "Intellectually we are still in some ways an 19th century puritanical society" one of the guests opined. "Our state endorses in effect a literal interpretation of the Bible since it is held to be the founding document of our civilization. We think we live in an anthropocentric world above which is God who must look like an old man since he created us in his image a few thousand years ago, There is only one inhabited earth in an otherwise non-living universe and all other intelligent beings are angels and demons. Any evidence which disrupts that long-held belief is regarded as unacceptable and ignored as much as possible. Our society admits scientific discoveries only as long as they don't directly contradict the judeo-christian paradigm."

We evoked various phenomena of popular American culture that since the nineteen thirties had marked the country, through the radio with Orson Welles's famous "Mars Invasion" broadcast which generated a mild panic in 1938, through the Buck Rogers strips, as early as 1930 and through the widespread DC Comics which had introduced the general public to extraterrestrial characters in futuristic scenarii such as Superman and the other denizens of the Krypton planet from 1936 onwards.

"In Europe our initiation was more literary" I pointed out. "Erich von Daniken and Peter Kolosimo among others were best selling authors and of course we have, like the Russians many Science Fiction authors, some of high quality such as Arthur Clarke."

"Lovecraft and Philip Dick are brilliant American visionaries. Isaac Asimov appeals to a broader public" Sigismond added "but for the young and the less educated the comics written by Larry Siegel and others and published by the duo of Donnenfeld nd Leibovitz were real eye openers, even if subconsciously so and I believe that they reflected the wish of some people in the Establishment to get the majority used to the Alien presence while cashing in on the topic. Adamski and some other well known contactees blazed a trail which drew quite a few scientists like Puharich and researchers at Stanford Research Institute, NASA and the NSA. Then in 1966 Gene Roddenberry started the STAR TREK TV series and in 1977 Lucas released the original STAR WARS movie. By then we were fully in the space age."

That made everyone in the group ponder the incremental but major change in human consciousness triggered by the dissemination of information, both factual and imaginary, about non-human intelligent beings from the outer universe. There was little doubt, one of the guests pointed out, that the widely reported statements by famous people such as General Douglas MacArthur, President Truman, Wernher von Braun and other political, scientific and military leaders had influenced the proliferating science fiction production shortly after the second world war.

"Apart from blockbusters of the time such as *The Day The Earth Stood Still* which came out in 1951, various branches of our government directly or indirectly supported the production of various documentary style movies on the UFO situation from the mid-fifties on" Richard Sigismond recalled. "I still have copies of them. They are based on data collected by the military but skeptics found it easy to claim that they are allegorical scare-films alluding to the evil Commies as Aliens. One from 1956 is called *The Truth about the Flying Saucers* but the most factually accurate one is probably the one, released in the same year and entitled *Earth vs The Flying Saucers* which featured a lot of input from the Pentagon, just as *Close Encounters* twenty one years later, included much feedback from the CIA, according to its director Spielberg. Not long before, in 1976 Disney produced a very informative and objective film entitled *Overlords of the UFOS* but, probably under pressure from above, aired it only once. Then in 1979

Sandler and Ermenegger updated their documentary based on authentic film footage and called it *UFOs: It has begun.* Long before that the Government or rather the powers-that-be had settled on a systematic policy of letting sleeping dogs lie and chasing away anyone who would disturb them."

The evening ended soon after, but not before I had taken an appointment with Sigismond at his home on the following day.

V
Entering the Maze

Let me see, then, what thereat is, and this mystery explore
Let me heart be still a moment and this mystery explore

Edgar Poe, The Raven

THE STATE OF AFFAIRS

Sigismond had invited me to share a simple lunch at his house on Ninth Street and I got there by noon as requested. It was an unpretentious clapboard villa fronted by a little garden which, in that season glowed with multihued blossoms. I complemented the owner on his talents as a horticulturist and he accepted my praise with quiet pride. He had, he confided, won more than once neighbourhood and civic awards for his flowerbeds on which he spent a good deal time of time every day for six months of the year. The inside of his flat was cosy but austere and paneled with books on science, psychology, philosophy and of course on matters related to UFOs and related topics. A quick glance at the shelves revealed that almost all the classics of the genre published since the nineteen fifties, from Keyhoe to Edwards and from Cathie to Berlitz were there in volumes which looked well used.

"It is increasingly difficult to keep track of the mushrooming literature" the host told me with a slight shrug. "Now dozens of books and hundreds of articles, not to mention documentaries and TV reports are being produced every year and even though I spend a fair amount of money on my library, I can't find everything and I am running out of space and also of time to read. Of course not all works are of good quality or bring new information but it is hard to know until you go through them."

We sat down for a wholesome meal whose ingredients denoted Sigismond's organic philosophy. While we ate he told me that much of his income derived from his activities as a mining consultant. A trained psychologist, he did not practice and spent virtually all his free time on UFO related research and on his garden.

"We have a big network throughout the country and also abroad" he said "and we keep in contact frequently by telephone, fax and mail."

I asked him about the mining business. He had owned a silver mine in the state and had developed great expertise in that field but I knew that the market price of silver had long been too low for small scale operations to be profitable. I asked him about the famous silver cornering scheme mounted by the billionaire Hunt brothers some years ago and about the ensuing crash which had ruined those Texan tycoons.

"I'll put you in touch with a friend who was very much a part of it" Richard said with a hint of a smile and a glint in his eye. "He'll tell you more about how our system operates. He is a Texan but he comes to Aspen every now and then."

We gradually moved back to the topic that had brought me to him. I inquired if his work as a psychologist had led him to get into the Ufosphere.

"There is a strong connection" he acknowledged. "The governments here and in other states such as the USSR have long been studying the phenomenon in relation with psychic sciences and the understanding of the human mind. In the fifties Allen Dulles the head of the CIA started the MK-ULTRA program aimed at developing psychological warfare techniques but it involved analysis of UFO evidence and attempts at contact and communication with Alien intelligences. That is going on within the Intelligence Community and the Pentagon. MK Ultra seems to have taken over the mind control experiments carried out by Cameron in the late sixties."

"What do you know about the Gondola Wish program?" I asked.

He peered at me almost slyly through his thick glasses. "That is a project hosted by Stanford Research Institute since 1977. It was started by the Army Assistant Chief of Staff for Intelligence. In 1978 it was renamed Grill Flame and its experimental facilities were moved to Fort Mead in Maryland, the headquarters of our most secretive intelligence organization, the National Security Agency, under INSCOM within what is called Detachment G."

"Yes" I conceded "It seems that the National Research Council has come down heavily on that research, claiming that it is mumbo jumbo carried out a great public cost."

Sigismond shrugged. "The NRC would make such an assessment. They are hand in glove with the professional debunkers of the Rationalist Association which deny and ridicule anything remotely smacking of the paranormal. They don't admit that much of our contemporary technologies would have been characterized as paranormal only fifty years ago since even their underlying principles had not been discovered."

That was obvious to me. I was familiar with the trench and guerilla warfare carried out by a large section of the scientific establishment against any allegation or evidence that contradicts its cherished dogmas. Sigismond and I traded quotes from Popper, Polanyi and Kuhn who had highlighted the natural corporate hostility that societies and especially their ruling elite nourish towards revolutionary changes which challenge their control over knowledge and belief.

"GRILL FLAME, now codenamed the INSCOM Center Lane Project or ICPL for short is a SAP, a special access program aimed at exploiting remote viewing and other 'paranormal' clairvoyant and telekinetic abilities for strategic and tactical ends of national defence" Richard patiently explained. "It is now headed by General Albert Stubblebine, the head of the army for Intelligence and not much is known yet about its real operations and results. You must have read the names of a few of the psychics it has employed. McMoneagle, Ingo Swann and Ed Dames among others. There are apparently not many. The project appears to be small although it has been well funded."

"How exactly did it originate?" I inquired.

"Partly in the wake of MK-ULTRA and other such long-standing research undertakings" he replied. "Then there was the pioneering work done at the private Monroe Institute which was of high interest to some people in the military and in the scientific community. There is a small group of very high level physicists who are also psychologists and neuro-scientists. They combine cutting edge knowledge in electronics and quantic physics with an expertise in mental processes and the investigation of consciousness. Some of them, especially Harold Puthoff and Russell Targ are based at Stanford since several years but there is a mounting conservative reaction here, in science as in politics and I think those frontier fields may have to be abandoned soon due to establishment pressure, unless the researchers go further underground to escape scrutiny. Targ is seen as a rebel of sorts because of his non-conventional research and ideas. You know that he married the sister of the great dissident and chess genius Bobby Fischer, don't you?.."

I did not know that. If anyone had illustrated the repressive nature of the US socio-political regime, it was Fischer, the only American to have risen to the very peak of the steep pyramid of world chess mastery.

I asked if he knew about the specific UFO-dedicated aspect of the Grill Flame program.

"In 1977 a young psychologist called Alfred Lambremont Webre was tasked by the Centre of Social Policy at SRI with the job of reviewing evidence related to UFOs and presenting some conclusions to the Carter White House which wished to have a better understanding of the facts. However the Pentagon intervened forcefully and declared that the project was unacceptable since there were no UFOs and hence nothing to investigate scientifically. At that time SRI received 25% of its budget from the Armed Forces and the funding was threatened if the CSP persisted with its plan. Reluctantly Stanford closed the project down in 1978 and Webre left the institute soon after."

"What happened to his sponsors, Targ and Puthoff?"

"They were not directly his sponsors because they run a separate lab dedicated to electronics and bio-engineering. They are still there but they have set up independent platforms to evade some pressure. Targ founded a corporation called Delphi Associates with two partners last year to pursue his research on the physics of consciousness. The main funding comes from the Defence Intelligence Agency and the CIA, which says a lot about its nature. However only the military and the security outfits are willing to invest in such areas. Civilian and private scientific entities are afraid to touch them because of the attached stigma."

"I believe the Stanford Research Institute itself has been heavily connected to the military industrial complex from its inception right after the last World War, in the year when the Tavistock Institute was started in England with funding from the Rockefellers" I noted. "SRI's founders had links with Lockheed. At least one of them, Ernest Black did and much of the initial research was defense related. They invented the ARPANET, the electronic network to coordinate advanced research centres and have worked, with the Naval Research Observatory on Over-The-Horizon Radar systems to detect and track fast-moving high altitude targets over very long distance by bouncing long wave beams on the ionosphere. This enables them to monitor if not intercept alien craft as well almost anywhere on earth."

"You have referred to the MUSIC and MADRE OTH arrays but there is a lot more far out work going on at SRI" Sigismond noted. "With the assistance of our friend Jacques Vallée they have begun to expand the communications grid to connect academic and government institutions through the three media of packet radio waves, satellite and ARPANET and they are far ahead in Artificial Intelligence development. One of their teams headed by Lawrence Pinneo and David Wolf has worked on building a EEG-based mind-reading machine. There is also a big push on stealth technology which makes aircraft and ships invisible to radar. The president is a man called Bill Miller. Between you, me and the lamp-stand I have reasons to believe that some of those technologies are being reverse-engineered or at least are inspired by observations and retrievals of UFOs. There may be even be some actual technology transfer, direct or indirect from certain alien beings."

MJ-12

That was startling though not entirely unexpected information and I had to find out more.

"What makes you say that?" I asked after taking s sip from the black coffee mug he had brought from the tiny kitchen.

"I have my sources" he said in a low voice "but if you look closely at how and when Allen Dulles launched MK ULTRA in the fifties and put Sydney Gottlieb in charge of it, you can see that it was partly triggered by a number of UFO observations and interactions which pushed some high-ranking government people to investigate the twilight zone of reality. Of course the fear of the Soviets played a role but the Cold War was also used as a cover to do a lot of secret and weird things. I don't think I am the first to tell you about MJ-12?"

I shook my head uncertainly. He proceeded to tell me that according to some new sources it was a top-level unacknowledged committee made up of civilian and military officials who reported directly to the National Security Council and were supposed to gather and analyse all information and material related to UFOs and related issues.

"MJ-12, short for Majic or Majestic was part of the reorganization of the national security structure carried out in 1952 by the Rockefeller Commission, under President Eisenhower" Richard further explained. "Nelson Rockefeller really controlled the country with his brothers and the family's network of experts and dependents. He took charge of the planning to respond to major challenges and threats, whether from Communists or Aliens as Special Assistant to the President for psychological warfare."

"This was the time when the Rockefeller system groomed and moved to key positions a number of people who were to craft and run American policies right until today" I commented. "Averell Harriman, Kissinger, Brzezinski, Gordon Gray who was appointed the first

Director of the newly created Psychological Strategy Board in 1951 and was succeeded by Nelson himself, Nitze, Frank Wisner, Richard Helms and even Allen Dulles who later became Rockefeller's opponent belonged to that network which was also an incubator."

My host nodded and added: "Don't forget Prescott Bush the father of our vice-president and a close friend of Nelson's, General Haig the NSA and the present State and Defense Secretaries Schultz and Weinberger, the men from Bechtel, a long term industrial partner of the Rockefellers's Standard Oil. The MJ-12 organization appears to have had its inception as early as 1947 under President Truman when the watershed National Security Act was adopted following the Roswell and other events. It was formalized on the basis of a memo written by General Nathan Twining, in charge of the Roswell investigation to Cutler, Eisenhower's National Security Assistant. Ike set up the organization as an unacknowledged, *ad hoc* thinktank that officially never existed, together with the Operations Coordination Board, the OCB. So this secret system which is de facto in control of all UFO related matters is more than thirty years old."

"I guess MAJIC, or Majestic must have accumulated huge amounts of data and material, given the number of cases we know and all those we don't" I pointed "but who does it report to?"

"Technically to the National Security Council which itself is supposed to brief and advise the President but does it really work like that? The chain of command is not clear and the hierarchy is so opaque that the White House is probably not in the loop. Rockefeller set up the Planning Coordination Group in 1954 with himself as chairman but it seems it did not work and was dissolved before the end of that year. It may however have subsisted in a covert form. In 1955 Nelson convened the Quantico Study Group which crafted the "Open Skies Policy" to establish exchange of information with the USSR on all things of interest taking place in the earth's airspace, officially to prevent a war by mistake between the superpowers. Then the following year he set up the Special Studies Project which was headed by Kissinger. Its official report was released in 1957 and led to an acceleration in the arms race but there are reasons to believe that there was a classified agenda which involved assessment of the UFO and Alien situation. So in fact, running through all those committees and cells you have a parallel unaccountable and secret government that can perhaps override the known one. An ominous aspect of that whole clandestine process was the conversion of policy makers to modern behaviorist theories of human nature" Sigismond explained. "Those were rooted in Ewan Cameron's socio-psychological experiments which saw people as biological machines moved solely by responses to pleasure and pain. Once you wipe out the spiritual side of humanity you reduce people to living systems that are not so different from ants and cockroaches so that you may use them freely and destroy them when desired."

I carried on: "Love then is only an emotional impulse triggered by the sexual drive which itself is a response to the genetic programming for reproduction. Any human feeling is viewed as a reflection of neural conditioning evolved for survival and multiplication or as Skinner puts it: 'there is no soul, only sets of reflexes' and his predecessor John Watson claimed that men are built and not born. In that light there is no virtue, no sin, no good, no heaven and no Beyond."

"Extreme Darwinism leads to some kind of nihilism" Richard nodded gravely.

"Deconstructionism is the literary equivalent. When people in power are converted to that ideology, they are capable of committing the greatest crimes."

"How could a country so steeped since its origins in Biblical beliefs accept such an opposite worldview?" I wondered aloud.

"Protestantism traces a path toward rational agnosticism" my host suggested. "By trying to reduce Christianity to a historic moral teaching it makes its followers question the very supernatural event which is said to be at its source. When people no longer have an esoteric doctrine to refer to they build theories based on the current state of scientific knowledge and then they drop Christianity altogether or restrict it to social rites in their lives because it is incompatible with their intellectual persuasions."

"Well yes" I conceded "but only if they don't heed the great mystical thinkers that have flourished within the reformed churches, from Boehme to Blake. That is where the great divide lies in America, between the Transcendentalists on the one hand and the promoters of boundless materialism on the other." I thought of Ayn Rand again.

"And the latter want to remote control people, through drugs and radiation to ensure their obedience and prevent disorder..." my host began.

A Call from Professor Hynek

At that moment the telephone interrupted the dialogue with a monotonous jingle and Richard picked it up. "Hello Allen" he said in his evenly soft tone of voice. "You'll have a long life, I have a foreign visitor and we have been talking about you."

He conversed for a minute or two and then held up the receiver to me. "Allen Hynek from Chicago" he said "speak to him about his work."

I picked up the phone and greeted the well known astronomer from Northwestern University who answered me with polite formality. I remembered seeing him as a pipe-smoking bearded and bespectacled cameo actor for a brief moment in the final stage of Spielberg's blockbuster *Close Encounters of the Third Kind* a few years earlier.

I told him about my interest in the theme to which he dedicated much of his professional life and stated that I had read some of his books and was aware of the importance of his contribution to the area of ufology.

"It was thrust on me" he said almost apologetically "I originally thought I would be able to unravel the mystery and prove that it was all due to a combination of natural phenomena and human ignorance but then, while participating to successive Air Force funded projects, SIGN, GRUDGE and then BLUE BOOK I found myself faced with an intractable enigma which in some cases had only one somewhat satisfactory explanation."

"You never seem to have fully accepted it however" I objected.

"As a scientist I cannot take anything as proven unless it is reproducible under controlled conditions" Hynek pointed out. "As an astronomer I can't make assertions that properly should come from zoologists or biologists but if I apply my common sense I have to admit that the events I have investigated, however puzzling, can only be caused by intelligent actors since they involve machine-like objects far more powerful and sophisticated than what *homo sapiens* is able to build so far. At times living creatures which don't look human have been observed by multiple credible witnesses. We can't keep denying all those facts in the name of our long-held ideas about the universe."

"What changed your mind from being a skeptic like most of your colleagues to an eloquent exponent of what you believe" I asked.

"Some very serious and precise testimonies" he answered with hesitation "such as Clyde Tombaugh's. He was an outstanding astronomer who discovered Pluto and he described the UFOs he saw through is telescope. Then I had talks with the head of the Foreign Technology Division at the Pentagon, Ray Sleeper and he told me that his staff was keeping close tab on the UFO situation because they realized that there was much scientific and technological information to be gotten from its study, contrary to the official statements from government sources that there was nothing to it. It struck me that that there was a policy of denial and that I too was being pressured to give negative opinion and deny or hide facts. The worst example was provided by the head of BLUE BOOK Professor Condon who was openly committed to denying and ridiculing any evidence that went against his predetermined conviction. I felt he was only following the rule of the game secretly set by the CIA in the Durant Report of 1953. Obviously that is not scientific and not in good faith. It is not skepticism, it is obfuscation. In 1975, Jacques Vallée, your countryman and I wrote *The Edge of Reality* to try to account for what I call a M&M technology, encompassing matter and mind, two years after I founded CUFOS. I am convinced that we can't figure out the UFO phenomenon unless we admit that it overlaps the fields of physics and consciousness. Is that technologically possible? Many scientists answer in the negative. I say "Not for us, men so far but will it always be science-fiction?"

I was well aware of CUFOS, short for Centre for UFOS Studies. I also knew that, as a adviser to the initiative sponsored by Sir Eric Gairy, Hynek had addressed the UN on the topic in 1978 on behalf of his fellow experts Vallée and Claude Poher. I asked him about the NICAP, the National Investigation Committee on Aerial Phenomena.

"It was a major initiative supported by very prominent officials" Hynek said "and its very creation proved how important the UFO phenomenon was. I knew Major Keyhoe and he was a man of great integrity who did not agree with the decision made by some higher ups to keep the whole issue secret."

I recalled that a former technical consultant of the Lockheed Aircraft corporation, Thomas Townsend Brown had co-founded NICAP and that he was reputed to have invented a new technology known as "gravific capacitance" which seemed related to the method of propulsion used by at least some UFOs. However he had resigned within a year in 1957 under pressure from Keyhoe and other military officers who had turned the organization into a virtual preserve of the Navy. Brown's discovery had come to nought unless it had been spirited away into clandestine military laboratories and withdrawn from the public. I told Hynek that I knew about it from reading William Moore's book *The Wizard of Eletrogravity, The Man who invented how UFOs are powered*.

"Yes, that is all very intriguing, TT Brown was a wealthy independent researcher who fought the scientific and military establishment for much of his life. He is still with us, you know though quite old. Although he was supported by General 'Hap' Arnold, the father of the RAND corporation, physicists tend to disagree with his theory and the prevailing view is that what he called electrogravifics is in fact better described as ionic wind propulsion or magneto-hydro-dynamics although the so called "Biefeld-Brown effect" he demonstrated has not been convincingly explained in current theory" the Professor commented "As for NICAP it has been long ago taken over by the Intelligence Community which lets very little information out. A Franco-Russian aristocrat, Nicolas de Rochefort, who was a high level CIA officer became its vice-chairman and that says a lot, given that many other disinformation and psychological warfare experts joined him at NICAP."

"Tell me, Professor" I inquired "why do you think the US government and other governments as well are so determined to hide and deny the facts, as you found out during your years of association with the Blue Book Project?"

There was a pause on the line. Then I heard "I am not sure if anyone can fully account for that policy. Our strategic decisions are often inscrutable from a logical point of view. I feel a mixture of fear, deep-held religious prejudices and beliefs, military paranoia and business concerns. Our officials like to feel they are in control and they need everyone to believe this. We must be bigger, faster, richer stronger, better, more powerful than anyone else to justify our existence. Anything that eludes control and is instead potentially able to control or destroy us is so disturbing that it is unacceptable and even unthinkable. Turning a blind eye, at least publically is considered the best way to avoid dealing with it. For sure neither political nor religious leaders want to face popular scrutiny on this and even if a few were willing to, they are overruled by the majority of the elites."

"We were talking about Thomas Kuhn shortly before you called" I said "and the current paradigm does not really allow much room for a higher intelligence form from anywhere in the universe outside the realm of faith which is itself regarded as irrational so that it has no place in science or public affairs."

"Well, anything that is not accessible to our established metronomic theories is seen as irrational" the Professor answered. "Jacques Vallée has done a lot of work on what he calls High Strangeness phenomena but his theories are regarded as curious speculations into parapsychology and yet parapsychologists study many allegedly supernatural events according to scientific methods and have thereby proven them to be real. I tend to favor Feyerabend's demand for unrestricted scientific inquiry, free from the inhibitions imposed by current authorities and prevalent theories."

I said that I was hoping to meet Vallée since I had read a lot of his work and found him very challenging and mystifying. It was agreed that an opportunity would be provided.

CATTLE MUTILATIONS AND OTHER ENIGMAS

After we had said goodbyes and hung up the telephone, Richard also volunteered to introduce me to a few of his fellow investigators. We ended the conversation by evoking the cases of unexplained cattle and horse mutilations in the rural South West that he had investigated in the late seventies along with other experts. "The FBI was watching us closely and writing reports on our work" Sigismond explained. "I was one of those who concluded that UFOs might be behind those nightly surgical interventions which left dead animals on the ground after extracting some of their vital and reproductive organs. Witnesses reported lights and even flying discs around those places and the carcasses showed traces of having been dumped from a height. Then there were unmarked helicopters flying about at very low altitudes shortly after some of these sightings. The man who gathered the evidence and testimonies was New Mexico police officer Gabriel Valdez. Of course no one seems to know as yet why those animals were killed like thousands of others around the country in the last fifteen years."

I left his house and took a long walk in the quiet neighbourhood of shaded streets leading up to the Chautauqua Park and the sandstone Flatirons which looked like five giant slanted slabs waiting to be written on by a titanic celestial finger. Two commandments for every slab I fleetingly imagined. The Mormons would have grasped at the symbolism and settled there if they had come first. I thought of the enigma Sigismond and I had debated. The collected data raised so many questions that they challenged all contemporary notions of reality. As Vallée and others had noticed, they crossed the line between the physical world and the psychic realms and they forced us to redraw the borders customarily traced between subjective ideas and objective facts, if indeed there were any such borders.

I knew that some people had lost their minds or at least had been regarded as insane when going too deep into the UFO mystery. Some, like MacDonald had committed suicide; there were rumors that top ranking officials who had been exposed to at least some aspects of the UFO secret reality, such as Secretary of Defence James Forrestal and CIA veteran Frank Wisner had put an end to their days unless others had done it for them. I had read of Paul Bennewitz, an engineer in New Mexico who was convinced that in 1979 he had found proof for the existence of an Alien underground base deep beneath the Dulce plateau near his home and had even gotten funding from Air Force Intelligence (AFOSI) for his work. He was said to have gone mad. Yet he had taken snapshots of flying discs seemingly hovering around the plateau and even disappearing into it or emerging out of it and he also had intercepted specific unexplained electromagnetic signals. He believed that they were targeted at chips implanted in a number of people in the area.

Back in the early fifties, a senior Canadian official, Wilbert Smith had investigated the evidence secretly gathered by the US Government on behalf of his superiors and come back with hard proof of the phenomenon and of its intelligent but 'meta-human' nature.

He left various thought provoking notes on the information he had gleaned over the years. I had read and reread one of his most significant messages and I could remember it almost literally: "*Some of the communications have been on a face-to-face basis but I have not been so honored myself. Some of the communications have been by ordinary radio, and I have received a few messages by this means. But by far the majority of the communications are by what we call Tensor Beam transmission, which uses a type of radio with which we are only vaguely familiar, and which I couldn't possibly attempt to describe now. However, the mental images of the person wishing to transmit are picked up electrically amplified and modulated into a tensor beam, which is directed to the person to whom the transmission is addressed, and within whose brain the mental images are recreated. The transmissions are therefore very precise, and independent of language. I have had some experience with these transmissions myself and can say that they are like nothing within the conventional experiences of earth people.*"
"The question might be asked—'if these people are our brothers, and they are interested in our welfare, why do they remain so aloof?' The answer is

available. There is a basic law of the universe, which grants each and every individual independence, and freedom of choice, so that he may experience and learn from his experiences. No one has the right to interfere in the affairs of others—in fact; our ten commandments are directives against interference. If we disregard this law, we must suffer the consequences, and little thought will be shown that our present world state is directly attributable to violation of this principle. When we enter this life, we do so to participate in certain events, the sequence of which were established before our birth, and if altered substantially would deprive us of experiences necessary to our development. We have built-in protection against altering substantially the sequences in that we do not seriously know of them. But these people from outside have a much greater knowledge than we have, and have a means of perceiving sequences, which must not be changed. Therefore, while they have every desire in the world to help, and stand by ready willing and able to do so, they are not permitted by cosmic law to interfere."

That testimony was consonant with several others. What Sigismond and Hynek had said pointed in the same direction. Credible analysts and experts believed that certain agencies in the government, particularly the National Security Agency, were electronically in touch with some of those non-human visitors and even that some physical meetings had been held.

There were connections between at least five developments that had occurred during the fifties and sixties: The proliferation of UFO sightings, encounters and reports had led to the enforcement of rules of secrecy from military and official authorities in the USA and in other countries while the American government was being reorganized in keeping with the acceleration of the arms race as an effect of the intensifying Cold War. Simultaneously UFO inspired literature and filmography was invading popular culture while political and military leaders such as General MacArthur were warning their citizens about the possibility of an Alien invasion and interplanetary wars. I could discern an underlying pattern behind those processes but it was yet too complex to be mapped. Would I succeed where so far all seemed to have failed or at least had not shared it with the public?

I felt that I had seized a few random strands from a vast cobweb-like network that spread far beyond the wildest reaches of imagination, across politics, advanced scientific research, high finance and into spiritual and paranormal dimensions. I did not quite grasp the size and scope of that maze but I was at least sensing its reality. I evoked fleetingly the image of Theseus stepping into the labyrinth holding one end of a thread. I could not fathom where it would lead me but I saw a ray of hope lighting the way towards the goal I had set myself and hoped Ariadne was unspooling the string at the cave's mouth, waiting for my return.

VI

A Supper at Higman's

I can't believe this is the land from which I came...
All I wanna say is that
They don't really care about us...

Michael Jackson, They don't Care About us

SKULLDUGGERY IN HIGH PLACES

By seven o'clock I was back at Higman's house and discovered its rather complex internal layout. It had been enlarged in stages over three decades at the whim of the owner who had taught himself architecture and carpentry in order to restructure his home according to his wishes. The many rooms were filled with heterogenous furniture, chosen more for comfort than for style and all sported telephone sets. "Seventeen in all" the host proudly said.

The walls were covered with paintings, drawings, etchings and photographs on every possible subject from landscapes and abstract figures to portraits and caricatures. The place had a cosy and studious feeling and I felt I was in the den of an Academic or, as Higman put it "a self-professed know-it-all." I knew his reputation as a polymath which provided a welcome relief from both the specialized and the deliberately non-academic environments that the country usually provided. Higman was proud of his eccentric salience which surrounded him with a mixture of awe and irony. His nasal voice and clipped accent (he had spent one year in a British university) could lend itself to a snarl or rise into the lion-with-a-cold's roar that characterizes an angry Briton. However when in a good mood, the old professor was the epitome of charm and he served me a drink and promised me *artichauds farigoule, fillet mignon* and *tarte tatin* as he was proud of his autodidactic talents as a French chef. I realized it would be a big change from the customary organic foods and healthy Japanese and Mediterranean recipes that were *de rigueur* in Aspen.

A few other guests were in the living room. Three or four were fellow professors at the University and another was Raymond Maurice whom I had met earlier in Aspen and who had put me in touch with his friend Higman. Maurice was the son of the homonymous famous photographer and his mother Eleanor Ingersoll was a noted painter from the distinguished New England family of that name. The lady of the house, Marion Higman made a brief appearance to greet us and vanished as she had an evening out. With her grey bob of hair she looked as reserved and prim as her husband, who boasted of a welsh ancestry, was loud and temperamental. I found out later that he was a staunch believer in all-male confabulations around gargantuan meals in which women might have felt out of place.

The discussion began in right earnest when I referred to Higman's past clashes with censorious public powers in McCarthy's era. In the fifties he had attracted the ire of the FBI's famous or infamous head, J Edgar Hoover after publically calling the Bureau a secret police.

"I never apologized" the professor testily said "I merely conceded that it was not a police but a church, which was probably even a worse thing to say."

"Yet, the FBI was acting like a secret police in the most reviled sense of that term" Maurice pointed out "They used viciously devious methods to discredit, tarnish, sully and compromise their targets, planting false news, writing anonymous defamatory letters, attributing documents and statements to their victims and spreading rumors about their private lives. No blow was too low."

"That was all part of CointelPro" Higman noted "and it was in parallel to the CIA's MockingBird Operation which spread disinformation in the media. Hoover had an obsession with homosexuality which he tried to attach to many of those he opposed but it turned out later that he himself lived for many years with a man and gave many other hints that he was a fag as well as a—hole." From his reputation and aspect I had gathered that the old scholar was prone to utter profanities.

"That is not surprising" quipped Professor John Murphy, a dapper white haired gentleman who was afflicted with multiple sclerosis. "The Nazis unleashed a campaign against homosexuals in Germany and yet many of their leaders and idols were of that persuasion. Roehm built up Hitler with his SA and Stefan George was one of the many open practitioners of what used to be called 'amour anglais' in France, I am told."

"Humor aside, the turn taken by our government soon after the Second World War was very disturbing" said another guest, Professor Merrill Adams, a gentle, bald, bespectacled and bow-tied former Harvard-educated pupil of Talcott Parsons (he looked vaguely like him) and Sorokin. "It took time for people to realize how closely they were being monitored and spied on and by the time they became aware of surveillance, it became broadly acceptable to most. It was regarded as a necessary protection from the communist peril and indeed there were many spies who vindicated the fear-mongers. As a result people have become used to disinformation and few try to critically analyse the kind of narcissistic nationalist propaganda that passes for news."

I had noticed at first sight that Professor Adams was a living image of that eminent type known as the Anglo-Saxon Ivy League Intellectual.

"Of course there were spies" said Higman "how can there be none when a society creates so much alienation amongst its members as ours does? The witch hunt generates even more dissent and when it becomes known that national leaders are planning to wipe out a entire part of the human race to sate their thirst for power, some people are likely to try to prevent that by informing the intended victims of the genocide. Take the Rosenbergs for instance. They copied files smuggled out of Theodore Von Karman's office from the National Advisory Committee on Aeronautics of which he was the chairman and passed them on to the USSR and then they obtained some documentation about the Manhattan Project through Ethel Rosenberg's brother David Greenglass who was employed at Los Alamos but that began during the War when Stalin was a US ally and people high up in Washington knew that the Rosenberg were members of a Communist cell, with Max Elitcher, Harry Gold, William Perl, Jacob Golos and others. Yet they were only arrested in 1950."

He went on: "The early fifties saw the rise of the anti-Marxist phobia and the country was on the warpath once again. By 1953, President Eisenhower himself was getting increasingly cut off from the Pentagon and Curtis Le May, the commander of the Strategic Air Command refused to let the White House in on his plans to nuke hundreds of Soviet cities and kill sixty million people at a first strike. The generals were out of control and the civilian leaders were not allowed access to the most sensitive military installations."

I thought briefly of what I had read once about Julius and Ethel Rosenberg. During their trial, it had transpired that they had referred to "airships of – or from – space" but that tell-tale hint had been ignored, probably for national security reasons and the Rosenbergs executed, taking their secrets with them. Was there fear in official circles that they might say more if they were allowed to live?"

"There was widespread outrage at the time that, despite the generous welcome the US had given Jewish immigrants and refugees before and during the War, most of those who gave or sold secrets to the USSR were from that community" Maurice commented. "They were accused of being ungrateful, especially since Stalin's regime was being so harsh on them."

"Was the Rosenberg case not an entirely jewish affair from both sides, beginning with Professor von Karman and the scientific leaders of the Manhattan Project?" I queried. "If I remember well, the Rosenberg's Soviet handlers, the American judge who sentenced them, the prosecutor, the defense lawyer and even the executioner at Sing Sing belonged to that religion or nation. Was that not the reason why they given the maximum penalty by their coreligionaries? Anti-Communist Jews like Roy Cohn would have wanted to make an example of traitors within the community."

"The Knight Kaddosh's dagger" Merrill Adams quipped. I was not sure whether all understood that evocation of Masonic symbolism.

"Let us remember that the Bolshevik revolution was led mostly by Jews" Higman retorted. "Stalin himself turned against them late in his life but he had saved vast numbers of them by waging total war on the Reich and he was replaced by Khruschev who restored the Jews to their former eminent status in the Soviet Union. Many of the top Apparatchiks had close American relatives in Brooklyn, as Winston Churchill noticed, and some of them are now at the pinnacle of the Wall Street and Fifth Avenue pyramids. The umbilical cord between the Jews and the Soviet Union has never been severed and many of them never wanted the US to be the sole superpower with a monopoly on the ability to exterminate mankind. I have spent a long time investigating the Alger Hiss espionage affair and there too you see a very strong Israelite ingredient. Hiss was of German Jewish origin and Whittaker Chambers, his accuser had long been involved through his wife Esther with an almost entirely Ashkenazi communist group in the US. The important members of the American Workers' Party and of the Soviet espionage network in this country belonged to it."

"What is almost eerie" Murphy commented thoughtfully "is that the development of nuclear weapons was completely controlled and mostly staffed by them. I am not only talking of Einstein, Fermi, Oppenheimer, Rabbi and Teller but also of well less known names like Ross Gunn and Philip Adelson or Oak Ridge's Research Director Alvin Weinberg. Our nuclear navy was since its inception in the hands of Admiral Hyman Rickover. I don't think there are many examples in history of a world changing military technology being created and controlled by members of a single ethno-religious group."

There was an instant of probably embarrassed silence. I realized we had broached a topic that was almost taboo.

THE BLACK SCIENCE IN GOVERNMENT LABS

"What do you know of psychological warfare techniques developed by the government?" I asked, orienting the conversation towards the theme of my main interest though I did not expect anybody to bring out its more covert dimension.

Heads shook around the table. "The Black Science" Raymond Maurice muttered after taking a sip of Cabernet Sauvignon.

"Disturbing stuff" Higman said, while taking his knife through the fillet mignon. "Some of the research began at the Allen Memorial Institute in Montreal. A professor Donald Cameron there carried out a project on behalf of the CIA, from 1957 on to induce coma for months on end through a mixture of drugs and what he called electro-convulsive therapy. The goal was to make dissident subjects become obedient and forget 'subversive opinions'. Of course it was all done under the label of medical research but it amounted to a follow up to earlier experiments by the Nazis in Germany and the overall objective was to achieve mind control."

"I think that those sinister tests began well before that, even before World War II" another guest said. "We all know of the CIA's use of LSD and other drugs for political purposes, tellingly alluded to as mind rape."

"Heard of *Operation Midnight Climax?*" Maurice put in. "It involved having unwitting men visiting prostitutes in CIA safehouses and being given LSD without their knowledge to find out the effects."

"Some in our government seem to have no dearth of macabre imagination" Murphy opined "and I am convinced that Richard Condon based himself on real facts when he wrote *The Manchurian Candidate.* One desideratum of the cloak and dagger agencies is to create perfect remote controlled assassins and I for one am keenly aware of the potentially nefarious use of the psychological tests that most Americans are subjected to as soon as they enter the education system. The data are stored and used to build profiles which are supplied to any government department or even, I suspect to major private corporations when needed."

"The State always invokes the excuse that our enemies are doing things that we must do too for self-defence" Maurice replied. "Since the Ruskies are allegedly practicing "brainwashing," we should be able to do it even better than them. People like the CIA spook Edward

Hunter pointed to the reports by Luria from Moscow in the nineteen thirties to argue that the Soviets had mastered the ability to hypnotically train agents to become criminals and Watkins managed to induce hallucination to similar ends in his subjects from 1947. Two years later, the recently founded Rand Corporation published Janis's Report on mind control techniques in the service of national security. We have never looked back since, in spite of the Church and Rockefeller Commissions."

"Just think of MK-ULTRA and its managers, Gottlieb and Abrahamson" Higman declared with a snort. "Gottlieb was mad as a hatter and enjoyed wearing a SS uniform in drunken private parties. Many of those programmes were run by barmy SOBS. No wonder they produced horror shows. That is what they had been picked and were paid to do." He emptied his glass with a flourish.

"Gottlieb was a model for the movie character of Dr Strangelove" someone else said. "Although Hermann Kahn is more often cited as the original, Gottlieb means 'God's love'...."

"I was told that after retiring in 1972, Gottlieb became a peace activist and a social worker in India and is now living in a farm in Culpeper, Virginia where he practices vegetarianism and takes care of the environment" Maurice said with a smile. "I suppose he figured that he has a lot to atone for."

"Many of our chief spooks and Frankensteins or their children went to India or embraced spiritual cults" another guest remarked while stabbing a carrot with his knife.

"Back to my question" I insisted "what about the history of psy-war in this country and why did it become so important?"

"The American government developed a dangerous addiction at the end of the war, following Hiroshima and Nagasaki" Higman said while holding up his glass to the light. "We thought that we could achieve total victory over anyone. After Germany the generals wanted to bring the USSR to surrender or destruction and all means were good to get there. In 1952, Whittaker Chambers's book *Witness* triggered widespread fear that the country was falling prey to communist subversion and motivated our current President to embark on a lifelong anti-commie crusade. The most dangerous weapon of the Soviets according to some was the psychological warfare arsenal so that effective countermeasures had to be developed."

"Early reports came from Seymour Fisher, at the Bureau of Social Science Research, under a contract awarded to RAND by the Air Force" Maurice recalled. "The technique combined electroshocks, hypnosis and drugs like paraldehyde and sodium amytal to induce amnesia—codenamed BZ—and control behaviour, either on people 'brainwashed' by Communists or on individuals who could be used as agents, assassins or saboteurs."

"I remember reading about the CIA's strategy of LSD warfare back in 1953" Higman interjected with a wicked grin.

"I think though that LSD lost its shine when it was seen that it made people question everything and embrace some fuzzy mystical ideas borrowed from Asia" I said.

"That is when they brought in heroine from the Golden Triangle to destroy people who could become dangerous dissidents" Maurice declared. "They were carrying out an agenda suggested by Gottschalk who advocated controlling citizens through addictions."

"I heard they stockpiled tons of those chemical agents at the Edgewood Arsenal among other places" another guest said. "Testing behaviour altering drugs on thousands of unwitting Americans and foreigners was big business. One of the CIA'S own people, Ted Olson killed himself in 1953 after being given a large dose of LSD without his knowledge, according to the 1975 Congressional Report. Usually though the targets were military personnel, university students, children or members of minorities such as conscientious objectors or seven day Adventists. It sounds almost funny despite it being horrifying."

"Have those practices been stopped?" I asked " I am told that more than hundred and thirty chemical products were synthesized and tested from the early fifties and into the seventies so there must be a considerable amount of information on what could be done."

"The official story is that it is all over" Maurice replied "but who believes official stories? Although MK ULTRA and ARTICHOKE are supposed to have been terminated I am willing to bet that other, more sophisticated programmes are going on under other names, in places like Camp Peary which is remored to be a CIA training ground for zombified assassins. Dr Gilbert Jensen who ran it for many years is said to have programmed both Lee Harvey Oswald and James E Ray who shot Martin Luther King. I've heard that the TV series *Mission Impossible* with its self-destructing messages was inspired by his methods, except he is said to have manufactured self-destructing killers as well."

"We have many cases of unexplained, extreme anger and violence among our patients" noted a professor of psychology at the table who had hitherto remained silent "and both government and private research labs have all along been testing drugs to combat mental illness but the border between health and military research is blurred. For instance I know of the experimental use of anectine at the Vacaville federal prison in California and it has been found that it generates uncontrollable states of violent fury in patients as an after effect. Correctional medical facilities have also been test sites through the Law Enforcement Assistance Administration for many other problematic substances like bulkocaptine which can cause schizophrenia. I and many of my colleagues are concerned about the unregulated or clandestine administration of such potent neurochemical agents."

"One of the most ominous project that I heard about was carried out at Bethesda Naval Hospital under the direction of one Dr Gaefsky" Maurice commented. "It began as early as 1947, lasted for several years and it intended to isolate drugs that could be used to penetrate and control the minds of individuals to force them to reveal all their secrets and carry out actions suggested to them, including suicide."

"I wonder if there is any connection with the suspicious suicide of Secretary James Forrestal in 1949" I said in lower tone. "He had fallen into a very strange state of depression and apparent incoherence and was taken into actual custody by military physicians, as you know. He was under twenty four hour watch. They separated and isolated him from his friends, family and even his confessor until he hung himself from his room window."

Nods and glances were exchanged fleetingly around the table. I was not going to say more about what I had heard regarding Forrestal's death as I felt the group might not be receptive. Merrill Adams broke the silence by opining that all those operations were related to the McCarthyist mindset and its focus on ideological warfare and repression.

"All for freedom and democracy" quipped the host.

"I still have my doubts about the efficacy, if I may use that term, of those sinister recipes" Murphy submitted with scholarly prudence. "Are many of those claims not manufactured by opinion makers on both sides to scare the public or the enemies? I am convinced that various secret societies play a very big role in our country and abroad, perhaps a decisive one but their most powerful weapon is fear and our government is one of the world's major fear mongers. However the substance behind all this is not necessarily what it is made out to be. I remember reading a book by an Englishman called Sir William Stephenson. The book is entitled *A Man called Intrepid* and it talks about the deployment and use of "zombie agents" precisely, by the Intelligence Service right from the end of the second world war but how much of it is novelized or at least exaggerated? The author may have wanted to impress the world with the superhuman powers of MI-6 or what it was called them."

"Actually, I rather believe that novels tend to lag behind reality. You may recall that famous quote: 'One reason to keep something secret is that it is incredible.' The Sunday Times back in the summer of 1975 carried an article quoting a Navy psychologist from the San Diego Neuropsychiatric lab, one Colonel Narut if my memory is correct, who confirmed that the navy performed audio-visual desensitization on certain prison inmates in order to turn them into fearless and remorseless killers. Those individuals were then sent to important posts like US missions abroad as Marines, members of

Special Forces or security guards." That was my rather lengthy retort to the old professor's argument.

"Yeah, I can believe some of the famous assassins in our recent political history like Sirhan Sirhan when he shot Robert Kennedy may have been programmed and drugged" Raymond pitched in. "After all we had in this country the famous Professor Estabrooks who conducted in-depth research on the criminal mindset and the possibility to harness it. His work was closely supervised by our military and Intel authorities. Also, one of the key men behind the conspiracy to kill JFK, George de Mohrenschild is reported to have shot himself under hypnotic suggestion before he could make further revelations about what he knew."

"I know that specific ultrasounds have been tested for their power to affect brain matter and modify consciousness" the psychologist said. "In particular, low frequency sounds can make people sluggish, drowsy and erase or dim their memories so that subjects are no longer in position to report correctly what they did or witness and don't develop remorse for their actions, which is a key factor in preventing confessions. That condition is also highly amenable to hypnosis."

"As always there is a context" Merril Adams argued. "If you recall the statement by CIA boss Helms in 1964, he claimed that the Soviet State was trying to create the perfect communist man through a combination of cybernetics and behavioural conditioning..."

"But he also said that the US was possibly ahead of the Russians in the mastery of some of those techniques" Higman remarked. "Of course not to build a communist man but rather to craft an obedient consumer and worker in the free market economy."

"Part of that work was carried out by W Ross Adey at the Brain Research Institute in LA in the sixties. One goal was to achieve some remote control over the brain without implanting electrodes" the psychologist confirmed. "Obviously that would be an improvement on the rather crude methods which José Delgado experimented on animals but the end is the same, the creation of a "psycho-civilized society" controlled by machines. In theory it can even sound laudable as it may be the only way to regulate human behaviour and prevent criminal and other disruptive acts which seem intrinsic to our species and to animal life in general but then, no one can tell what we are getting into."

"Eric Fromm warned us about that in his book *The Revolution of Hope*" Murphy mused. "The dream of an ideal society can rapidly become a nightmare as we saw time and again in history."

ANECDOTES FROM A WORLD AFFAIRS CONCLAVE

We had reached dessert which consisted in Higman's renowned tarte tatin and fueled by the flowing wine, the hitherto heavy though loud conversation took a lighter turn. We went over the history of the Boulder World Affairs Conference, our host's best known achievement and he related a few amusing incidents that had taken place since its inception.

"As you may have noticed, I have a soft corner for the French" Higman said with a wink directed at me. "When I started the WAC in 1948 Boulder was a corral and there was no tradition of debate on international affairs and culture. My first speaker was a French official from the UN, a Monsieur Louis Dolivet who wowed all the good local people. From that tiny beginning it grew and grew and now celebrities are vying to be invited even though they are not paid and are not even reimbursed their travel expenses. This is fairly unique in our country where time is money."

I had glanced earlier at the long list of famous names that had participated, from Eleanor Roosevelt to Henry Kissinger and Timothy Leary and from Arthur Muller to Buckminster Fuller and Ralph Nader. All political and ideological tendencies had made an appearance in that liberal platform which was viewed as a predominantly leftist talking shop. One of its most assiduous guests was indeed Adam Hochschild, the founder of *Mother Jones*.

"I still recall getting phone calls from Mrs Arthur Miller for her husband" Higman said with a glint in his eyes. "Of course she was Marilyn Monroe. I wish she would have come with him but I resisted the temptation to start a conversation because I realized that she did not particularly want to be recognized."

The evocation of the most famous star of her day brought to my mind her tragic end on which I had heard reports that connected her with the main theme of my investigations but I did not bring it up.

We had gone though the copious meal and Higman gave the signal to rise and move to the drawing room where he wanted to make us see a documentary of the espionage trial of Alger Hiss to which passing references had been made at the table.

"Imagine the impact on our country when a high ranking bureaucrat who was the main architect of the UN and had represented us at Dumbarton Oaks and San Francisco was accused of being a Soviet spy!" the old professor explained. "As a young man I remember combing the newspapers to get every bit of the unfolding trial."

"It really rebuilt a fence or rather dug a pit between two Americas" Merrill Adams remarked "the internationalists and the conservative isolationists."

"Well it combined the issues that fascinate and concern Americans" Maurice added, "the totalitarian peril, treason, espionage, high class privilege, the destiny of the US and homosexuality which Chambers confessed to publicly."

AMERICA IN THE EYES OF ITS WRITERS

On the next day I had been invited by Professor Murphy to lunch with him at the University Faculty Club on Baseline Road whose dining room, with its white tablecloths and napkins and uniformed staff preserved the gentility of olden days on a campus known for its informality and whose main student cafeteria was called the Alferd Packer grill, after a notorious gold prospector from the Wild West era who had turned into a cannibal to survive a bitter winter storm in the high Rockies.

A biopic had recently been made about that sinister figure whose grave lies not far from Boulder in Littleton. I could not help feeling for a fleeting meeting that Packer and fellow gold-diggers who had become his victims symbolized a particular aspect of America's history; "how the west was won." He had indeed become some sort of folk hero and the University Grill beckoned patrons with the macabre invite 'Have a Friend for lunch.' Fortunately Murphy had not called me there.

My host had the demeanour of an Anglo-Saxon gentleman of the Old School, complete with bowtie and tweed. While he walked with difficulty due to his illness he was remarkably agile intellectually and proved to be a brilliant and humorous conversationalist. Like many of his generation he soon evinced his concern for the future of the country.

"For anyone brought up on our Classics, from Washington Irving to Henry James and from Hawthorne to Whitman, the evolution of our society offers a sorry sight" he noted with a pained expression on his pale, lined and expressive face.

"Are you one of those who see the fulfillment of Poe's cryptic forecasts in current developments?" I asked, knowing that I could expect an expert comment.

"Not only his" Murphy replied instantly. "He was uniquely profound and prophetic but some of our founding fathers saw the problems inherent to the social theory they embraced and to the system of government we had set up. Jefferson and Franklin both distrusted the extreme mercantile materialism of British liberals as well as the Puritanism of the Plymouth Rock Pilgrims while Hamilton was wary of divorcing certain traditional European institutions in our yearning for utopian republican freedom. In later years Emerson and his followers rejected industrial capitalism as a way of life and Henry James went into voluntary exile in Europe to flee the rootless race to riches of his countrymen."

"I think Tocqueville as an outsider from the Old World was perhaps the most perspicacious observer of your country" I added. "He foresaw the likely effects of ruthless individualism long before the concept of social Darwinism was invented."

"Success here is contingent on self-promotion. One of our heroes is Barnum and another one is Houdini since our society functions as a circus. Even a great writer like Mark Twain had to perform a mystifying theatrical act for much of his life in order to win fame and wealth" the professor pointed out, smiling wryly.

I was given other instances of his humor when he quipped that the current president of the university had "met culture once by chance" and when he opined that the average American was "a Holden Caulfield wanting to be John Galt," thereby linking two emblematic characters of modern national literature.

He was more serious when we discussed some of the great writers of the past, Poe, Melville and Pound.

"I think that Poe, in his dark and tormented broodings described the United States in the allegory of the *House of Usher*" he mused. "The year 1839 was a difficult time for the country, particularly trying for him as he was suffering more than others in the aftermath of the major economic panic two years earlier. He foresaw the coming conflict between the increasingly industrial North and the agricultural, slave-owning South and depicted it through the sly and deadly animosity between the possibly incestuous Usher siblings Frederick and Madeline which leads to the apparent death of the sister whom Frederick buries even though she is still alive. He himself is mentally ill, an opium addict and finds not a moment of peace which is also the state of our nation. The United States in Poe's days was cleft in two over the issue of slavery just like the Usher mansion through which runs a crack from the roof down and which is doomed to fall apart at the end of the story."

"Yes" I nodded "the mysterious illness that Madeline suffers from may be seen as a symbol of the possession and trade in slaves, though of course it may be a mere psychological portrait."

"Yet, her entombment does not settle the issue as she soon emerges from the coffin and murders her brother" Murphy retorted. "They die together and the family house colapses and burns. In a way you know I think that our Civil War, a quarter of a century after the book was written, led to a premature burial of the South which has not healed yet from the devastation and the humiliation. Many of our current problems stem both from the arrogance of fratricidal victory in the North and the bitterness of the defeated side which has fed the lingering fires of racism, lynching laws, vigilante justice and colonialistic attitudes. We are indeed a divided house as Poe saw it."

"He was also a lucid observer of the character of this country's government" I noted. "The physician of the Ushers is a bumbling and enigmatic character who is said to have been inspired by the then president Martin van Buren, nicknamed "Martin van Ruin" by some. By that time it was obvious to many that the presidency was more of a façade for the real powers behind the scene and its holders were often ridiculed.

Personally, I was tremendously impressed with Poe's novel *Eureka*. In France it was translated by Baudelaire a few years after its first publication. The author condensed in it his scientific visions about the future which are far ahead of the knowledge of his time. He was perceptive enough to critique the scientific method by singling out one of its main flaws: an excessive reliance on procedure at the cost of intuitive freedom and acceptance of evidence."

"I agree" the professor responded with a euphoric expression. "Poe was a mystic in the sense that he could sense and understand the ways and mysteries of nature. He perceived the cyclical character of creation, the expansion of the cosmos and the principle of relativity."

"And he realized that time and space are inseparable" I added. "He even guessed that there are many universes around and within the one we know about. What Jules Verne was to technology, Poe was to science."

"Yet he exhibits a troubling facet of the racial beliefs on which this nation was founded" Murphy objected. "His *Arthur Gordon Pym* is read by some as a rather gothic allegory of the American national quest for identity and discovery on a dark and lurid journey which features various massacres and even cannibalism. Our country is a product of seafaring, from inbound and outbound explorers, traders and adventurers. The dichotomy between the allegedly ugly, cruel and deceitful blacks and the whites is epitomized at the end of the novel in the discovery of another world and the vision of the snow-white shrouded figure which closes the book. Is that not a reflection of the ultimate American utopia: an all-white, anglo-saxon polar race ruling an ideal other world—or inner earth—yet to be found?"

"We can't entirely blame authors for sharing some of the almost universally held notions of their time" I cautioned "but I agree that vast numbers of Americans have not necessarily moved away from those prejudices. I am also fascinated by the strange insights of Herman Melville, another visionary writer who in some ways depicted the United States allegorically in *Moby Dick*. The central characters of the novel have biblical names, in keeping with the country's Calvinist neo-judaic roots but the wide mix of people and origins reflects the "salad bowl" of the American population. The seer of the story is an Indian Parsee, Fedallah and the captain is a fanatic devoured by the desire for revenge, rather typical of those who believe in the law of Talion but some of the other important figures are African or Polynesian, like Queequeg whose coffin, made of American wood is the only object that remains on the surface after the sinking of the whaling ship, as if the indigenous peoples were to be the sole survivors of civilisational collapse..."

"Not to forget that Captain Ahab's ship is called the *Pequod*, after the New England native tribe" I inserted.

"And that he can only be killed by hemp according to Fedallah's prediction, which seems to hint at the nefarious and decisive function of drugs in the American society. Moby Dick is also a very enigmatic beast. He is seen as an embodiment of the devil by Ahab who expresses our typical colonizing attitude towards nature, whose wild animals are vermins to be exterminated. Everything that escapes man's control must be killed but in the end Ahab is carried into the abyss by his nemesis, the sperm whale, as if to warn us that nature will take us to our grave if we try to destroy it. Moby Dick becomes a living hearse in the words of the novel."

"So there is a really strong current of ecological thinking in the American tradition" I commented. "This is how people like John Muir, Gifford Pinchot, Walt Whitman and others laid the foundation of the natural conservation movement."

"Fortunately, there is a great wealth of thought and pioneering experimentation in our history" Murphy argued with genuine passion. "It is linked with the great mystical current in England that adopted or produced Swedenborg, Shelley, Blake, the Lakist poets, Coleridge and Ruskin. I am an admirer of our great philosopher John Adams. Yet our heroes have by now lost the intellectual war to the utilitarians, pragmatists, liberals and other children of John Locke. The romantics of our literature are studied less and less and replaced by the cynical authors of the last half century like Joseph Heller and Company who leave little room for hope and idealism."

We had reached the stage of coffee at the end of the meal and we both had to go.

"I really enjoyed our conversation" I said. "As Howard Higman told you, I plan to enter the University and do a PhD in sociology but I look forward to gaining further insights from you."

As we stood up, he shook my hand and took a few unsteady steps towards the door and then half-turned around, looked at me and said: "I tried to give you my perspective on our nation but I feel there is a deep, dark mystery at the core of our present state and I see you want to explore it. I wish you luck but be careful."

"It is like a Moby Dick" I replied "but I don't wish to kill it, just understand it."

VII

Over the Mountains

*"Over the mountains
Of the Moon
Down the valley of the Shadow
Ride, boldly ride
The Shadow replied -
If you seek for Eldorado"*

Edgar Poe, Eldorado

THE JET SET PARTY

Scott and I drove back to Aspen on the next day as we had both done what we wanted in Boulder. On the way we were surprised by a sudden storm whose violence struck me. Torrents of rain morphing into a a hail of pingpong sized icicles poured out of a dark ashen sky. To protect the car from the relentless pounding we stopped under the awning of a gas station and waited for the mercifully brief deluge to end. "The extremes of the climate help explain the violence and even the craziness of the American mindset" Halazon suggested, half-jokingly.

On the next evening I was invited with Nancy to a great party thrown by one of the wealthy denizens of Aspen. The host's house was on the outskirts of the town in the direction of Aspen Highlands. By the time we arrived at dusk, amidst a tide of imposing SUVs, customized jeeps, boxy range rovers and road-hugging sports cars the sprawling timber and stone mansion was full of the habitual elite crowd, some of which had recently landed in private jets flown in from both coasts. A band played nostalgic Country and Pop tunes from the seventies in alternation. I heard Southern drawls, mid-West twangs and Texan accents emerge from the symphony of voices which also included the high pitched San Fernando Valley upspeak and New York's nasal intonations. Two or three Mexican oligarchs were recognizable by their tawny complexions, despite the ski slope and surfing tans of blonder guests, as also by their more fastidious elegance. Somebody whispered me that one of them owned a ranch bigger than the State of New Jersey while another controlled a large share of his country's GDP.

We were greeted by the casually dressed hosts and, leaving Nancy in a conversation with old family friends, I walked out, drink in hand to the illuminated pool surrounded by a zen-inspired rock garden. The sunset of a limpid glowing day was fading out of a cloudless mauve sky. Around us the pistachio hued leaves of the ubiquitous aspens fluttered in the breeze. I was looking for Elizabeth and Joy I soon spotted them, talking to a tall graying but athletic man whose designer cowboy boots reminded me of the Texas businessman they and their friend Richard Sigismond had wanted me to meet. Elizabeth introduced us and added: "Lowell, I told Côme about your experiences with the Hunts and I think he'll like to hear your story because we all share an awareness of the way things are...."

He shook my hand in long bony fingers while his steel grey eyes surveyed me impassively.

"Nice to meet you" he said, in a deep low voice. "So, you heard about the story of the silver bust, eh?" He indeed hit on the rs, as expected from a Texan.

He was not wasting time in polite chatter.

"Yes, I was told that you were involved in it and the entire story attracted much interest abroad too" I confirmed.

By then the two women had stepped aside to chat with other guests. We moved slightly away from the thickening crowd and he took a sip of his Bourbon, awaiting my question.

"It appears that the government moved fast to stop the Hunts and their syndicate from cornering silver in the markets" I suggested.

"Well, yeah. You see Bunker and Herbert, the Hunt brothers, like many others saw that the US federal currency is not supported by anything other than the belief people have in the Fed and in the country's economy. It is *fiat* money and the government on various occasions has struck against metal as when they declared silver not to have reserve value towards the end the last century or when FDR confiscated privately held gold. The final blow was Nixon's, delinking the greenback from gold. Some people have never agreed with that and I am one of them. It is a rip off."

"So the Hunts started buying all the silver?" I insisted.

He looked at me quizzically and asked: "Have you read Ezra Pound?"

I did not expect him to invoke the controversial American poet and essayist although I immediately saw the connection.

"He was an early critic of the US financial system" I acknowledged "and he denounced the privatization of the economy and even of currency for the benefit of the big banks. Did you know him?"

"No" he said with a hint of regret in his eyes "but I spent a great deal of time talking to one of his last confidants, Eustace Mullins, an authority on the Federal Reserve system and he explained to me how it really operates. Pound was right on this. He saw through the crooked 1913 Congressional Act which authorized the Fed as a private monopoly to control the economy but there is a lot more to it."

"I read something of Mullins and I know a bit about the Fed" I clarified "but tell me more about what has happened with the Hunts and the Saudis."

"It is too long a story for this occasion" he retorted with a brief, hard smile "but if you are free tomorrow around 5, we could have a drink at the Ajax Tavern and I'll tell you more."

That sounded promising. I felt that he was almost eager to give an inside account of the story and I promptly agreed. We plunged into the fashionable huddle and I was introduced by the few I already knew to some of the guests. The socialite Christine Aubale-Gerschel, a relative of the Lazard clan from France was chatting with the elegant Adams couple. Nancy Oliphant, a thin, impish local heiress tested her passable French on me and soon resorted to the inevitable song line that had fired the American imagination when she took my arm and whispered with a wink "*voulez vous coucher avec moi ce soir?.*" I opted for a mock "mais oui," treading the thin line between courtesy and flirt.

A tall, statuesque valkyrie with a cascade of white gold hair and arctic blue eyes turned out to have two PhDs and to have written the same number of books on themes related to psychology and the dawning new age; her name was Patricia Hill and we began a conversation on science's encounter with oriental gnosis. We paused to greet George Gradow and Barbie Benton who had just arrived. The former Playboy idol and Country singer Barbie shone with the platinum of Beverly Hills beauty and wealth at the side of her real estate moghul of a husband. I was told they had built a huge house called The Magic Mushroom on Buttermilk mountain where Gradow indulged his passion for fitness during no less than three hours every day by swimming in his Olympic sized pool, jogging, running, lifting weights, doing yoga, judo and aerobics. There was, as usual in Aspen a sprinkling of film stardust over the crust of entrepreneurs, landowners and financiers.

I was by then used to the typical American way—can it be called protocol?—to start a conversation with a first name introduction, gather a few facts about each other and move on, at times citing the need to meet other guests. There is a purposefulness in this procedure which reflects the national culture's craving for systematic efficiency. Even leisure and socializing are carried out like work. The glitterati of Aspen who mostly knew each other may not have had as much desire to "network" as their less fortunate countrymen but they kept the habit and newcomers attracted their real though superficial curiosity.

The party was very pleasant, the hosts gracious and the food and drinks delicious. I experienced again the almost miraculous sense of lightness imparted by the clear cool night at 8000 fee. The swinging tunes being played increased the heady exhilaration derived from the presence of several attractive women. One truly felt like being on top of the world and I understood why many of those present believed that it belonged to them.

THE WALKYRIE AND THE MONROE INSTITUTE

I woke up late the next day as I had stayed up well into the night. Nancy Pfister had dropped me back to my duplex at Fasching House and driven on to the family ranch. I had taken an appointment for lunch at the Nature Food store's cafeteria with a friend of Scott Halazon who owned the Isolation Tank Spa in town.

Ingrid J. was, as her name foretold, a tall, quiet and sensuous looking girl of Swedish origin, usually wearing a corduroy shirt and a short leather skirt with long boots, who had settled in Aspen some years earlier to practice alternative therapies. She had trained in various oriental techniques, such as Chih Gong, Rolfing and Tai Chi Ch'uan and had become an adept of the Monroe Institute's methods to explore human consciousness.

My awareness of the said Institute's work was purely theoretical. I knew that it had developed since 1974 under the direction of radio broadcaster and owner Robert Monroe as a research centre dedicated to the expansion of human potential, in the Blue Ridge Mountains of Virginia, not far from the national capital, on the basis of a patented technology called HEMI-SYNC binaural soundtronics which reportedly produced altered states of consciousness in the experiencers. It had links with a technique explored by John Lilly, mostly for achieving inter-species communications between humans, dolphins and other sea mammals.

Lilly's research led to the perfecting of what was officially called REST as an evocative acronym for Restricted Environmental Stimulation Tank. A Hollywood feature film titled *Altered States* had been released in 1980. It was a Sci-Fi thriller based on the insulation tank technology which could supposedly regress the human subject to a primal or animal state of consciousness. Lilly had noted that it was loosely inspired by his own book manuscript *Dyadic Cyclone* which documented the psychic and chemical effects of ketamin absorption combined with a prolonged session in the tank.

The scientists involved in the study of the practice had concluded that, absent the drugs abundantly tried by Lilly, the REST experience produced a commendable state of relaxation and released endorphins that temporarily wiped out the pains and aches affecting most of us at one time or another.

The basic tool was a sealed tank, supplied with air through a filter, filled with saline water at body temperature on which the subject floated in complete isolation from the sounds and other sensorial inputs of the outside world. The programmed sonic stimulations were then provided in a state of total relaxation to send him or her into a series of gradually ascending "focus levels," beginning with number 1 which corresponds to the usual earthly stage of existence and perception.

While we sipped Celestial Seasonings tea in flower painted rustic cups, Ingrid answered my initial questions in a calm, curiously high pitched voice that I did not easily associate with her voluptuous shape.

"The focus levels are clustered in groups of 7" she explained "Focus 21 is like a bridge to other dimensions and at Focus 22 one reaches the planes of the after-life. So you are in conscious or subconscious contact with the world of the departed." She said it with strange casualness, holding my gaze in her dreamy pale blue eyes.

"Does everyone reach that state in the tank?" I inquired, a bit incredulously.

"No, the mind must be completely still and empty of thought. Eventually the brain waves migrate from Alpha or Beta to Theta. Many people don't get there because it is too difficult for them to get rid of anxieties and ideas. In fact many people can't even take it in the tank for more than a few minutes. They are claustrophobic and panic when in total silence and darkness. They ask to be released and the session ends right away. By the way at the Monroe's retreat centre on the East Coast they usually put you not in a fluid-filled tank but in what is called a CHEC."

"Which is?"

"A controlled holistic environmental chamber but I use the tank since I am also following the protocols set by Lilly."

"What happens beyond level 22?"

"You keep rising and encountering other kinds of consciousness or beings if you prefer. All in your mind of course but it is not separate from the world. Above levels 34, many dimensions come together as if you were in touch with different universes at once. That is when you attain what we call the I-There or consciousness of the monad. Then you can go ever higher and connect with being that exist in all sorts of parallel worlds. We call level 44 the Sea of I-There Clusters because you attain holistic consciousness."

"How does the supervisor of the process know that the subject has reached such states and not merely hallucinated according to what he was told to expect" I probed, dutifully playing devil's advocate.

She did not hesitate as she had surely been asked that question many times. "There is a system to watch the progression by monitoring various physiological signs when in a control or experimental procedure" she clarified. "Some signals are given by skin temperature and the Direct Current potential voltage measures. You know that Theta waves are of two sorts. The ones recorded in the hippocampus of the brain reflect REM sleep in humans, when we are about to wake up or dream. The cortical Theta waves, from our cortex are specific to meditation. Scientific tests have shown that the effects of the Hemi-Sync waves on the brain are not acoustical but electromagnetic. They trigger what we call a Frequency Following Response in the form of binaural beats. It is like a third sound generated by the two that are beamed into your skull as in a stereo recording."

"So I have read. It all goes back to Galvani and his detection of body electricity" I commented "but I assume that the ultimate test is the subject's awareness that he has indeed gotten out of his normal condition, a bit like Plato's prisoner when he emerges from the cave. Yet, can he get there without taking some psychotropic drug? In

Altered States the main character, Jessup I believe, consumes the ayahuasca plant in a solution"

"Yeah, we like to say that it is a doorway to the Otherworld which is usually called spiritual but we don't use drugs. Lilly and others did because they were experimenting with chemicals to produce DMT but the brain makes itself naturally" was the response. "You should come into the tank and do it. Scott told me that you are into UFO and ET studies. I think that you'll gain new insights for your research."

I had no reason to decline and we agreed that I would pay a visit to her centre in the coming days, but not before asking her what level she herself had reached while carrying the practice. She smiled almost coyly and said that she knew for sure she had visited Focus 27, usually described in Monroe's nomenclature as the "reception centre" on the threshold of higher realms. "It feels and looks like you are on earth but not in this body" she explained "rather in the second one, used for Gateway voyages."

Ingrid gave me her card and told me to call for an appointment. "The tank is in a spa facility out in the country" she said "but I can drive you there if you come to my home which is downtown, close to your place."

When I walked her to her car, an old clunky bottle green Chrysler, she picked a book lying on the front seat and handed it to me: "I am lending it until you come to the tank" she explained. I peered at the cover. It carried the title *Journeys out of the body* and the author's name: Robert Monroe. When I thanked her, she conjured a dreamy smile with dawn-colored eyes and full lips and waved while driving off in the quiet Sun-drenched street.

Texas Tycoons, Saudi Princes and the Silver Saga

By 5 pm I had made my way to the popular Ajax tavern on the ski slope and was soon joined by Lowell, the Texan who was, on that cloudy and nippy day in a dark blue cashmere sweater and jeans.

He ordered a Coors beer and I settled for black coffee, despite my justified skepticism about the merits of the usually insipid and diluted American brew which claims that name.

As I expected he spent little time on preliminaries and came straight to the point.

"I've heard you are doing some research into our country and trying to get the real picture" he stated, while his eyes rapidly surveyed the surrounding tables. "Elizabeth told me you are well informed about things few people know. I assume you think that the whole episode about silver was just a wildcat speculative venture gone wrong? Yet there is more to it."

"I have always thought so, from the little I learnt" I confirmed "although I never took the Hunts to be altruistic angels. They are investors and entrepreneurs after all."

"If you are a bit familiar with the way our people settled America, you know that many were adventurers and risk-takers and some horse thieves and gunmen who could also be clergymen at times. The Hunts, like many families including mine are a bit of all this. I knew them since the fifties when we were all young oil men. Their father, old H L Hunt was a poker player, a womanizer and a wildcatter."

"I read that he raised three families from three different women who bore him fifteen children" I noted.

"Yep, he was bigamous for years, unbeknownst to both his wives and at the same he made and lost two or three fortunes like many others in his day. He was like Paul Getty and several other tough SOBs who lived life kingsize even though they did not really care about luxury and loved driving beat up pick up trucks, drinking with ranch hands and listening to Bluegrass on the radio or LPs. When he died in 1974, his sons had already made their own fortunes. In 1961, Bunker found himself at 35 the richest man in America when his oil concessions in Libya were estimated to be worth seven billion. He used that leverage, more than the cash itself to purchase millions of acres of land, including a huge station in Australia and a thousand thoroughbred racehorses in Kentucky as well as interests in sugar and other commodities while Herbert developed Houston real estate. In the sixties and early seventies there seemed to be no end to the growth of that fortune. I was in some of the ventures and I can say that I did extremely well too."

"The typical American success story" I commented while sipping the coffee which was tastier and stronger than I expected. Aspen standards!

"Yes but all things that are too good can't last. In the seventies Colonel Gaddafi nationalized the oil fields and the US Government did nothing about it, which made all of us very angry. That was a time of crisis here. Washington was engulfed in the post-Vietnam crisis and the Nixon scandal which weakened the White House decisively. Interest rates kept going up, inflation was eating into the value of money and Nixon took us off the gold standard. The oil shock during the Yom Kippur war put an end to western growth."

"I know that the transnational banking elites accepted the consequences of the OPEC embargo and the subsequent price rise" I interjected. "Kissinger used the situation to set up the so-called petrodollar economy by entering into a secret agreement with the Saudi Royal Family which gave the greenback a monopoly on the fossil fuel trade."

Lowell nodded and went on: "The Hunts and we, their partners were well aware of what was going on and we felt that the Rockefellers and their gang in New York and Washington, controlling the oil majors were the ones wreaking havoc with the economy for their own high stake gambles. Bunker was openly saying the dollar not supported by metal was mere paper backed by promises from the tooth fairy, as he liked to put it. By the mid-seventies our syndicate had acquired a lot of silver and we kept on buying since we saw a big crash coming. The Hunts predicted that the Wall Street cartel would bring about some kind of socialism, meaning that they would not allow any fortune to remain outside their ruling circle."

"I know that the Right Wing here tenaciously believes in a coming world government controlled by multinational banking hidden elites" I said.

"That was Hunt's creed" my informer confirmed. "He would say very controversial things about the Kikes—The Jews—and their plans to rule the planet and enslave everyone else. He had read Henry Ford who was one of his heroes and he believed in much of what David

Duke says. He was also a committed evangelical who tried to discover the Ark of the Covenant in Armenia, financed the film on Jesus for the Campus Crusade, funded Jerry Falwell and Pat Robertson, did not drink or smoke, went to mass on Sunday, unlike his father, although he liked women as much as the old man and also married thrice and had fifteen kids."

"It seems like a very biblical way of life" I said with a smile.

"You see, that's the spirit that pervaded American inland society until recently, especially in the South. We were all raised, a bit like the Mormons, reading the Good Book and trying to be like the patriarchs of Old, gathering money, land and houses, breeding children and spreading around the land. Yet we and the Jews tend to see each other as competition. They don't like redneck goyim trying to be like them and we don't trust their money creating and shuffling tricks. Do you know about the origin of the Dollar?"

I nodded assent but waited for him to tell me as he visibly was eager to have his say:

"It was a currency coined in the Habsburg Empire in the sixteenth century from silver mines in Bohemia, at Joachimsthal. First called the joachimsthaler, the name was shortened to thaler or daler and was emitted by the great Augsburg banking families, the Fuggers and Walzers to finance the religious wars of Kaiser Charles the Fifth who happened to rule the recently colonised Americas. So that currency, the "pieces of eight" invaded Europe and the new world and were known as dollars, Each one amounted to a little more than 24 grams of standard silver and believe it or not, the silver dollar remained in circulation until 1965 when it was removed. However for our generation it was the silver that guaranteed the value of our money. Remember that since FDR's financial coup Americans have not been allowed to own gold. So much for the land of the Free."

I remarked the irony. "So that is why Bunker decided to get much of the silver in the world and thereby make the prices rises?" I asked.

"Yes, but he wanted physical delivery as he did not believe in certificates. He knew our financial system all too well. Back in 1973, he had sent forty million ounces—I said forty—in three 707 Boeings to Switzerland to hold it in safe keeping away from the prying hands of the Fed. Then in 1975, he got the Saudi Royal Family to partner with us on this and our holdings grew to 55 million ounces. By the end of 1979 he and his parterns owned a billion troy ounces, over three thousand tons and the profits on those transactions, with silver at 34 Dollars a troy ounce amounted to over two billion Dollars."

The figures were staggering even though I had heard of those astronomical amounts before.

"Did Hunt not try to bring the Shah of Iran into the deal" I inquired.

"Yes, he went to Tehran on the introduction of one of the Emperor's brothers who was in touch with Bunker. That did not work out but the Saudi King was receptive and arranged for some Sheykhs to act as representatives of the kingdom's sovereign fund in the deal."

I asked him if he thought it coincidental that King Faisal had been bizarrely shot dead by one of his nephews who had just returned from studying in Colorado at the time.

Lowell looked away pensively at the green slopes of Ajax mountain bathed in the radiant light of the late afternoon.

"Who knows?" he said, shrugging. "The young man might have been brainwashed by some operatives here, with a mixture of psychotropics and lectures about human rights and democracy, our favourite drug. However the cooperation began when the International Metals Corporation was set up in Bermuda. We also had a Brazilian partner."

"I think that the Federal Government became really worried by then about your plans and began to intervene" I pointed out.

"Well, all in all on the new year 1980 our group through its various holdings has accumulated some hundred and thirty million ounces of the stuff and we had contracts for another ninety million. We controlled about a third of all known silver in the world and we had done nothing illegal."

"Maybe but it still looks like a huge money making scheme rather than a paradigm changing initiative" I objected while he took another sip of beer. "Was there a grander intention behind all this?"

"Of course money was a goal" he conceded "but the idea was to bring silver back up to its original level before the Government had artificially depressed the price and destroyed a big part of the economy in the Rockies by walking out of the bi-metal standard. The intent was to bring the metallic dollar, the real McCoy back from the grave and it could have worked."

"Had not a big part of the operation failed in the Philippines earlier?"

"Oh you know about that too?" Lowell said. "President Marcos was an incredibly sharp guy and he knew about the US monetary shenanigans. He was open to taking countermeasures to protect himself from the Americans who were thinking of pulling him down so he agreed to start a trilateral commodity swap in oil, sugar and silver with us and with the Saudis. The IMF stepped in, quite illegitimately I should say and forced the cancellation of the deal. From then on Marcos was no longer in the good graces of Washington but our silver purchases continued and were really giving the Treasury and the Fed a run for their money literally speaking."

"Anyway, that was not to be" I commented.

"The brothers had underestimated the Fed, banking and Exchanges cartel. On 7 January 1980, COMEX, one of the two main exchanges we used to buy adopted Bullion Rule 7 which restricted drastically the margin purchase facilities. This was an *ad hoc* regulation targeted at the Hunts and they rightly complained that it was unfair as others were allowed to get away with similar operations, though not quite on that scale and the authorities at COMEX had a conflict of interest as they were mostly short on silver futures. However we could not get our way and two weeks later, COMEX simply suspended the trade in silver."

"That was the beginning of the end" I remarked.

"Not quite, contracts had been signed and in early February our group received another 26 million ounces. By then the entire financial and monetary apparatus of the government was on the case and the official reactions aroused fear in the market so that the prices plunged precipitously to a third of their highest level. Before the end of March

Bunker saw that he could not fight the federal system and he suspended the purchases. 27 March was the infamous Silver Thursday which saw a temporary stock market crash. It was like a second demonetization of metal. Not only our syndicate but the entire Hunt family were devastated. They had to default on the margin calls and to save the market from a panic the Fed Chairman Volcker lent them over a billion but the repayment of the debt gradually forced them to go bankrupt while they were under several judicial investigations as they had to pony up some eight billion in value of collateral. Thank God for their trust funds which could not be touched. Otherwise they'd have been left without a roof on their heads or food on the table."

"That almost never happens to the very wealthy" I reflected skeptically. "The elites protect their own."

"The goal of the powers-that-be was to wipe out their ability to change the system" Lowell retorted. "Once that was taken care of, they were allowed to play with a few remaining millions. Two of the major brokerage houses Bache Halsey and Prudential which had been our main conduits to get the silver were also in big trouble and merged in order to recover from the blow."

"Do you think that the Reagan administration which came in about that time could have saved the Hunts?" I queried.

"Reagan and some of his advisers were not too far from our ideas regarding the Fed and the value of money" he clarified "but once a president assumes office he is bound by the system and can't really change much. If you read what Reagan said, or was made to say when he was a younger politician in California about restoring the American republic in the spirit of the founders you'll see what I mean."

"Don't most politicians go through that process? They often start with ideas and ideals, propagate them to become known and then they get elected and toe the line. Why did you ask me about Mullins at the party?"

Ezra Pound, The Rockefellers and Senator McCarthy

He shook his head and gave him another one of his sharp stares: "Look, I am not into attacking any community and I don't believe in races or thousand year old conspiracies as Mullins does. I think that he has gone astray on that. He was too influenced by Pound who was a fascist romantic, terribly impressed by Mussolini who flattered his writer's vanity. However Mullins did serious research and got it right when he analysed the real nature and origins of the Federal Research Board and Bank. Heck, it was set up in secrecy and passed through Congress stealthily at the behest of a few major banking families who logically enough wanted to control the economy. You don't have to believe me. See how the Fed operates and read Mullins's newly republished and updated *Secrets of the Federal Reserve*. When he tried to bring it out first in 1951 he was fired as a researcher by the Library of Congress and told by at least one publisher that no one would agree to print it. It was practically self-published and it is very well supported by facts and figures. The fact that it drew such a vicious reaction from the system's apex confirms that he had exposed something very sensitive."

"If I remember right the basic thesis of the book" I said "it argues that the Fed was set up as private money printing and lending monopoly to the government by the Rockefellers, Rothschilds, Warburgs, Schroeders and their associates in collusion with Colonel House, the grey eminence behind Woodrow Wilson."

"Yep, that is the gist of it and the structure is part of that wider system which includes the other Rockefeller creations, the Economic Stabilization Fund, the Council on Foreign Relations, the Trilateral Commission and the Bilderberg Group among others. There is nothing implausible about that map. Powerful people want to keep their power and extend it. They form alliances with their peers and try to keep them secret in order to avoid hostility and scrutiny. Trouble is that they often harm others who are not in their gang and that happens to be the vast majority of us."

"I know from good sources that the Oil Shock was anticipated and the petro-dollar strategy was worked out in a meeting of the Bilderberg group in May 1973 at a spa in Sweden, months before the Yom Kippur war" I pointed out "David Rockefeller was present of course but back to Mullins, didn't he work with Senator McCarthy to find and expose Soviet agents shortly after the war?" I inquired.

"He was interested, like McCarthy in finding the funding sources for the Communist movement in America and lo and behold, he concluded that much of it was supported by the self-same transnational elites which control power in the US. I still believe, like so many in this country that McCarthy was a patriot who may have saved America from an even worse situation than the one we are in."

"That seems a bit contradictory in my view" I argued "you have reasons to complain about the oligarchic system which you say controls America and much of the world but were Communists not fighting it as well?"

"Or just helping it come to the stage we see now" he replied unhesitatingly. "The Atlanticist World-Government power group, the secret government if you will, uses both communism and capitalism and supports the Cold War mitigated by détente to build global hegemony. They are quite cosy with the Soviets for what suits them and are indifferent to religion in general, although some of them are basically hostile to Christianity and we even believe that they worship Satan, as the prince of this material world.

It is order to fight that system that Bunker supported the Western Goals Foundation and the John Birch Society. They are both portrayed as nutty far-right wing organizations by the mainstream, system-controlled media. We see them as conservative, patriotic, Christian associations which resist the hegemonic power."

I was perplexed and not convinced . He noticed it from my silent expression.

"Back in 1958, when he set up the John Birch Society Robert Welch already talked and wrote about the New World Order and One World Government as the goal of the transnational rule socialist elites secretly allied with the Communists. You will find those very words in many official documents and statements nowadays and our current Vice-President and CIA veteran George H W Bush is a great advocate of those ideals, which is why Reagan can't have his way. His administration has been infiltrated by the enemy. So we are not conspiracy loons inventing stories. Now, as to charges of anti-semitism, the John Birch Society has many members from the Jewish,

Black, Hispanic and other minorities. Its fight is against Bolshevism and its allies and agents of any origin, not against a religion or an ethnic group. We even have Masons and Mormons amongst us. Of course there is a love hate relation between Christians and Jews which started a thousand years before the birth of the USA. There is theology and business competition in the mix but it is not racist. Likewise, the Western Goals Foundation was started in 1979, when Carter was in to power, by General John Singlaub who as a veteran Intelligence officer and military commander knew that Carter, a nice enough guy by himself, was a liberal puppet of the Rockefeller clan."

"I certainly acknowledge that his mentor was Brzezinski, a Rockefeller protégé from the CFR" I pitched in.

"Here you go. Singlaub who is an undisputed patriot also reorganized the Council for World Freedom but he is not a war monger as such. He, like Welch and the Birchers are opposed to American military interventions abroad and we believe in keeping the troops home to protect the motherland. We want to fight Communism with information and public mobilisation but not in a world war."

"Your people prefer to stir up and support insurrections against left-wing governments in other countries though" I interjected mischievously.

"Well, if there is an invasion of another country as in the case of Soviet troops entering Afghanistan, we think that people have a right to fight foreign occupiers" Lowell said looking at his watch. "I am sorry but I have taken another appointment."

"That's fine" I replied "thanks a lot for your time and all the information. I found this conversation very helpful."

"My pleasure. I hope I have made some things clearer for you. You see, even amongst our like-minded supporters there are disagreements on many things. After all we believe in freedom. Some of our religious stalwarts are strong supporters of Israel for confessional and strategic reasons. Others are unhappy about Jewish control of the financial, cultural and media sectors which ensures the hegemony of the globalist liberal cabal. We usually have no problem with religiously traditional Jews who also oppose the liberals in their community. Our common ground is faith in the US Constitution and Bill of Rights and the rejection of the erosion of the rights of states in the Union which goes together with the creation of a super-government for the planet. That is not what America was about. Our founding fathers did not want the subordination of the people to a global banking cartel or even to a huge central government. Jefferson fought the concept of a central bank which he saw as a harbinger of tyranny."

We both stood up and shook hands. The light still shone with solstitial brightness over the slopes in that summer day. I had now heard the other side in the ongoing power struggle in the country. The Old Right Wingers were being tarred with the brush of fascism by the liberal faction but they saw themselves as Constitutionalists fighting for the original American identity against socialistic One-Worlders.

I did not see either of the two groups as entirely white or black but I saw the threats looming in both the apparently lofty-minded ideologies. However it seemed to me that the patriotic conservatives were no match for the formidable coalition of the globalists served by the secret weaponry and mind control paraphernalia I had been told about on previous days. If there were conspiracies, they existed on both sides but the "East Coast" elite, allied to Hollywood looked like it was winning the battle in the governments and in the minds. The Hunts had been crushed by Wall Street and Reagan had not replaced the real leadership of the country although he had brought some new policies and attitudes. He was a symbol of what many regarded as the original United States in a modern garb but he did not call the shots. Those who stood against the globalist liberal juggernaut were being increasingly marginalized as dangerous reactionaries, out of touch with current aspirations and technologies. The "home of the brave," the nation of supposedly free individuals had been caught in the net of an anonymous corporate spider using the state as its mask and all others looked like mosquitoes, either glued in its web or buzzing helplessly around it.

VIII
Pieces of a Puzzle

*"Is all that we see or seem
But a dream within a dream?"*

Edgar Poe, A Dream within a Dream

NEW AGE PIONEERS

In the following days I went to meet Amory Lovins and his wife Hunter at the Rocky Mountain Institute set up by them in order to learn more about their work. They had recently moved to Aspen where the Institute was located in sylvan surroundings.

Amory Lovins, despite his relative youth, was already regarded as a pioneer of the revolution in energy policies that had only begun. A Harvard alumnus and Oxford Don and dropout, he was a leading expert in the field of alternative power generation, particularly from solar sources, and an influential and convincing critic of nuclear fission which he had famously called "brittle power" in his book of the previous year. He was a bespectacled man in his mid-thirties, of middle height whose light build and soft spoken studious manner bespoke his academic upbringing. Hunter who was a forester by training looked more in tune with Aspen's casual outdoor culture. They had recently married and their constant togetherness attested to the freshness of their bonds.

I began by asking them, over cups of Celestial Seasoning, whether they found a receptive audience in Reagan's America which was under the overwhelming influence of fossil fuel companies and where the pro-nuclear lobby still had a strong voice, in spite of the Three Mile Island and other atomic plant accidents.

"This administration is of course very close to the Seven Sisters" Amory conceded "but there are many people who see the environmental writing on the wall. Oil makes us far too dependent on foreign imports even though we pay it in dollars printed for that purpose and we must think of the time when it will not be as readily available, for environmental or political reasons, and will therefore become too expensive. Two years ago I wrote a book which made the case that we needed to become independent of nuclear power in our energy generating policies if we want a peaceful future. I call that an ethical strategy."

"We also like to define it as a soft path" Hunter added. "It goes with our overall prescription for natural capitalism.... Imitating the freedom of nature but also its economy of waste and its genius for synergy."

"We are also warning of the danger of atomic war that this Republican administration has much increased" her husband commented.

I told them that I was aware of their soon-to-appear work entitled *The First Nuclear World War.*

"To whom do you owe your primary inspiration?" I asked. "You are seen as members of the New Age revolution sweeping the country and affecting every aspect of life."

"We are on the conservative and moderate side of New Age thought" Amory said with a faint smile. "We are able to reach out to a lot of mainstream people and institutions which would not readily interact with the Institute of Noetic Sciences or Esalen to name only those two. However in one of my recent books *A Golden Thread* I show how our work is in line with the ecologically sound technologies of ancient civilisations."

"But we know we are all tending towards the same goal" Hunter pointed out "an ecologically sound and viable society endowed with technologies which enhance human life and the quality of our environment instead of damaging them."

"In the end that is the realistic approach to national security in the long term" was Amory's concluding remark.

I thought about this conversation on my way back to Fasching Haus. In the last few days I had been exposed to the power structure of the country and to the oligarchic plans for ever tighter global domination but I had also heard about some of the initiatives that were aimed at building a different kind of society, both at the level of consciousness and in the political domain. The Lovinses had cited the Institute of Noetic Sciences or INS created a few years earlier in California by the NASA astronaut, scientist and philosopher Dr Edgar Mitchell and headed by Willis Harman, an electrical engineer who coincidentally came from Stanford University, close by the Research Institute of the same name that Sigismond and I had talked about in connection with paranormal and UFO studies. The INS belonged to the intellectual family of the Monroe Institute and of several other such think-tanks.

Mitchell reported having experienced a transcendent enlightenment of the type described as *Samadhi* in ancient Indian scriptures during his space journey back to Earth on the Apollo 13 Moon mission. That had convinced him that Hindu and Buddhist sages described a real phenomenon in their mystical writings. Both he and Willis had scientific and technical backgrounds. I understood why Amory Lovins had referred to their institute. Harman had published last year a book on the future of energy for mankind and they worked in the same area.

The Esalen Institute was another famous incubator of new ideas that I was somewhat familiar with although I had not visited its Big Sur campus on the California coast. The brainchild of two rather affluent friends, Michael Murphy and Richard Price who had both dabbled in oriental philosophies just after the War, it was dedicated to alternative humanistic studies inspired by the spiritual traditions of Asia and by contemporary scientific insights. Its academic godfather was also a Stanford professor, Frederic Spiegelberg who taught among others Sri Aurobindo's yogic doctrine and co-founded the California Institute of Integral Studies.

Price had also been initiated into Zen Buddhism by Alan Watts. Since its foundation in 1962 Esalen had hosted some of the most eminent thinkers of the western hemisphere, from Aldous Huxley to Gregory Bateson and from Abraham Maslow to Joseph Campbell. It also played a role in the international political sphere since, in the last two or three years its mentors had initiated a process of citizen diplomacy, called Track Two, between eminent American and Soviet individuals. In 1982, this initiative had resulted in the launch of what was called a Space Bridge between the superpowers in the form of a dialogue platform. These and other programmes manifested a design to end the Cold War and bring the world together on a new and shared perspective. I could see the synergy between Walter Russell's university, Windstar, the Rocky Mountain Institute, Esalen, the Human Potential Movement and others but what was at the core of this expanding nebula whose atoms all came from one central source?

I needed to find someone who could reveal more links between the New Age theories and the clandestine research being pursued in certain scientific facilities, according to the various testimonies I had collected abroad and since my arrival in the USA. I had to get back to Sigismond as he was my best prospect for gaining further insights. I called him that very evening. He told me he had just finished dinner but assured me that I was not disturbing. I rapidly explained my quest:

"Where do you situate the starting point of the transition that we are going through?" I asked "and can you see a link with the UFO enigma, if you wish to define it in that way?"

He cleared his throat and took a moment before replying: "It is almost impossible to locate the origin. Too many things have happened since quite some time, during and after World War Two, if not before. Of course you have to factor in the introduction of eastern wisdom in our culture since the days of Vivekananda and later Yogananda, Coomaraswamy, Huxley, Suzuki, Alan Watts and then so many gurus like the Maharishi and Chogyam Trungpa Rimpoche here in Boulder. But at the same time one can notice the impact of George Adamski's testimonies. Have you heard of Van Tassel?."

"It rings a bell somewhere but I am not sure."

"He died in 1978. Since 1947, the year of Roswell, he had been living in a cave-home under a rock, appropriately called Giant Rock in California. That location had first been settled by a German immigrant who was held to be a spy during the war and who died there in unclear circumstances while state troopers besieged Giant Rock. In 1953, George Van Tassel claimed to have met a being from Venus while he was in deep meditation. Mind you that was the year of the Robertson Panel convened by the CIA which decided to systematically discredit and ridicule all reports of UFOs and alien visits that flooded the airwaves and the popular media then. Van Tassel claimed he was told to propagate the transcendent knowledge given by his alien guide and to build a device called an integraton. He founded a "ministry of universal wisdom" and wrote a few books which are in my library. One of them is called *I rode a Flying Saucer* and another *The Council of the Seven Lights*.

"Did he build the Integraton?"

"Almost but he died before he could complete it. However you can see the unfinished structure which took him many years as it was hard to raise funds. There used to be big annual conferences on UFOs and the future civilization that is to emerge from our increasing contacts with them. It all sounds weird, like all Alien-related things but Giant Rock was a shrine of what we call the counter-culture which sproutedout of California."

THE DESCENT OF ALIEN SCIENCE

"All that reminds me of Andrija Puharich and the Round Table Foundation in New York State" I commented. "He began his research on the paranormal at the Edgewood military research lab around that period and became convinced that superhuman aliens had visited Nikola Tesla and given him access to new knowledge."

"Yes and you may be aware of the connections with our TV and movie industries. Gene Roddenberry conceived the *Star Trek* series on the basis of alleged outer space channelings to Professor Puharich's group which much later included John Denver . Separately George Lucas began to write *Star Wars* after reading Joseph Campbell's essays on ancient myths and eastern cosmologies. The first part of his trilogy came out in 1977, thirty years after the return of Admiral Byrd from the South Pole, the Arnold sighting, Roswell and all that jazz. On the same year Lucas's friend Steven Spielberg, a UFO literature fan brought out *Close Encounters of the Third Kind* which was a blockbuster and in 1982, *ET The Extraterrestrial*, another huge box office success. I feel that was part of an incubation period. So-called science fiction precedes or closely follows actual events with which it often intersects. I would bet that those mass-appeal films were promoted by forces within our government or above it in order to get people used to what our future looks like."

"I remember that Puharich entered into contact with the cosmic entity he calls The Nine back in 1952 through a Indian sage called Maharishi Vinod" I added. "1952 and the early fifties were really a period of intense activity in that field. Many seeds were being planted And flying discs just kept hovering over Washington DC."

"You might put in that list Arthur Young's Foundation for the Study of Consciousness which also came into being in 1952. I don't have to tell you that, while pursuing scientific research Young, a Jungian, was a student of yoga, theosophy and astrology. I recently read his recent book *The Bell Notes* which is subtitled "A journey from Physics to Metaphysics" He was a member of Puharich's RoundTable but by 1953, the government clamped down on ET related matters and decided to deny and dismiss it all. It was too dangerous for the system."

"What about John Lilly and his work on communication with dolphins and other species?" I asked.

"He started in the fifties and in 1961 he was a founding member of the Order of the Dolphin set up at the Green Bank observatory to establish communications with Extraterrestrial entities. He used yoga according to the teachings of Patanjali to reach that goal so you see, there is a continuous relationship between Eastern knowledge and the exploration of consciousness and the cosmos in our century."

"There you have it!" I exclaimed. "A tidal wave of new inspiration was sweeping over the intellectual landscape, possibly in the wake of the discovery of atomic fission and in the shadow of imminent nuclear world war."

"That is the message we are getting" I heard him reply softly. "We are on the brink of self-destruction since several years and we must change direction. Otherwise the adventure of out species will come to an abrupt and tragic end."

"Can you put me in touch with some other people involved in this process?" I asked. "I need to get deeper into it."

Another instant of silence was followed by a cautious promise: "Let me see. Puharich is now based on the Virginia estate of the Reynold family, the owners of the tobacco empire. An heir to the fortune is a believer in spiritual philosophy and a promoter of ecological causes. I may be able to set up a meeting with someone who has worked with him or with Lilly nearer to these parts."

H promised to call me back and we wished each other a good evening.

I did not have long to wait. Sigismond rang me two days later and gave me the name and number of an acquaintance of his who was a researcher at the Capstone Institute which he described as a "frontier science" facility located in a rural country of Colorado, not far from Boulder.

"Bruce Adams is a pioneer in the area of free energy research" Sigismond clarified. He worked with Puharich for years at Ossining, until Puharich left for Mexico. I don't know if he is still in touch with him now but he was familiar with his ideas."

I called the Capstone Institute's number. A receptionist took a message for Dr Adams who was not available and told me I would get a return call soon.

In the afternoon Adams called. He had a pleasant voice and the name of Sigismond produced a cordial reaction in him. I went straight to the point and told him I was doing some research on the scientific work of Andrija Puharich. I felt in the response that he was on his guard: "What is it exactly you wish to know?" he asked with sudden coldness.

"Dr Adams" I said "there is much to discuss and it may not be so convenient to do it on the phone. Could we meet?"

There was a second of hesitation before he somewhat reticently suggested I visit him at the Institute.

"I could come and see you in the next few days" I volunteered. "I believe we are only a couple of hours apart by road."

"Three hours at most by car he replied. You'll excuse me if I don't offer to meet you in Aspen or somewhere halfway but I don't often get out of here. Too busy."

A Thinktank in the Wilderness

We agreed on a day and on a time, in the afternoon and on the given date I duly took the direction he had indicated on state highway 13 until I reached US 40 and went on towards White River National Forest.

By three pm, an hour and a half after stopping briefly for lunch at a small rural roadside bar and restaurant run by a friendly middle aged and obese couple I turned, as instructed on a narrow paved road to my left which led me to a stone wall cutting across the ponderosa pine forest. A closed steel gate flanked by two square stone pillars stood in front of me. The name Capstone Institute inscribed on a discreet plate told me I had come to my destination. An interphone was nestled in the right-hand pillar. I pressed the buzzer and an impersonal voice resonated in the silent woodland: "Yes?"

I gave my name and mentioned Bruce Adams.

"Straight ahead. Main building" said the metallic voice.

The gate slid open quietly. The car proceeded slowly for two or three minutes between two rows of conifers. I could see a few low and unostentatious stone and timber buildings scattered in the tree dotted glade. The campus was large. I did not know how far it spread on all sides but I estimated the distance to the central edifice at no less than one mile.

I alighted in front of an austere but pleasant stone, slate and glass structure that might have been built by Frank Lloyd Wright. A man of average height with a graying short collar-beard and a moustache and wearing jeans and a chequered shirt greeted me at the door. He was the first person I saw in the compound.

"Hello, I am Bruce" He said, shaking my hand and sizing me up carefully. "I hope you did not have trouble finding the place."

I assured him that, thanks to his instructions, I had not gotten lost.

"Let us go to the conference room" he intimated before preceding me into a large entrance hall and through a corridor that led the back of the building. There were doors on both sides, some closed and some open. In the offices I noticed two or three people sitting in front of Apple computers, the novelty of the time.

My host's own office was spacious and well lit by a wide bay window offering a view of a rolling wooded slope that gradually descended towards a creek meandering below.

"I am grateful for your time" I began after we both sat down around a low, irregularly shaped table carved out of an oak trunk. "I have a long-standing fascination with Dr Puharich and Sigismond told me you are the best person to learn about him."

"I called Richard after we talked" Adams said without letting out any impression of what had been said "and he said that I could be open with you. You may know that Andrija and his research were always controversial."

"I thought as much" I confirmed. "Was he not perhaps the first scientist to be employed by the government to work on ESP, telekinesis, remote viewing and other paranormal abilities?"

"I am not sure about that" Adams responded "but he definitely is one of the early ones and the most gifted. His Round Table Institute in Maine attracted brilliant people from many disciplines and also some powerful folks from the Du Pont and other noted families. Arthur Young, who is in some way the inventor of the modern helicopter was one of the members."

The conversation had begun well and I felt the ice was probably breaking despite Adams's natural reserve.

"You see" I explained "what fascinated me, among other things, about Puharich is that he followed, more than any other investigator in the footsteps of his compatriot Nikola Tesla and carried out together the science of nature and the study of consciousness. He was seen as very unorthodox, naïve or even irrational by many of his conservative colleagues but he had no problem accepting that Tesla for one had benefited in his discoveries from the information imparted by Extraterrestrial guides."

"Or what John Lilly would call Ultraterrestrials" Bruce pointed out with a faint smile.

"And yet" I remarked "in spite of the official taboo on that entire subject, he continued for long to work under government patronage."

"Semi-covert government support. The Defence Department and the CIA through proxies. One of his early advocates and supporters was former Vice-President Henry Wallace."

I was only half-surprised. I knew that Wallace, a one-time member of the Theosophical Society and patron of the metaphysician and artist Nicholas Roerich had maintained a strong interest in spiritual and frontier-science matters. After serving as Commerce Secretary under President Truman until 1947, Wallace, had gone back to private life as a millionaire agronomist and idealist although he unsuccessfully ran for the presidency in 1948. He would have been a natural backer of Puharich's work.

"I believe that Puharich focused for a long time on the quest for a magic mushroom that could open the doors of consciousness into a wider, more real universe ... out of Plato's cave as it were" I ventured.

Adams assented impassively. He had calm, hooded brown eyes that projected a detached, speculative gaze. A true scientist's attitude to the world.

"He thought that he found the sesame, the Stargate if you will in the fly agaric which some indologists equate with the soma, the magic brew of the Vedas but he also built a machine which actually raised the ESP in people who used it, as far back as 1952" Adams commented. I realized that he knew more than just his discipline and had been exposed to Eastern knowledge.

"So what happened to his research? Was it related to the CIA's MK-Ultra and other projects connected with drugs, mind control and so on?"

I had touched a raw never. Adam flinched slightly and shook his head: "The CIA and other government agencies will use any research they can get their hands on for military and political ends" he conceded calmly "but Andrija is an idealist who only looks at the big picture, at the ultimate goal. He became a suspect to the Cold Warriors who took over policy under Truman and then Eisenhower. It is true that some of his work was funded by the Psychological Warfare Department but then as you may be aware, most of advanced research in this country is sponsored in one way or another by the Intelligence and Defense apparatus. There is no escaping that."

"That would have placed him at the time under the ultimate supervision of Nelson Rockefeller" I pointed out. "Do you think that Puharich was uncomfortable with that patronage which must have many string attached and that the Round Table Institute closed down for that reason in 1958?"

Bruce frowned slightly and caressed his carefully trimmed beard: "I must tell you that a decisive change in Puharich's research began when he met a visiting Indian Guru, Maharshi Vinod from Bombay on a train between Boston and New York and was very impressed with the Maharishi's psychic channeling abilities. You must have heard of The Nine, haven't you?"

I nodded. "I am told that it is a group of very advanced Beings who claim to be the Ennead of the ancient Egyptian cult at Heliopolis and to guide mankind in its evolution. Is that correct?"

"Yes and as long as Vinod was alive, the connection was kept with the Nine through him. After his death there was no more contact and the Round Table Institute lost its main purpose although the information received was used in many ways."

"Such as Roddenberry's blockbuster TV series which opened people's minds to the existence of a interplanetary federation of intelligent beings and to mankind's cosmic destiny" I interrupted.

Bruce assented with his eyes and resumed: "and also when Uri Geller was 'discovered' and brought to the USA for testing his paranormal abilities scientifically—he made with his fingers the sign for inverted commas—but many years later in 1974, when I was already working under Puharich a medium called Phyllis Schlemmer living in Florida turned out to be inspired by the Ennead as well.

Andrija was convinced by the uncanny correspondence between what messages she relayed and what had come from Vinod, which she could not possibly have known according to Puharich. Since then the communication goes on even though most of it is rather confidential among the people who are in touch with her. However Stuart Holroyd wrote a book about it a few years back."

"I am aware of that book" I interjected. "I think it is called *Prelude to the Landing on Earth* or something like that, published in 1977, the year of *Star Wars* and *Close Encounters* but was there not an interruption when Puharich abruptly left for Mexico in 1978?"

Adams paused for a moment and appeared to ponder how much he should tell me. He eyed me with a hint of suspicion and probably decided that he might speak freely:

"You see Andrija pushed far ahead in his research at the frontier between matter and mind. He was on tracks of Tesla and some of his work was about new energy generation technologies based on the real structure of the universe. That potential discovery would be a game changer."

"A paradigm shift" I commented.

"So you can imagine that it attracted some unwelcome attention. He came to believe that the book he was writing would disclose some very closely guarded secrets and upset the current global system and he got some rather worrisome warnings."

"Such as?'

"One fine day in August 1978 his home and study in Ossining burned to the ground and the police registered as a case of arson which has not been solved so far. This, after various anonymous messages to cease and desist convinced him that his life was in danger he moved to Mexico for more than three years and gave up publishing his book."

"Yet he came back last year?"

"He was tired of life in Mexico, facing financial difficulties, far from his children and he was assured by the CIA that they would not harass him. In fact they offered to sponsor his investigations into bio-electromagnetics and apparently apologized for past mischief."

"So, he made a deal?"

Adams shook his head: "No, I told you he has integrity. He said no and he is now pursuing his research with funding from a very wealthy individual instead."

"Josh Reynolds" I added, to show him that I had done my homework without betraying my suspicion that the name might be a cover for the very agencies that Puharich had shunned. "Let me go back to Geller" I continued. "Why do you think Geller ceased to cooperate with Dr Puharich and appears to have distanced himself from him?"

Adams shrugged, almost with annoyance.

"The problem is probably that Puharich put Geller under hypnosis and made him regress into his past. Then Uri let out that he was under the control of a supercomputer in a spacecraft located many light years away and placed there by Extraterrestrials" he explained, regaining his impassivity. "That story made Geller *persona non grata* in many circles and turned him in an even bigger target for the rationalist debunkers such as the magician and professional skeptic James Randi who had a field day with him. As you know our government systematically encourages ridiculing anyone and anything related to the ET issue. Geller is very interested in money and he wanted to grow mega-rich thanks to his abilities. He realized that he could do that provided he did not bring UFOs and little green men into his story so he cut his losses with Puharich in the mid-seventies and dedicated himself to public performances and book tours, remote sensing gold placers from aeroplanes for wealthy investors and so on. Simple explanation."

It made sense indeed. Geller had probably not enjoyed the adverse and derisive publicity generated by the reports on his alien connections. There was one more thing I wished to clarify. "What papers could I read related to Andrija's scientific research?" I asked. "Especially his more recent work?"

"Much of what he is doing now is not published or not available" Adams replied. "I am in touch with him because our institute here is working on related subjects. His focus is electromagnetic low frequency radiation and its effects on biological systems. He has set up a company called ELF Cocoon Corp. to fund and commercialize his research."

"Do I take it that he is off UFOs and off drug-related investigations?" I inquired in a skeptical tone.

"At least publicly" he replied with a light wink which surprised me from one who had so far kept a rather distant attitude. "I can tell you that he was very interested in an ongoing wave of UFO sightings that has been taken place in the Hudson Valley area since over a year now, with multiple witnesses. That was his neck of the woods when he lived at Ossining."

I had not heard of that and asked him to say more.

"Since the very end of 1981 there have been thousands of reports of craft silently gliding low in the sky over the Hudson Valley and hovering about the Indian Point nuclear power station which has had its share of technical alerts and incidents by the way. Since it is a heavily populated area, a sort of extended suburb of New York inhabited by many wealthy and important people, it has attracted particular concern. Gee, the Rockefellers and other tycoons reside right around there at Pocantico, Tarrytown and so on. The vessels are usually described as boomerang-shaped or triangular, as large as aircraft carriers and they are lined with rows of multicolored bright lights. They are almost entirely silent and can cruise very slowly, remain motionless or take off at tremendous speeds. You can guess that all this is up Andrija's alley and he is in contact with quite a few of those who researched the matter. These things are still being seen on an almost weekly basis and nobody has been able to account for them as natural or man-made phenomena. The government has mostly kept mum on it or feebly attempted explanations that were quickly shown not to bear scrutiny. The local press every now and then carries reports but predictably the big media try their best to ignore the stories. We who know better are aware that our friends from above are giving us all those shows although we can't really tell why."

"They must be trying to demonstrate their existence once again to all those guys who rule the world, or think they do around the Big

Apple" I quipped.

He opened up his palms and raised his eyebrows: "who knows?" he said.

"Are you doing UFO research here?" I inquired. I still knew next to nothing about the purpose of the place I was in.

"No. Our work is in the area of new energy" he replied. "our main sponsor is a venture capital company called Ventures for Humanity."

"Who is behind it?"

"A few wealthy patrons but the founder is Rennie Davis, of the Chicago Seven fame."

That rang a bell in my memory. Rennie Davis, the son of a high ranking official of the Truman presidency had become well known as a leader of the student rebellion against the Vietnam war. The last I had heard of him was that he had become the confidant and spokesman for the Hindu teenage spiritual leader Guru Mahara Ji and his Divine Life Foundation.

"Is this connected to his Foundation for a New Humanity?" I asked.

"In essence yet, although this is a technology oriented organization. You may see the FNH as a source of inspiration for what Capstone tries to accomplish."

I felt he was not willing or ready to give me more specific details. Like many scientists he was probably secretive about his work and Capstone looked like a secluded, quiet and rather mysterious facility which did not seek publicity. I had seen no sign of workshops, machines or engineering activities. Were they located elsewhere on the estate or outside?

I wanted to collect some more information or at least a lead. Just as I was about to leave I asked him if he could direct me to someone close to the government who could answer questions on the state of the research carried out formerly under the psychological warfare department.

He raised his eyes to the ceiling and for a second I thought he was going to plead ignorance.

"I can put you in touch with a friend in Aspen" he finally said.

"She may help you to meet an uncle of hers, a retired general who should know a few things. Let me give you her number."

He flipped through a rolodex on his desk, found a page and wrote on a post-it a name and a number which he handed to me. I glanced and read Mary-Jean Dartmoor above the seven digits.

I thanked him for his time. He walked me back to the door. "We should meet again to continue this conversation. I'd like to hear more about your work on power generation" I suggested as I got into the car,

He nodded non-commitally. "Let me see when I get to Aspen next" he said.

The long drive home in the luminous and prolonged summer dusk was uneventful. I got a glimpse of an elk in a clearing just next to the road. The Capstone Institute was an enigma but it seemed to be part and parcel of the larger mystery I sensed deep in the innards of the United States. I was trying to piece together a few fragments of a very large puzzle. In a way I felt like a paleontologist imagining the shape of a dinosaur from a few tiny bones. This dinosaur however was very much alive though hidden in the shadows.

The Geller Mystery

On the next day I called Sigimond to give him my account of the visit to Capstone. He listened to me attentively and when I brought up the matter of the Hudson Valley sightings he interjected that Allen Hynek was carrying out a systematic investigation of those cases by interviewing eye witnesses and collecting documentation.

"Anything more you heard from that area that may be relevant?" I inquired.

"There is something very strange coming out of the greater New York area, specifically Long Island" he replied immediately. "We don't know if it is genuine or made up but it is worth investigating."

"What is it about?'

"Some alleged first hand reporting about a former US secret experimental facility located at Montauk, controlled by the Air Force and NORAD, the North American Aerospace Defense Command, where advanced work in radar communication and electronic warfare was carried out."

"And you think that is related to the craft over the State of New York?."

"I can't tell but apparently the giant radar set up there as part of SAGE would have interfered with UFO propulsion systems and, according to one story, ripped a hole in space time. It all sounds bizarre and could be fictional but at this point, knowing what we know, we can't dismiss anything out of hand, no matter how incredible."

He said that he would try to find out more and would talk to Jacques Vallée in order to get his views.

I had a hunch that the general to whom Bruce Adams had referred might be of help and a day or two later I called the number for Mary-Jean Dartmoor. I heard a message uttered by a singsong voice with a soft southern intonation inviting callers to leave a message which I did with some elation. The sensuous voice conveyed a subliminal promise of antebellum, indolent and carefree "Gone with the wind" nostalgia.

I could not help waiting for a reply with some impatience but that afternoon I received an unexpected call from Lowell, the Texas businessman.

"I told you I would put you in contact with people who have some more information on what we talked about" he said simply after the shortest of greetings. "There is someone I want you to meet when you go to Denver. I'll call him Steve for convenience and here is the number."

I somehow felt from his intonation that I should not ask more questions about the person he was referring me to. I agreed to telephone him when I would find the time to travel to the State capital.

I had taken few books with me to America and in those days one did not have the facilities of the worldwide web. However there is a well appointed municipal library in Aspen and I made it a point to go there once in a while. On that particular occasion I looked for books about Uri Geller. I found his 1975 autobiography *My Story* and, although Puharich's account *A Journal of the Mystery of Uri Geller*, listed in the bibliography was not there, I located another book from 1976, Colin Wilson's *The Geller Phenomenon*. I was thus able to acquaint myself better with his strange case. Not much was written on his alleged extraterrestrial connections about which Geller himself seemed rather elusive. I saw however the reference to the statement made under hypnosis about an alien spaceship called *Spectra* inducing superhuman powers in him.

Like most people with open minds I was left puzzled and skeptical about Geller. He might be an exceptionally clever magician able to fool, with tricks and sleights of hand millions of people, including qualified scientific investigators; after all many scientists have been found to be at least as gullible as the average member of the public but how had he achieved such mass publicity? Magicians were many and some of them, like the implacable James Randi had spent a good part of their lives trying to expose him as a fraud but that had not convinced all those who had witnessed his demonstrations or been affected by his powers. Geller had made millions from his craft and he probably worked as a spy for at least one if not a few governments.

The story that emerged from those various versions, including his own, strongly suggested that he was used by the Mossad and probably the CIA as well. The connection with Puharich's lab, the Stanford Research Institute and other parapsychological research facilities linked to the US Government's psychological warfare programmes supported that thesis. That did not however prove that Geller's paranormal abilities were genuine. It would not have been the first time that a state had used an gifted trickster magician to gain access to privileged circles and gather sensitive information. Obviously, the extraterrestrial link was not required and could be explained either by a genuine belief on his or Puharich's part or by a desire to obfuscate the enigma even further but would that not make Geller's claims even harder to believe?

The Belle from Mississipi

As I was pondering that question the telephone rang and I recognized the soft southern drawl of Mary Jean Dartmoor.

"Hello" she said "I am returning a call from a gentleman, Carpentier."

I promptly introduced myself again and confirmed that I had been referred to her by Bruce Adams. I also mentioned that he wished me to meet her uncle.

"How sweet of Bruce" she intoned mellifluously. "It's been quite some time since I saw him. My uncle Robert O'Kennan comes in the summer and he should be here in a few days. How long will you be in Aspen?"

I explained that I would be there for quite some time.

"Lovely" she purred. "I hope we can meet sometime."

I wasted no time to propose a drink at a café downtown on the next afternoon."

She delayed the appointment by one hour, explaining that she had "chores" to do and ended noting that it would be a pleasure to "visit with me."

"Goodbye Hon" she said auspiciously before hanging up. Delighted, I realized that I had just experienced the old southern effusive charm.

On the next day we met at a quaint little watering hole located in what was then Aspen's only covered shopping gallery.

Ten minutes after five I saw a thin but shapely woman of middle height, dressed in black and white tones with the elaborate elegance that one would have rather expected in a big city. In the relaxed and sporting local environment, it was striking. When I stood up and introduced myself, hoping it was her she flashed milk white teeth between deep rouge lips and held out a long, manicured hand.

"How lovely!" she drawled, "I am Mary Jean Dartmoor. She supply slid into her seat and glanced at me between half closed mauve lids. That is when I took in her beauty; an oval face, white as young ivory lit by dark violet, almost black pupils beneath long thin eyebrows on the edge of a small limpid forehead, all framed by wavy jet-black hair. Perhaps partly out of expectation I felt like I saw Scarlett O'Hara, or rather Vivien Leigh across the table.

"It is very kind of you to meet me so readily" I said, repressing a faint bout of self-consciousness. "Bruce wanted to put me in touch with the General and it appears that you are the guardian angel to that gentleman."

I was trying to be humorous but I realized I might sound gauche. She seemed to enjoy that comparison but then she had almost not turned off her smile since she had come. She was apparently one of those Southern belles who knew that a radiant disposition is the best cosmetic over and above all others.

"Uncle Bob is a darling" she stated, somewhat unexpectedly and he should be here in the next few days but why don't you tell me about what you do...."

Before we continued a pink-faced, flaxen haired and eager waitress came to ask for our order. I subconsciously wished Mary Jean to ask for a mint julep but she instead ordered a mimosa and I went for my habitual tea.

"You'll excuse me" I said "but it is the five o'clock." She giggled softly in response.

We talked for almost an hour on my interests and my past and she told me a little about herself. She had moved to Aspen two years ago from Mississipi as she was an interior decorator and there was greater demand and a more affluent market for her trade than in her mid-sized hometown where her mother, a widow lived with four cats – two Persians and two Siamese, she emphasized - and one maid who must have been black. Her two brothers and one sister had moved away, on the east coast and in the great lakes region. She mentioned proudly in passing that her family had produced a state governor more than half a century ago, apart from her eminent military uncle who was in fact properly her cousin, being a son of her father's aunt. However due to the age difference she had always regarded him as her uncle.

During one of my forays in the municipal library I had looked for the general in the *Who's Who*. I had learnt then that his middle initial stood for Dartmoor, his mother's name and that he was born in 1930, had been to West Point and the War College, had won a PhD in international relations and a degree in Russian Studies from Brown and Columbia and was acknowledged as an expert in Soviet and Eastern European affairs since spending two years at the US Embassy in Moscow. After holding visiting professorships in two Ivy league universities he had joined the National Security Council under the Carter administration and had been promoted to his second star in 1980 before joining the Defence Intelligence Agency in a high position. Thinking about all that I wondered whether and why he would even want to talk about anything strategically sensitive. Why had Bruce Adams thought that he might open up to the foreigner that I was?

However meanwhile his lovely niece or cousin had no such constraints and she displayed the mock coyness that made her flirting allusions all the more exciting. I did not miss on the opportunity of suggesting a second meeting which she mischievously called a date, before asking me to call her on the following week to set it up and we parted in delightful terms, I with high hopes and she presumably with the mixture of satisfied pride and doubt that women usually experience in such situations.

IX
Some Veils are Lifted

"Prospero:
The fringed curtains of thine eye advance
And say what thou seest yond'"

Shakespeare, The Tempest

JOHN LILLY'S TANK AND DOLPHIN DREAMS

I felt time had come to take Ingrid up on her offer to experience the isolation tank and I called her. She readily assented and on the following day, an uncharacteristically cloudy morning, I went to her home, a modest white clapboard house with red roofing, more like what is known as a cabin in that region. I knocked at the door which did not have a bell although a Tibetan set of copper wind chimes melodiously jingled in the sighs of breeze. "Come in" a voice I recognized called from within the dwelling.

I opened the door and stepped into a small, thickly carpeted living room lined by a couch and separated from the narrow kitchen by a bar counter. Two doors were on the opposite side: a bedroom was behind the open one.

"Sit down. I am coming" the voice said through the closed door.

I noticed the low tune oozing out of the cassette player. I recognised the soft melancholy voice of Joan Baez in *Sweet Sir Galahad*. As I looked around, the closed door at the back opened and Ingrid stepped out, stark naked and holding a towel in front of her. I got a sneaking glance at her flushed face, heavy bosom and long thighs before she shut herself in the bedroom after flashing a smile which conveyed the characteristic mixture of embarrassment and elation that the female gender experiences when revealing itself. I was still holding the vision when she reemerged sportingly but fully clothed and gave me a quick hug. Joan Baez had given way to Pete Seeger's *Turn, Turn, Turn* on the cassette.

"Let us go" she intimated "the drive lasts about twenty minutes."

We stepped out, got into the bottle green jalopy and off we drove at the leisurely pace that Americans mercifully tend to keep on the road where rules on speeding are far stricter than in fast-motoring Europe. We chatted lightly until we got, not far from the small town of Basalt to a low timber building on a meadow edged by conifers. An unobtrusive sign read "Rest Research Center." The place was rather attractive despite the sparseness of the architecture. Ingrid unlocked a metal door and let me in a long room. floored and paneled in pinewood and lined by three bay windows on one side. On the other there were a few doors.

"Sauna, tanks, shower rooms, dressing rooms and rest room" she said, gesturing at them. "Patrons are requested to have a shower before using the isolation tank. While you do that, I will fill your tank. The water we use is filtered with UVs and we add a specific amount of Epsom salt."

I went into the first shower room, took my second ablution of the day and emerged clad in a thick white bathrobe that I found inside.

"The water in the tank will soon reach the required level" Ingrid explained coming out one of the other doors. "You can come and take a look."

I walked into the windowless room and saw the smooth grey ovoid module which exuded the soft hum of flowing water.

"It is made of glass reinforced resin and inside there is continuous water convection. We call it a REIT for Restricted Environment Isolation Tank" Ingrid explained.

"I guess you add magnesium sulfate inside to make bodies more buoyant inside" I ventured.

"Yes and also for the skin to absorb magnesium from the water which must be at the same temperature. When you are ready, you can get inside and I'll close the door but I am on call whenever you want the experience to end. There is a little plastic buzzer which you can press on to let me know you want out. Otherwise, I will keep you in for an hour and a half which is minimum to experience good results. You will be naturally afloat without effort because of the high salt content, as if you were on the Dead Sea. There is a heating ring outside the tank to feed a warm water convection that keeps you motionless in the middle so that you don't brush the sides. Here are earplugs. We won't use the Hemi-Sync equipment because we only want you to achieve the intense relaxation which leads to the brain generating theta waves that echo deep meditation."

I motioned that I was set to go in. Ingrid pulled up the upper part of the light eggshell-like capsule by lifting a handle on the ledge. I got out of the bathrobe and glided into the tank. The lid fell back silently and I found myself in dark and liquid silence. I had previously fitted the plugs into my ears so that I was as completely isolated from sound as my eyes were deprived of light. However I am not claustrophobic and find the obscurity of night restful and comforting. For a fleeting moment I thought of the haunting air on The Music of the Night in the *Phantom of the Opera* and then of the aria of the Queen of the Night in Mozart's *Magic Flute*. It was as if my mind was reacting to the uncanny quiet by suggesting all sorts of familiar musical and visual images in order to occupy the vacuum but I knew I had to let those evocations flow away as one should in meditation. "Neither resist nor consciously pursue those fleeting figments of memory. Don't feed your imagination. Instead accept and absorb the void outside and become one with it."

I likewise let the body shed its instinctive, habitual reflexes and twinges and after resting my attention on every part of it from the feet to the head I felt consciousness drift spontaneously on a lake of flickering, evanescent and fuzzy impressions until it stretched in concentrical circles as if it were the wave generated by a fallen stone and appeared to fill an increasingly wide three dimensional space. I was neither asleep nor awake and had no grasp of the passage of time. Only breathing, hollow and even like the rise and ebb of a distant ocean on a flat shore kept an intermittent link with my physical being. I had read earlier that this state of complete relaxation releases a tide of endorphin which smoothes and smothers all the discomforts, itches and occasional pains that keep the awakened body on edge but I was not thinking of this or of anything else, as far as I can recollect. I was immersed in the emptiness and silence and watching it in me and myself within it, absent any border between the inner and the outer.

I am not able to tell around what moment I became subconsciously aware of a rising luminous presence in the indeterminate area that encompassed the closed space and my physical self as an egg includes its embryo. The sensation of separation between me, the water and the infinite empty expanse that I felt I was had vanished but now instead of pitch black I perceived a dim white glow through my eyelids. Then it was as if a very tall radiant form stood in front of me or was it in my heart, in unison with which it appeared to faintly pulsate? It was a strange, very serene and yet awesome sensation which persisted until the cover of the tank was lifted again and I opened my eyes to the penumbra of the chamber in which I saw the shadowy outline of Ingrid's silhouette.

She did not speak but waited for me to find my feet and awkwardly climb out as I was in state of complete relaxation, akin but not tantamount to sleepiness. Because of that I did not react to the fact that I was unclothed in the close presence of an attractive woman whom I knew little and I was neither discomforted nor excited by the realization that she was only wearing a thin bathrobe which let me guess her nudity beneath it. When we got out, she told me she had gone into the sauna while waiting for my session in the tank to draw to a close.

"How was it?" she asked simply once I had put on the robe back on and stepped into the main room of the building.

"Very promising" I said "I sensed I was on the threshold of higher dimensions but I have practiced meditation in various ways for quite a few years."

"Then that must be easier for you" she noted approvingly. "You are past the stage of fear and discomfort that many feel at first and have trouble overcoming."

I went for another shower to wash out the Epsom salt that had settled on my skin and hair and we drove back to Aspen. We hardly spoke on the way as I was not eager to break out of the bubble of oceanic, embryonic serenity that I was still wrapped in. I realized that my exit from the womb-like tank brought to mind the act of giving birth and that Ingrid had been a symbolic midwife. And then gradually awoke in me the realization that the white form perceived in my state of suspended contemplative animation evoked the immaculate shining and towering beings envisioned by Poe in the final passages of his enigmatic novella *Arthur Gordon Pym*.

Ingrid dropped me at my residence. We kissed and I thanked her for the experience and we agreed to remain in touch.

"Tell me whenever you wish to get into the tank again" she told me smilingly as she drove off.

MARY JEAN AND THE GENERAL

As the summer set in the mountains I settled in my habits and enjoyed the majestic and serene nature I was surrounded with. The swimming pool provided a welcome relief from the bright sunshine and I took advantage of the opportunities for trekking, horse riding and exploring the area. I met Mary Jean again. She came for tea to my condominium one afternoon, tantalizingly dressed in bright red and wearing black fishnet stockings and gloves. We conversed and flirted happily, trading piquant innuendo which made me discover an eccentric sense of humour that contrasted with her ingénue appearance. She displayed an almost exaggerated femininity, in the manner of Southern Belles, as if to disguise an inner strength which belied her seemingly childish bubbly naiveté. I formed the impression that she would retain that pre-adolescent freshness even in her old age.

She invited me to dinner at her apartment. It matched her personality which set it apart from the alpine chalet or western ranch style of most Aspen dwellings. It had colourful silk rugs, piles of embroidered cushions on soft sofas, pale pink walls half hidden by paintings of flowers and fruits and by lithographs of American birds by Audubon. A low table at the heart of the living room carried family photographs. in colour and black and white displaying earnest young men in West Point, Navy and Air Force uniforms, smiling debutantes in ball gowns, white haired seniors in tuxedos and clustered clans of Dartmoors and relations posing against the backdrop of Antebellum plantation houses. A tape of Dolly Parton's nostalgic ballads could barely be heard in the background.

I complimented her on her taste which I said advertised that the flat was occupied by a very young and pretty woman. As a reply she drew me with a hooked finger and a naughty smile to the threshold of her bedroom to show me the innumerable stuffed bears and other creatures of all colours that littered her bed. "Do you still like my taste?" she snickered.

"They take space that one would like to occupy" I replied with a deadpan face.

She coyly guffawed with a hand on her mouth and assured me that her bed was only meant for one person, herself.

"If I ever have to put you up, I'll have to sleep on the couch and leave all those teddy bears to your care" she declared with mock magnanimity.

"I would only ask you to put me up if I could cause you pleasure and not discomfort" was my pat reply.

"What if you have no choice?" she simpered with a dramatic expression. "What if pretty Nancy does not want you?"

I did not expect that cut but I realized that gossip circulated instantly in Aspen, especially when it was inaccurate.

"Nancy is a very good friend thanks to whom I came to Aspen" I said "but that is all and I only stayed at the ranch for a few days when I arrived." I did not thank I needed to say more about the past.

"I was making fun of you" she retorted smirking wickedly. "I think I know the story but she is a stunner and it is hard to believe you don't feel more than friendship."

"If you know her, you are aware of Nancy's unique personality. I don't think she is looking for or willing to adjust to a relationship in the traditional sense. She is one of a kind and that is what many like in her."

Mary Jean dropped the subject; we sat at a candle lit table and shared a delightful evening. At one point we evoked Scott Fitzgerald and Zelda, those American *Enfants Terribles* wandering and partying on the French Riviera and what followed could be entitled like Fitzgerald's novel "Tender was the Night."

Two days after General O'Kennan arrived Mary Jean called me and after exchanging the usual pleasantries around her coquettish hints, she said that her uncle would be willing to meet for breakfast at the Aspen Club on the next morning. I was by now familiar with the American predilection for confabulations around early bird meals that in much of the world are treasured as private moments at home preceding the call of outdoor obligations. In America time is money and none is to be lost for business even if the latter is of a non-monetary nature. The time given was 8.30 which must have sounded late to a military man but which was decent enough in the mild august weather. I promptly agreed and asked my favourite caller if she would be present.

"No honey" she said with mock contrition "you'll discuss big men's stuff that goes far above my little head and I don't like getting up so early anyway. I am not a soldier." I realized that the General must not have intended to merely have a social conversation. He apparently meant business.

The morning after I was there exactly on time. It was shaping up to be another dry and blazing day of blue sky and light wind. The healthy air made one impervious to the relative poverty in oxygen at that altitude so that one felt hardly shorter of breath than in places located a mile below. I walked from my condo to the Club on West Main Street, not far from the Jerome Hotel.

There were quite a few patrons in the sunny breakfast room but I recognized the General by the agreed signs for recognition. He wore a dark blue polo shirt and brown corduroy trousers and had put a copy of the *Rocky Mountain News* on his table. When I approached he stood briefly to shake my head and gestured for me to sit opposite him. He was a thin, fairly short, nearly bald man with a ruddy complexion. His pale blue eyes watched me intently behind large glasses.

A mug of black coffee stood in front of him. I ordered another and some bread, butter and pancakes with honey while he called for toast, bacon and eggs and orange juice.

"Mary Jean told me a lot about you and I spoke to Bruce as well" he told me while slowly turning his spoon in his mug. "I gather you are interested in understanding how our country runs." He finished the sentence with an ambiguous half-smile.

"First I would like to say that I am grateful that you are willing to spend the time to meet me" I began, wishing to warm up the mood. "I know that you are in an important position which makes you privy to matters that you cannot share with outsiders but I have experienced the basic openness of most Americans."

"Call us garrulous" he replied with a hint of sarcasm. "That is the spirit of our democracy even if many in the State spend considerable time and energy trying to keep too many things under a lid and confusing people about things they can't hide, but tell me what exactly you hope to accomplish?."

To his direct query I tried to give as straightforward and complete an answer as I could muster. I went into my background and cited the names of a few people whom he might have known and who were favourable and helpful to my quest. He listened impassively but nodded once or twice to signal that he was aware of certain things I said or approved of my views. He seemed particularly attentive when I pointed out that the US's secret policies and plans in certain areas aroused many misgivings abroad, some of which might be unjustified and could be dispelled by throwing some light on what was really going on."

"The reason why Bruce gave you my name is that I have followed his work for a few years. He knows my opinions. I am one of the guys in our military pushing for a reform of our defence and security policies since the end of the Vietnam war."

That was a promising opening for me to move forward.

THE SHAMANS, THE YOGIS AND THE WARRIORS

"How did you and some of your colleagues get influenced by New Age ideas?" I asked.

He looked up briefly as if to evoke the past. "Oriental concepts were in fashion" he reminisced. 'Our armed forces were emotionally broken after Nam. I was a youngish officer like many others who noticed the gloom and the hopelessness in the military after that awful war. Some people were teaching Indian and Chinese meditation techniques and martial philosophies based on yoga, bushido and kungfu. Integral studies and TM were very popular with the educated middle and upper classes. In the seventies, while the Church Committee investigated and put a lid on MK-Ultra, Monarch and the like a few of the top brass decided to explore those avenues for rebuilding the morale of the forces. We had to show we could do good. Colonel Jim Channon started his First Earth Battalion at Fort Knox in 1979 and his methods were highly successful and were reproduced in several other places. I am one of those who got involved and Boy, did it open up our minds!"

While he spoke our order had been served and we began to eat when he finished his sentence. I was captivated by that account which revealed a side of American military history I had only suspected hitherto.

"So Colonel Channon was the pioneer of all this?" I asked.

"He played a big role because he is an elite soul and studied Aurobindo, Irwin Thompson and the other folks at the California Institute of Integral Studies but this was all tied to experiments with ESP and other paranormal abilities in various labs under government supervision."

"You mean Puharich's Round Table Institute and such?"

"Yes. Among others. As a young guy I was exposed to what we would now call parapsychological ideas. I and some of my peers like many of our contemporaries, we read Yogananda, Alan Watts,

Timothy Leary and the Tibetan Book of the Dead. I met General Dornberger, von Braun's mentor and a godfather of the space programme. He started experiments on telepathy and remote viewing at Bell Labs. Remember that our nation has an old connection with oriental philosophies, going back to Whitman and his contemporaries. Even FDR was interested in the occult and eastern theories, General Bradley was called Omar by his parents to honour the Persian poet Khayyam. General Hap Arnold who set up RAND supported Townsend Brown's research into electrogravifics and UFO technology. In my West Point class we have a few students of Chinese and Hindu texts and we were impressed with the martial but flexible wisdom of the Bhagavad Gita and Sun Tzu which teaches that violence is the ultimate recourse that successful methods can make unnecessary. Just this year at Fort Leavenworth in Texas Colonel Frank Burns has formed a Task Force Delta of military psychics. Channon's motto is "uniforms without uniformity, structure without status, unity powered by diversity." He wants soldiers to be shamans, diviners and psychics attuned to the natural environment and to the psychology of native cultures. Quite a revolution for the forces."

"Quite!" I noted with some amazement. "And the top brass is behind this?"

"Yep, so far. General Stubblebine is the current head of INSCOM, the army's Intelligence and Security command and he is very much into it. He belongs to the group that worked with Channon and Burns, went to ESALEN and is a specialist of electronics and psychology and a driving force behind the Stargate Project. He is convinced of Uri Geller's abilities and claims he can bend spoons too and do quite a few other supernatural things so he supports Channon's ideas about training superhuman soldier monks."

"What about the other branches of the military?"

"I am revealing no secrets when I say that the relations between us, the Navy and the Air Force are rather competitive and at times adversorial so they don't share many of their findings with us but Admiral Bobby Inman is into some rather esoteric stuff as well I think and he is not the only one. The Navy prides itself on being even more scientifically sophisticated and exotic than the Air Force but there is always a bragging contest between them."

"That is a fascinating insight" I said while munching on a raisin muffin "but is it not a bit confusing and even destabilizing for a military force which after all has to carry out destruction and killings. Those oriental philosophies are pretty subversive in that context. They teach you to disregard material goods and question all certainties while instilling compassion for all living beings and concern for the planet as a whole; not exactly a recipe to make a perfect warrior."

"I had the same objections" the General replied quietly after taking another sip of orange juice. "Channon wants his special forces to be in the service of the earth and that can pose a real problem for a national army which is sometimes called to fight another country but then if you absorb the Japanese Bushido doctrine, it makes you serene and determined about what you have to do according to the code of honour, to the point of sacrificing your life and if you read the Gita you see how Arjuna was told he had no option but to carry on with the war until the ultimate victory, whatever the costs. You need that kind of conviction and will power. Otherwise you are just a mercenary trying to reduce your risk while killing for profit. Anyway it's an old instinct here. Remember Kennedy and the Peace Corps? This is a mystical version of it."

I could see his point. The Americans were trying to imbibe the indomitable spirit of the Japanese and Vietcong who had fought them so ruthlessly with much lesser weapons and means but I had trouble envisioning a yankee kid, raised on a diet of television serials, hamburgers, coke and peanut butter in a self-indulgent society, as a samurai or a vedic knight. Meanwhile however O'Kennan's thought took a different direction.

"I must say that we are not all of one mind on this business of spirituality in the forces. I am much more concerned about the Soviets than Channon and some of other officers who tend to think all can be settled with love and light. I am a cold warrior by training" he noted." but not one of those who just want to be tough and mechanical, killing machines if you will. They are like the Vulcans of the movie and they view all people, at least those outside their group, as cattle to be controlled with propaganda, electronics, psychedelics or any other means. Then there are the Evangelical Christians who say that anything outside their Church is satanic. I was born in an Episcopalian family and we are tolerant so that I have no problem with other philosophies and religions when they teach good things. I see the oriental martial schools of wisdom as close to European traditions of chivalry."

"I have no difficulty grasping that what some of you are doing is disturbing to Old Style Christian or agnostic mindsets" I assured him "but are you getting good results from your trainees? I guess success is what can best deter critics."

"We surely take care of many habitual mental issues and problems in the recruits we build up" the General said decisively. "The whole concept is to give them higher objectives than just fighting if they have to in order to keep getting paid until they are honourably discharged and find another job. We want them to feel that they can change the world for the better. I have long been concerned about the influence of civilian spook agencies like the CIA and the NSA on our people. They do the job they have to but many of their guys are twisted bastards" he said ruefully, staring hard at me. "They play by a dirty playbook and that is contrary to the military code. I don't want soldiers turning into high-tech fiends and using treachery and deception against either friend or foe. Even the Soviets keep their defence personnel away from the KGB."

I felt his anger. He clearly resented the "Black Op" mentality of the civilian agencies which was percolating into the armed forces. However I did not want to remind him of the nefarious chemical, biological and radiological experiments carried out by the Pentagon on unsuspecting civilian populations in the USA and abroad. That might simply make him shut down and end the conversation. On the other hand I could guess the rivalry and the mutual suspicions at play between the various outfits operating in the realm of Intelligence. The ruthless power games of undercover operations was not compatible with the planetary ecological awareness that the First Earth Battalion instilled in its personnel. Those were irreconcilable as far as I could see and I told him so.

"You are surely aware that most people can't see a clear difference between what Channon and you, among others are advocating and the CIA-driven experiments to build remote controlled soldiers and operatives fighting under drug or psychically induced hypnosis or utilizing such drugs and techniques to subdue hostile soldiers or civilians. "Non-lethal weapons" is a nice reassuring expression but we are still talking about arms that can give total victory without causing physical casualties. I have heard about MK Delta, a project to research and plan the use of biochemical agents in military operations."

"I have to admit that" O Kennan said "you see. There are many links between apparently contradictory movements in American society. The concept of the First Earth Battalion is to resort as much as possible to traditional psychic techniques, known as occult powers, and function in harmony with nature. On the other side is the neuropsychiatric behaviorist gang which wants to implant electrodes in people and induce hypnosis with chemicals and VLF waves but there are crossovers and overlaps. The Beat generation and certain government agencies maintain not-so-obvious connections. Think of Lilly, Leary and the CIA regarding LSD and psilocybin. They share certain objectives such as improving the human condition, at least in their perception or to their advantage, with the help of drugs and electromagnetic emissions. We are a medicalised society, don't forget that."

"I know" I reflected aloud somberly "where to stop the testing and use of drugs, mind-altering or otherwise when the entire healthcare system is based on the use of chemical products and radiations? The only difference is between those things that are allowed by the State and those which aren't, and that is pretty much the border between what is for civilians in peace time and what is intended for enemies at overt or covert war."

The general once again smiled a joyless smile "The point is that the mind-altering drugs may get you lost in Lala-land, as materialists declare, or they could really enable you to expand into other, usually hidden dimensions of the world, at least as real as what we perceive every day. The shamans of ancient cultures stand by the second opinion and modern society tries desperately, and not very successfully to prevent people from finding out for themselves. Of course there is usually a heavy price to pay in terms of physical health."

I could see that his personal view on this sensitive issue was mixed but I did not press him to make his stand clear. I grasped at that moment the ambivalence of many American decision-makers on the role of drugs in their culture.

The Vulcans and the Others

"I have a sense that the people you refer to as Vulcans are working on dehumanizing people and computerizing society in the name of progress" I ventured. "Would you agree with this interpretation since you told me you see a great danger in their activities?"

He nodded approvingly and only added: "I'll put you in touch with an institute near Washington DC where you will find answers to your questions. Since you know about RAND, you can see the picture. They belong to the same category and I know them well."

I made a mental note to get back to him one way or another about that when going to the federal capital.

Breakfast at an end, the plates and glasses had almost vanished from the table. I seized the opportunity, before the meeting drew to a close, to bring out another subject related to Leary.

"I won't pretend that I am taking you into unfamiliar territory" I started. "You probably know much more about the reality behind the UFO phenomenon than I do and you must also know what Leary, Lilly and others wrote about that. I hope you are not one of the generals who refuse to talk about it."

As I predicted he did not flinch or betray any feeling.

"I told you. I am someone open to facts" he replied. "I share the attitude of some officers I respect like MacArthur, Hillenkoetter,

Arthur Trudeau, Doolittle, Sanford and Ben Childlaw who spoke publicly about UFOs and sometimes paid a price for not lying. This matter is of great concern for our national security but we are instructed to ignore it or, if we can't, trivialize it as much as possible to keep the population quiet. I don't necessarily agree with that strategy dictated by civilian Intel agencies but I understand that the economy does not take well to uncertainty. The state's job is to keep people feeling reasonably secure in a familiar world."

I was relieved by his frankness. He understood the futility of giving me the official position on the "alien" question. What would I ask next? There was so much to be discussed that I did not know where to begin and there was not much time left. It seemed difficult not to mention the seminal and loaded Roswell mystery. As soon as I said the name he gestured, as if to indicate that he expected it to come up. "Affirmative" he said "the Army was instructed to deny the story and witnesses were told to keep silent but it was not a great surprise at the top. Both the Pentagon and the White House knew of the Alien presence even before the war and an incident was expected, especially since the installation around Los Alamos of high power radars which interfere with electromagnetic propulsion systems.

General Twining prepared a classified report for Truman to update him and afterwards the president kept getting weekly briefings from his military aide, Colonel Landry. We knew the visitors were particularly interested or possibly concerned about our atomic programme."

"What about the Soviets?" I put in "You are an expert on that country."

"The Russians are a major reason why we keep this as quiet as possible. We don't want to tip them about our vulnerabilities nor our abilities and they behave in the same way. We know that they face the same issue."

On a hunch I brought up the case of Grenada.

"Are you familiar with the campaign led by Sir Eric Gairy?" I asked.

He kept a deadpan face but his comment was unhesitating. "We were informed when he came to the White House and met Carter in 1977. My boss then, Brzezinski was present as National Security Adviser and some of what was said was analysed in the NSC."

I did not hide my excitement. "That is when Gairy began lobbying to have it taken up at the UN?."

"More or less but he had seen a crashed UFO and perhaps been shown the body of an Alien at Grenada a few months before. That is why he had a missionary zeal about this."

"And the US stopped him?"

"Not just us but other leading western countries as well. We had told the UN Secretary General U Thant in the sixties not to pursue the matter and we did the same with Waldheim. Still Gairy had a General Assembly decision passed in support of his appeal...."

"Decision 33/426 from December 78 which called for setting up a UN UFO affairs agency" I cut in.

"Right you are but it but it could not get through to the Security Council so the matter pretty much died."

"Because Washington had him overthrown while he was in New York arguing the case?"

The General slightly shook his head: "Not the US as a whole but the faction in the CIA that is hellbent on keeping the secret. Gairy was seen as a dangerous alarmist because he believed that the aliens posed a clear and present threat to humanity. That could have raised hell internationally. We in the Pentagon believe that the boys at the Company made the Cubans kick him out through Maurice Bishop and his socialist gang. Good cover and easy deniability. Gairy was seen as rather Far Right. He was getting some military cooperation from Pinochet in Chile so it made sense for Castro to support the opposite faction in Grenada. Officially America was neutral and we did not mind Gairy despite his quirks."

I took a second to digest the stunning implication.

"So, you are telling me that the CIA can work with Cuba's communist regime?" I asked.

"Well, don't you know how much pressure we can put on Castro?

If we wanted him gone nobody could keep him in power for so long. When something is also in his interest why would he not help?"

Indeed I was not the only one to wonder about Castro's seeming invulnerability all those years despite the many alleged plots hatched in Washington and Miami to get rid of him.

"Where is Gairy now and what happened to the ET body in Grenada?" I queried almost by reflex.

"Gairy is living quietly in exile in San Diego under surveillance from the Puzzle Palace—I was aware that this was a nickname for the NSA—and the Agency. He is still hoping to return to his island home and reclaim power. You may not believe me but I have no information on the purported alien corpse."

I did not in fact quite believe him. I thought there was a limit beyond which he would not allow himself to speak the truth but that was just my impression. I realized he had said a lot without revealing anymore than what was known or at least strongly suspected in many quarters but, as long as no proof was produced his was only a personal statement with which his superiors and colleagues were free to disagree. The UFO issue remained in the shadows and I inferred that he had not broken any pledge or rule by stating what I had just heard which skeptics could always label as disinformation.

"You have been wonderfully open, General" I said while he glimpsed at his watch and stood up slowly. "I am grateful to you and Mary Jean for speaking in confidence."

"Son" he replied with a hint of irony underlined by that familiar address which he used for the first time "Shakespeare was right: *There are more things in heaven and earth Horatio than are dreamt of* ... is written in our philosophy. Even when we look like we know it all, we are just learning like all others, just a few classes ahead of them and the body of what we don't know grows as we move forward."

X

From Mysteries into the Mystic

Then magnificently we will float into the mystic.

Van Morrison, Into the Mystic

INTO THE RABBIT HOLE

The summer in leafy, alpine Aspen is splendid and I was not eager to leave the town even for a few days. By then I had a growing circle of friends and I was often drawn into campfire parties in the mountains, potlucks in the town's understatedly opulent homes and in neighbouring ranches. Nancy had left for Molokai but Mary Jean and I often drove around in her shiny black little Rover. I also began to give weekly talks on Eastern philosophies and esoteric knowledge to an audience of amateurs and dabblers in mysticism. There was every reason to be happy but I did not lose track of my goals and spent a lot of time researching and reading materials connected to what I was looked. When Richard Sigismond called me one afternoon to announce that he would host a few experts in his field of work that weekend for a fact-checking session, I instantly accepted his invitation to attend it.

"Some confidential information will be shared between us and we would not like it to be spread around" he warned me. "I know you are prepared to hear it and are aware that it is not for the general public."

I assured him that I was not acting as a journalist and that I understood it would not be easy to be taken seriously by average listeners so that certain things might as well be kept private. I remembered to call Lowell as he had suggested and told him I could call on the person he thought I should meet. He phoned me back a bit later, told me he had spoken to that individual and gave me a Denver number. "It is less than two hours from Boulder as you know" he said "and Jerry can probably drive up to see you if that works out better."

I thanked him and left for Boulder two days later. I would be enjoying once again Howard Higman's informal hospitality as he had insisted that I should stay in one of the many bedrooms of the family home.

I got there on a Friday early afternoon on the now familiar route through Leadville. The rendez-vous at Richard's was set for Saturday at 3 pm. Higman was out when I arrived but his man-Friday let me him and took me to my room. I took a walk to the nearby Boulder Mall and stopped for a snack at a greek café called Taverna Tertzakes. I called the number Lowell had given me from a payphone. A woman's voice answered and asked my name in response to my request. She told me to hang on and after a relatively long time, I heard a somewhat muffled man's voice: "What is this for?"

"I was told about you by Lowell up in Aspen" I explained. "He must have called."

Jerry did not confirm that he had heard about me but simply asked: "How long are you here?"

"Two or three days" I replied. "How are you placed this weekend?'

"If you come to Denver on Sunday, I can meet you."

"Alright" I replied "Let us say Sunday afternoon."

He gave me the name of a coffee place in Central Denver and we agreed on 4 pm. His laconism had not given me any hints about what he did but I had a vague idea from the way that Lowell had referred to him without wishing to get into details. I guessed he was somebody who kept a low profile for good reason. Not somebody I would wish to get close to but I wanted to hear his views and understand where he came from.

I took that afternoon off for a long walk in the Chautauqua park which spreads at the town's western fringe all the way to the top of the Flatirons. The last part of the tour entailed a rather steep climb of wooded slopes upto the foot of the massive slanting rockfaces and on my return at dusk I saw a brown bear at a distance of less than a thousand feet. The hefty beast reminded that wild animals, including the occasional mountain lion still roamed the area.

"They are attracted to the city's garbage and come to forage in the dumps at night" Higman explained at dinner that evening. "Fortunately for you there are no grizzlies here because one could have had you for supper. There is no way you can outrun or fight them unless you have a firearm. Brown bears are rather timid and prefer to feast on smaller animals" he commented with his trademark gallows humour.

As usual for him, we ended the evening watching political documentaries about the sixties and seventies, his favourite period of American history. The film we saw made references to Garrison's *A Heritage of Stones*, about the Warren Commission on President Kennedy's assassination. The book explains the author's conviction that the said Commission was set up to cover up the real circumstances behind the crime in order to protect its perpetrators. Both my host and I agreed that it was difficult to form a different opinion.

"I met George de Mohrenschild" Higman recalled while sipping his brandy. "He was in the circle of CIA operatives and Far Right characters who somehow were in touch with Lee Harvey Oswald shortly before the assassination and he also happened to be a family friend of our current Vice-President and ex-CIA director George Bush. In fact I heard that a few years Mohrenschild wrote to Bush to ask him for help against people whom he said were threatening him because of his alleged role in the plot to kill JFK."

"Mohrenschild has a brother, Dimitri who lives in Auroville, the New Age community near Pondicherry in South India" I noted. 'Both the brothers were known as white Russian reactionaries who had strong links with the more conservative and anti-communist sections of the western Intelligence community. Of course George may have been told to meet Oswald without being given the true reason. He is Russian and Oswald had lived in the USSR, spoke Russian and was married to a Soviet woman so that it made sense for US Intelligence operatives dealing with the USSR to interact with him. If you ask me,

Oswald's Soviet connection is a red herring. It made him the perfect suspect and allowed those who pulled the strings to trace the murder to the Kremlin and Cuba, whether or not Oswald fired the gun on that day."

"The plots hatched by the powers-that-be are so convoluted as to be impenetrable" Howard reflected aloud, gazing at the ceiling and slowly rocking his glass. "You can never find the truth and if you think you have, you can't prove it. Too many people giving contradictory stories and most of them lying or repeating other people's lies they believe in."

That summed up the evening's theme and brought an end to the after dinner session. I had not told him that the same rule applied to issues even bigger than a president's public execution in broad daylight.

The next morning, I visited the vast campus and the library of the University of Colorado on Pleasant Street. It gave me the impression once more that American academic enclaves are miniature countries which live largely outside the national ecosystem in bubbles of their own making. While the studious find in them the freedom and congenial environment to pursue their work undisturbed, most students live a strange make-believe world of classes, examinations, drunken parties and often promiscuous co-ed mingling. Unsurprisingly, average citizens have little confidence in the allegedly wise advice proffered by university types whom they regard as impractical eggheads. The suspicion extends to graduate students, generally held to belong to the privileged classes since higher education is too expensive for the poor who cannot secure a scholarship. In 1983, tuition fees were not nearly as high as they have grown but were already out of bounds for the bulk of hourly wage dependent families which make the vast majority of Americans, unless they are willing and able to contract heavy debts in order to pursue a degree.

THE FRENCH PRODIGY AND THE AMERICAN INVESTIGATOR

I had lunch at the cafeteria in the Regent's Building, thanks to Higman who had given my name to the reception office and afterwards I leisurely walked towards Sigismond's home. I got there shortly after three and from the little front lawn garden saw that his other guests had already arrived. When I came in I recognized Robert Desbois's pensive, sharp featured face, keen glance and thick, disciplined hair from the photos I had seen on his books' back covers. Here was a true French intellectual figure, at once a novelist, an essayist, a mathematician, a physicist and an electronics inventor, carrying the noble baggage of a long history on his lithe, thin frame with the thoughtfulness and reticence typical of those who have read and pondered too many things not to remain lastingly perplexed, so aware are they of the world's complexity.

Desbois's two decades in the United States gave him an easy-going informality which affected only on the surface his European upper class reserve. I instantly felt a great sympathy for him because he exuded unbridled intelligence and also because I could relate to the blend of influences from the old and new worlds I was exposed to as well.

The other visitor was introduced by Richard as Laura Glendale Hollyfield; younger than Desbois, she must have been in her mid-thirties and remarkably attractive with wide sparkling blue eyes, curly jet black hair and a ravishing smile. I knew about her from her 1980 documentary *Eerie Culling* for which she had been awarded an Emmy. The biography I had read somewhere indicated that she had been a Beauty Queen in her native Montana and had entered the 1963 Miss America Pageant—a woman could not let these facts be forgotten. She was a producer at a Denver television channel.

After a brief exchange of greetings, we sat down in the now familiar small living room cradled in book shelves and got into the thick of the intended topic.

I had so many questions to ask Desbois that I could hardly contain my impatience while Richard, magistrally ponderous as was his habit, retraced our respective backgrounds and explained that we were trying to exchange updates about the overall UFO issue in its various implications.

"Robert is a leading analyst and interpreter of what all the data amount to" he pointed out "while Laura has also accumulated a considerable amount of information and has seen documents and heard testimonies accessible to very few others. Côme on the other hand brings some insights from abroad and a background in eastern religious philosophical studies which can provide a wider perspective on the matter under consideration."

"That leads me right to what I was eager to find out from Dr Desbois" I said. "I have noticed that in your last writings, you have moved away from the usual explanation for UFOS and related sightings. You say they may not be beings and craft coming from other planets but rather creatures and phenomena from other dimensions, tied to the very structure of the universe. I am fascinated by that but wonder why you lost faith in the common ET thesis. Is it not pretty obvious by now that a universe consisting of an unlimited number of Suns like ours must contain many earth-like planets and hence quite a few lifeforms as advanced as ours or far more developed. Why discount this?"

"Not discounting it in principle but merely drawing conclusions from a number of facts that cast doubts over that superficially compelling hypothesis" the Frenchman replied guardedly. His gallic accent was nearly imperceptible.

"I have read your objections" I retorted but they sound, if you allow me, as anthropocentric as the claim that you dispute about "aliens" being humanoid creatures from another planet or solar system. For example you argue that there are far too many visits and passages for the explanation that the visitors are scientifically surveying the Earth and us to hold true and you rightly show that they have been seen for centuries and perhaps millennia so that they cannot be regarded as newcomers trying to find out about us. Yet how can you impute to them our own logic without knowing what they really are about?"

"I don't" he responded "but I attempt to get past the simplistic ideas propagated by so many ufologists who describe the "Others" as opposite numbers of our astronauts, that is a bunch of alien scientists and military types trying to find out what this planet is like and what we are about, either to conquer us or to add human specimens to their museums of natural history."

"I agree that we must look at all possibilities that come to our minds" Richard interjected "and not remain limited by the prevalent ideas but I am not sure that Robert can hold on to his claim that some of the ETs described by many witnesses, the little Grays are not physiologically fit for space travel. Given how little we know about outer space, about UFOs and about the aliens who come in many shapes and sizes, it seems a bit premature to come to such a conclusion."

"It is not a conclusion but a valid point for discussion" Desbois corrected. "It was almost meant as a provocation to dogmatic researchers who sometimes can be as intolerant of other perspectives as the classical scientists who ridicule or ignore them. The fringe must not set its own limits. By definition it is the limit and that can expand as no one knows where it ends."

"I am fascinated by Dr Desbois's speculations" Laura said in a mellifluous voice which denoted her gift as a radio and television host "but I have gathered enough facts to feel that, like many other investigators, I possess circumstantial evidence that we are dealing with at least a few different non-human highly intelligent and technically advanced lifeforms that travel and dwell in space. Several credible and well known members of scientific, military and Intelligence organizations in various countries, and especially in the United States have expressed the same conviction and have even said to have proof of that. It is a solid basis to accept or reject hypotheses and guesses as to what else may be at stake."

"Yes, I have read top level CIA official Victor Marchetti in an interview on *Second Look Magazine* of two or three years ago acknowledge that the matter of UFOs is a top priority concern in the Intelligence community" I pointed out.

"Marchetti has not really said much except that it is a very secret and deeply embarrassing subject of which everyone is afraid to talk" Desbois objected. "My question, given the record of dissimulation and deception within all state agencies tied to national security, goes like this: is the silence kept by governments a proof of anything beyond the fact that they don't want to say anything or don't know what to say because perhaps they don't know much and feel frustrated and powerless, not a position that any state likes to be in?"

"So you think that the main secret, to be kept at all costs, is that the government is clueless?" asked Laura.

"That is often the impression I get" Robert responded. "Further, we all agree that UFO-like phenomena have been reported and sometimes depicted in art or historical documents since the beginning of history so that what we are witnessing is not new and appears never to have been understood, perhaps because it is too complex and above our heads, literally and figuratively to make any sense, outside mythology, religion and mysticism."

"I have seen and heard reports from military and advanced research institutions, that the mystery craft are staffed by small humanoid, grayish chlorophyll-fed beings who have mastered the control of space time, matter and energy and are monitoring us as if we were their creation or at least the result of genetic manipulations carried out by them" Laura stated matter-of-factly. "At some levels, certain experts know a lot more than is publicly admitted and there are probably good reasons not to broadcast it in view of the confusion, turmoil and unpredictable reaction that could ensue in the population."

"The bigger problem would be for the authorities to explain why they lied and hid so much and who gave them the authority to keep all this out of sight from tax-paying citizens in supposedly open, democratic societies" I added. "We are not living anymore under the ancient theocracies in which the chosen ruling elites alone were entitled to commune with the gods. By the way, Laura, I am very interested in finding out more about some allegedly classified Air Force Grudge report, given that others in the series have been made public long ago and were dismissive of the extraterrestrial reality of UFOs. They attributed sightings to mundane events and natural phenomena."

"John Lear, a CIA operative and son of the famous aeronautical inventor and designer, wrote a report in 1977 from notes made by a military officer called Bill English" Laura replied "but I have no proof of the existence of the original."

Musings about the Nature of Reality

"We are now assuming that what Laura and others heard or saw from top secret informants is true and not disinformation" Desbois resumed "and that raises a number of problems such as the extent of the government's cover up and the reason for it, which could be that the truth behind UFOs is so disturbing that it could deal a fatal blow to human societies or at least upset the fragile socio-political order. However I still want you to consider the possibility that the source of the UFO and related experiences even farther above us, in the very underlying structure of reality which, for all we know could well be a conscious network influenced by transcendent minds or intelligent organisms. As you know I am a computer scientist and am involved in the quest for artificial intelligence, which is the attempt to mimic the natural operations of cognition and consciousness.

Following the work we did at Stanford some years in the PLANET project ago to network scientific databanks through the ARPANET with funding from the National Science Foundation we are soon going to have a global gridwork of computers which will bring together the world's intellectual and technical resources at the click of a key and at the speed of electricity. I talk about that in a recent book. That tells me that such super-intelligent organizations must already exist since a very remote past and that they may well intervene in our daily reality by temporarily or gradually altering the laws of physics in ways that we cannot even begin to comprehend or predict."

"I have a question for you, Robert" Sigismond said "You told me once that as a young man in France you witnessed a pretty convincing demonstration that your government was hiding scientifically recorded facts from the public. Did that not make you suspect that there were indeed non-human creatures out there that were moving about in our orbit?"

"Sure" came the reply. "You are referring to my story about a retrograde satellite being tracked at the French National Aerospace Committee in 1961 by a team of which I was a part. In my presence and in the presence of my colleagues a higher official erased the tape so that no visual proof would remain of that observation. No state on earth to my knowledge was able to launch a retrograde satellite at the time; it could not be natural so that it must have been put up there by someone who had a higher technology than any human agency and, clearly the French powers-that-be did not want to have to explain that baffling fact to anybody. I remain convinced this was a real craft of some kind but I also believe that the UFO phenomenon is in fact a multilayered array of events and processes that are not necessarily related and may not be traced to a single cause."

"That is fair enough" conceded Richard "but you will agree with me that the many reports and technical studies that are presented at seminars like the one that Dr Leo Sprinkle convened at the University of Wyoming at Laramie in 1980 converge towards the recognition that some of the encounters and observations at least prove the existence of broadly humanoid or at least higher intelligent animal beings endowed with powerful technologies. I belong here and one of the early public testimonies on UFOs came from a famous son of Boulder, astronaut Scott Carpenter who spent his childhood near here, at the crossing of Aurora and 7th Avenue. He confided that during his 1962 Mercury orbital flight he had been escorted by some shining objects and was even mysteriously helped to reenter the atmosphere and touch down at sea unharmed despite overshooting the target and running too low on fuel. After spilling his guts he was reprimanded by NASA and not allowed to go into space again. This is all very real and Carpenter is not prone to spiritual flights of fancy."

"And I am told that many other credible witnesses, including some rather high level experts and officials will come forward with more information in the coming years" Laura stated.

"I have no doubt about that" was Robert's response "but I also know that eminent people in all times and civilizations have testified to similar experiences which were assigned divine causes in the past when civilizations were not as technically developed. That takes us to the source of mythologies and religions and the borders between God, divine beings, angels and alien space travelers becomes blurred. Is our universe or at least what we see of it created by those mysterious watchers, the *egregores* as the Gnostics called them just as we build computers or television networks? As a matter of fact it is customary in NASA to allude to unidentified objects in space as *Santas* to highlight their supernatural or mythical features. Astronaut Lowell during the December 1968 Apollo 8 mission famously said on the radio to Houston once 'we have a Santa' when his module reemerged from the dark side of the moon. Obviously this was a coded report, meant to keep all non-insiders in the dark about what he meant but the choice of metaphor is significant."

Laura shook her head: "Let us not forget that we have some insights in the public domain about concrete aspects of the UFO phenomenon such as the saucers' propulsion system which was presented at a conference in Florida by William Hamilton a couple of years ago. They seem to use anti-gravitation technology."

"I have read about that for quite a few years" said Desbois "and also about electro-magnetic propulsion and others but until we can demonstrate one of those theories in practice, we are not sure whether they really operate as claimed by a few. Remember that in France the government has been more forthright than in America about admitting the fact and trying to unravel the enigma. The French Aerospace Agency has already plainly stated that the flying saucers and other mysterious aircraft must come from outer space but I still think that there is more to it and even the story of explorers from another planet may be a false flag. That does not make me popular among my friends in the ufological community or with some people in the military but I stand by my hunch until proven wrong."

"If UFOs and their makers originate in this universe, they must be able to come close or perhaps even exceed the speed of light which would imply that they harness principles of physics we have not discovered yet. Otherwise they may come from a parallel reality, a superspace in which there may be no distances and no time as we experience and measure them. We'd be dealing with Kantor's transfinity that Borges wrote about and that the late Jacques Bergier loved so much."

"Shall I tell you what I heard some years back in Washington?" Laura said. "It is well known that President Carter was keen to find out everything he could about UFOs since he had seen one in his younger days in Georgia. He asked Ford's Director of the CIA, now Vice-President George Bush to brief him on the matter. Bush wanted to retain his position and tried to negotiate an extension with the new commander-in-chief in exchange for his cooperation but Carter had already tapped Admiral Turner for that job and Bush refused to speak, claiming that the President had no need to know because of the exceedingly high classification of the subject. Imagine this, the commander-in-chief being stonewalled and having no power to break through."

"What such stories tell me is that we are dealing with an area that passeth human perception if I may paraphrase the Bible" the French scientist commented with a thin smile. His voice had lowered almost to an awed whisper. "The recognition of an entirely different architecture of the cosmos is a far bigger breakthrough than the discovery of the heliocentric universe by Copernicus and Galileo. It blows to smithereens much of our physics and biology, not to mention religions and psychological notions. Again, it might take a long time for our species to recover from this revelation. Governments don't like such upheavals which can sweep them away into the dustbin of history."

The silence that trailed his words was proof that we all were pondering his words that resonated in each of us.

"I still feel there is something very tangible in a nuts and bolts sort of way" Sigismond articulated in a soft but firm voice. "We have all heard here from good sources that some of the materials and technologies that UFOs use or are based upon are being studied and even replicated in some military and big corporate labs. They are not apparently dealing with parallel universes and psychic phenomena but with metals, alloys, energy devices and in other cases, flesh and blood beings, even if the flesh and blood are not like ours, though often not so different! I am told that anti-gravity propulsion was experimentally achieved in 1971 at the S-4 compound at Groom Lake of Area 51."

I nodded support. "I suppose you all know about the Lockheed chief aeronautical engineer Kelly Johnson" I added. "He is not the only one to have acknowledged that he studied the shapes and propulsion systems of certain craft not made on this planet. He was a hard-headed mechanic, not a mystic or an astrophysicist."

"There were many allegations of the same order revolving around the Hughes Aircraft corporation and its owner, the mysterious Howard Hughes" Laura recalled. "He was supposed to have been briefed about some of those finds in order to reverse engineer them."

"It is a fact that ex-GOP Republican candidate Senator Barry Goldwater spoke out about his knowledge of a secret vault at Wright Patterson Air Base in Ohio containing recovered flying discs pieces" Sigismond continued. "The Senator did the rounds in the Intelligence and Military leadership to try to get access to it and reported that General Curtis Le May blew his top when he raised the question and told him never to bring that up again. Even the doughty and usually obstreperous Goldwater was a bit shellshocked by the violence of the reaction."

"I am rather familiar with all that" the French scientist retorted "but then secrecy and even paranoia are hallmarks of the military, especially in this country and mysteries can also be created and used to keep people away from truly sensitive strategic matters like new weapons that violate international agreements or may outrage public feelings. If you read some of the documents prepared and confidentially circulated by generals such as Le May or Westmoreland, you will notice that they plannned or at least envisioned top-secret operations to destabilise, confuse or spread false beliefs among the targets which can be the public of allied nations or even the domestic audience. So there is more than one possible explanation and often the less obvious or logical one is true."

"After reading Phillys Schaffly's *Kissinger on the Couch*, I am quite willing to believe in the seemingly unlimited ability of some people in power to weave very complex yarns and keep everybody else guessing" Laura conceded "but I think that attributing all the very bizarre and otherworldly aspects of the UFO reality to some security-obsessed Strangeloves strains credibility far too much. After all there are thousands of reported abductions of people in the US alone and for the last several years I have analysed multiple accounts and seen physical evidence of cattle mutilations or rather clinically precise anatomical excisions which can hardly be pinned on State agencies or private corporations."

Shadows from the Past and Lights from Above

"If there is disinformation and deception, it stretches back to the second world war and earlier" Richard Sigismond noted. "The first director of NASA's Kennedy Space Centre in the early sixties, the German Dr Kurt Debus is known to have told a few people, just as his more famous contemporary Von Braun, that Hitler's space programme was inspired by the technology of a superhuman civilization from outside the planet and Debus cannot be taken lightly. He was one of the designers of the V2 rocket technology."

"That is perhaps why Hitler described to Rauschning his nightmares caused by his encounters with what he described the superman or the new man: intrepid and cruel. He confessed he was actually afraid of him" I quipped.

"We can go far beyond the last world war in history" Desbois resumed after taking a sip of coffee which Richard had timely produced to revive our sagging energies. "I like to pore over old books and records from antiquity, left by long vanished civilizations and they often evoke interventions by unknown creatures and powers far mightier than us puny humans. Closer to us, take the testimony of the great alchemist and astrologer John Dee who worked at the court of the Habsburg Emperor Rudolph II in Prague in the late sixteenth century. He writes somewhere that he was visited by a little man, who glided about without his feet touching the ground in some kind of fiery cloud until he suddenly went up in a pillar of fire. Dee indicates that a lot of what he knew about nature and the future came from this small, rather misshapen creature. We may think that this was an allegory borrowed from some religious and occultists texts but how can we know for sure? In times past, they would call him a goblin or a gnome. Now we might regard him as a small Gray Alien."

Laura picked up the thread of the dialogue: "Most Americans have some Irish blood in them and when I read some of the legends of that island, I can't help but compare them to the reports I get almost every week from diverse witnesses. The divine invaders of Ireland, the *Danann* are said to have come across the skies in clouds of mist thousands of years ago and landed on the hills of Connaught. Their high kings had many miraculous powers and supernatural weapons and tools and one can find that kind of story in every ancient literature."

"We all agree that this sort of divine or at least 'higher' interference in earthly event has been recorded for millennia" Desbois pointed out "but I go a few steps further. We know very little about how our universe is built and much of what we think we know may turn out to be inaccurate. So we are in no position to assign specific origins and features to whatever is behind all those prodigies and oddities. The cosmos could be like a pile of pancakes of which the part we are able to see and consciously experience most of the time is only one layer. What is below and above is anybody's guess. Think of a jellyfish floating on the sea's surface. Is it aware of the depth of the ocean below and of the unlimited space of the sky above? Another analogy is that of one versus two and three dimensional spaces. A hypothetical unidimensional creature could only notice or conceive of dots and horizontal lines. I wish us to consider the possibility that there are things and beings, including intelligent forms that live in other dimensions and sometimes erupt into ours. Their mental operations and sensory perceptions would presumably be so different from ours as to be impossible to grasp, even if they send us signals which for us make no sense at all.

Now I will throw in another possible factor which adds to the riddle. Modern psychic research as well as physics force us to realize the fundamental role of consciousness in nature or at least in nature as we can see and know it since most of modern science is based on sight, and much less on other sensorial impressions. What if the element which accounts for all we see, including UFOs and other strange phenomena, related and unrelated to them, is consciousness? It is impossible to rule out the hypothesis that the consciousness which makes life possible and makes us human, the operating system of our species as it were, instills in us visions and experiences perhaps dictated or inspired by our collective desire to evolve higher intellectual and mental abilities. We could not tell the difference between real material events and collective or individual psychological impressions, akin to mystical visions."

"What about the concretely physical evidence felt and collected?" Laura asked in an incredulous tone of voice.

"Any phenomenon of a higher order could and indeed should be both physical and mental" Robert replied. "A square may be a two dimensional shape but a section of it can be apprehended in one dimension since it includes it in each of its four sides. Likewise we are sometimes impacted by experiences perceived by various senses as well as our minds. Those are recorded in religious literature as miracles or as paranormal occurrences in a rationalistic context. I am not denying or rejecting any part of the UFO phenomenology. Rather I bring it all into a broader framework because I believe that the conventional view that space is simply a large container in which suns and planets sit like islands or rather swim like fish in a lake is simplistic."

"Thanks for clarifying your view on this, Robert" Sigismond said with a humorous sigh of relief. "More than one fellow researcher has told me that he found your apparent rejection of the straightforward theory of interplanetary visitors confusing or even offensive.... Superficial readers and those who reject the reality of UFOs claim that you are one serious expert who has dismissed the existence of alien beings."

"Alien means stranger to us" Robert emphasized. "Those aliens could come from inside the earth, from hyperspace, from a twin universe that is the shadow of our own – unless we are its shadow – from our collective unconscious or from our own future. There is no way to tell as they may be connected to all of the above. My apologies to those who like to keep it simple but I think we cannot ignore the notions and analytical tools provided by parapsychology, semiotics, hermeneutics and cybernetics."

There was a palpable sense of bewildered awe in the room. I felt that the meeting was drawing to an end and brought it back to the present: "President Reagan has launched the massive SDI or so called Star Wars programme earlier this year. It is, as you know a hugely expensive undertaking which those not in the know tend to see as a white elephant."

"I see in it a gigantic public investment programme in the tradition of FDR's New Deal, but in the aerospace sphere which will generate employment and spur technological innovation" Desbois retorted. "Unfortunately much of mankind's novel research has historically been oriented to military ends. War spearheads material progress because it challenges and raises the survival imperative. There may be an ET factor behind the SDI but if I apply Occam's razor I find enough justification for it without invoking the UFOs."

Report from Iron Mountain

I seized the moment to bring up a matter that had intrigued me for long. In 1967 a small publishing house had released a book called *Report from the Iron Mountain*. It purported to be a secret document prepared for the US Government over two years by fifteen anonymous high level experts from various major banks, corporations and universities who had had their first meeting in 1963 in an underground facility located in New York State, in the Hudson valley. The final text was submitted to President Johnson and his National Security Council by that "Special Study Group" in September 1966 as a classified report but it was leaked by one of its unnamed authors two years later. It created a commotion and rose to the top of the *New York Times*'s Best Seller list.

In 1972, one of its reviewers, Leonard Lewin claimed to have authored it as a satire of thinktank output but not many believed that reassuring explanation and the leading economist and diplomat John Kenneth Galbraith vouched for its authenticity as he had been consulted by the working group. He suspected Dean Rusk, Kennedy's Secretary of State and Robert McNamara, the Secretary of Defense of being the coordinators of the panel. Some other credible sources reported that Lyndon Johnson had been vastly upset by the unauthorized publication and that official authorities, faced with public outrage, tried to control the damage by claiming it was a spoof. The story reminded me of the scandal generated by the Protocols of the Wise Men of Zion which had been similarly debunked. Lewin and the individuals who had earlier published and promoted the Report from Iron Mountain belonged to the same community. I pointed out that one of the recommendations made by the Panel was for the Government to invoke an Alien threat as part of a policy meant to keep people under state control. It also emphasized the importance of war as a tool for continued elite dominance and prosperity and advised strict birth control measures, especially in poorer countries."

The three participants in the conversation knew about the Iron Mountain book but had different views about it. Desbois saw it as another trial balloon tested by the military-industrial complex as part of the unceasing search for policy alternatives in the American ruling circles. Laura felt that it reflected the perspectives of a group of Cold War hawks of the Kissinger kind who appeared not to have even been aware of the reality of UFOs. As for Richard he was cautiously agnostic about its validity.

"Yet" I argued "the US official policy about UFOs and other issues is consonant with the Report's recommendations, not to mention the infamous US Field Army Manual 30-31 Supplement B which was approved by General Westmoreland at about the same period and which was all about deceiving and confusing civilian populations through covert operations."

"In the media and even in government controlled channels the existence of unidentified spacecraft and non-human visitors is vaguely reported and ridiculed at the same time. It looks as if the State wants to keep people in the dark, worried but not too afraid. Scary theories and images are widely publicized and people are given hints that evil space invaders may have to be fought with old and new weapons. Also, think of the timing of the Iron Mountain report. The process began while Kennedy was still in power or just after his assassination, when Johnson became president and changed many of the policies, by escalating the conflict in Indochina with the blessings of the oligarchy. It seems that the first session was held in March 1964 whereas the report was finalized during the period of Vietnam war protests not long before the 1968 massive civil unrest in the US and Europe. It looks as if the Special Study Group expected trouble to erupt and was looking at ways of deflecting or harnessing the threat to the advantage of the ruling class. The fear of socialism was widespread and American hegemony was already being challenged."

"The method of assembling clandestine research groups and making them work outside public view on problems and prospects is a well established American tradition" Sigismond noted; "so there would be nothing uncanny about this particular one if it were not for the proposal to restore slavery under other names.... Even if some thought on that line, I can't quite believe that they would put it in writing in a high level policy paper."

"Why not? Don't they state in black and white that they believe that war is necessary and peace is rather undesirable because of its effect on the polity and the economy? That in itself is pretty shocking" I retorted.

"You are probably right on that" Sigismond reluctantly admitted. "The government includes people who are cynical or pessimistic enough—I leave the choice of words to you—to voice very unpleasant opinions. The character of Dr Strangelove is indeed based on real people unfortunately."

"In any event" I said "one of the key recipes found in the report is to launch huge projects that can mobilize economic and social resources by channeling people's energies towards long-term, perhaps unachievable goals. It seems that Star Wars is one such pie in the sky or at any rate a national initiative similar to the construction of the Great Wall of China or, in the recent past, the space race to land a man on the Moon. Your statesmen seem to be stealing pages from the Iron Mountain Report, whether it is an official document or a mockup, like that other red herring *Silent Weapons for Quiet Wars* allegedly produced by the Office of Naval Intelligence which transpired at about the same time, in 1965."

"Star Wars in itself is a fascinating idea" Richard remarked. "Reagan oddly has invited the Soviets to cooperate in it, which seems to negate its alleged intent as a space shield against Russian missiles. Is it rather a defense system intended to keep unfriendly aliens out though obviously that can't be acknowledged by governments?"

"An anti-UFO array of weapons has been proposed since the days of Roswell" Laura pointed out. "A number of more or less eccentric inventors tested new types of weapons for that. One of them was Wilhelm Reich in the early fifties in Arizona. He tried to use his orgone energy cloudbuster batteries and claimed to have shot a few of those flying cigars but by then he was quite mad so that few took him seriously and the fact that he went public about it in a self-published book did not endear him to the authorities."

"He believed that the Aliens were evil and wanted to destroy the planet" Richard noted, shaking his head.

"His judgment is far from credible" I retorted. "He was after all a deeply disturbed, sexually obsessed predator on women and children so that he cannot be regarded as a moral authority, rather the opposite."

"In any case" Robert Desbois concluded "we have been exploring an area to which Nietzsche's category "beyond good and evil" must surely apply."

I looked out the window, past the house's manicured flower beds into the quiet street. Evening had dampened the summer light and looming dusk wrapped the sky. Mentally we had also wandered into the twilight zone in which all things lost their sharp outlines, I thought silently.

XI

Death has Raised Itself a Throne

It is a monstrous thing for this great nation ... to have its destinies presided over by a traitorous government board acting in secret concert with international usurers.

**Congressman Louis T McFadden,
Chairman of the House Banking and
Currency Committee (1934)**

EUGENICS AND DEPOPULATION

Back at his home, I found Howard Higman at his feisty, grumbling cheerful best. Before dinner we sat down for drinks (obviously not his first of the day) and chatted about current events. I briefly referred to the topic of our confabulation at Sigismond's, wondering if he knew him. He gave no sign of it, although in that small town Richard was something of a celebrity but his eyes wrily narrowed and his head shook slightly.

"See you are into mischief and wizardry, ha!" he snapped humorously as he slapped his glass down on the low table next to him. "Watch out, this country burned witches not so long ago."

"If that is what you call it" I said.

I saw that, like so many others I knew, he was not going to comment any further. His friendly, rubicund, deeply lined face showed no expression as his palate basked in the Bourbon. I decided to move on to more familiar territory. "The subject of the Report from Iron Mountain came up" I mentioned. "I guess you must have discussed it at one of your World Affairs conferences."

He instantly warmed up to that, as an eager puppy when thrown a bone. "Yeah, I picked that up almost as soon as it was published" he stated proudly. "I am still convinced that it is a genuine article, or at least a good copycat work of the original stuff. If you notice the worry about overpopulation and the recommendation to bring birthrates down in poorer regions, you can make the connection with the massive publicity generated around Paul Ehrlich's book *The Population Bomb* only one year later and the associated sterilization and family planning campaigns targeting countries like Nigeria, India, Bangladesh, Mexico, Brazil, Pakistan, Indonesia, Egypt and Ethiopia, all cited in the Iron Mountain papers."

"I was in India when under Emergency Rule, Indira Gandhi's government started a nationwide sterilization and abortion drive" I pointed out "but she was not pro-American and fought US influence so there is no obvious connection politically."

"That does not mean that she had not bought into the theory that people in third world nations and especially the poor people there had to reproduce less if we were to avoid a global Armageddon" my host said crossing his arms. "We also heard and saw from here that the family planning crash programme was mostly carried out by her son Sanjay who I heard, had some channels of his own to our government. He may have seen himself as the enlightened and modern man who gets things done according to the latest ideas from God's very own country. Mind you I am also worried about overpopulation and all in favour of people being induced to limit the number of children but forcible sterilization by paramilitary means is quite another matter although I am quite sure that there are many people in high places, here and abroad who won't complain or object when that happens."

We both knew that eugenics was since the beginning of the twentieth century a popular concept in many scientific circles and had long enjoyed funding and support from the Rockefeller and other major institutions. When Hitler had made it a principle of state policy in Germany he was merely officialising an ideological trend on the rise on both sides of the Atlantic. Higman cited the work of the Special Commission on Population Control set up by Laurance

Rockefeller in 1972 which led two years later to the recommendations issued by Henry Kissinger and Admiral Brent Scowcroft in the National Security Study Memorandum 200. "It was entitled *Implications of worldwide population for US security and overseas interests* if I remember right" he recited, closing with a snort.

THE VETERAN

Next morning was uneventful and I left for Denver so as to leave plenty of time to acquaint myself with the city which I had only passed through until then. I took a stroll around the State Capitol in the drab downtown which, I was told became perilously seedy at night as is the case for many American cities when offices close and the middle classes retreat to the suburbs. Along the habitual glass-honeycombed concrete hives occupied by banks and corporations, I reached East Colfax Avenue and went up to the stately, soberly ornate Brown Palace Hotel, the heart of Denver's high life and official events which was situated not far from where I was to meet Jerry.

A few minutes later I slowly made my way to East 15h Street and spotted the bar on a corner that he had selected for our appointment. The Sun was shining bright and the temperature was ideal in the soft cool breeze so that I chose to sit outside. There was hardly anybody else and I quickly concluded that he had not arrived yet. I ordered my now habitual Celestial Seasonings tea and used the time to reflect on what exactly the next conversation might be about. I realized that we had not agreed on any tips for mutual recognition but I concluded we were unlikely to miss each other. As a European I stood out in a Midwest American population, so true it is that the US way of life, attitudes and sartorial styles have made most citizens of that country quite different from their 'Old World' cousins. During my musings I heard the remote insinuating melody of Boy George's hit *I am a man*, playing inside the bar. I noticed in passing the irony of that ambiguous song in the context of the meeting I was about to have.

Shortly after 4 I saw a middle aged man with a short beard and a moustache walk by, holding a muzzled dog on a leash. I noticed that it was a pitbull terrier, one of those stocky, muscular and steely jawed canines whose fierceness and resilience has made them favourite combat animals. As I watched the broad chested tawny beast trek purposefully its owner stopped next to me and asked: "Are you Lowell's friend?"

I got up and stretched out my hand. After a split second of diffidence he held out his. I noted the strength of his grasp. While he sat down across the table from me I rapidly surveyed his impassive face and sharp grey eyes. Although he could be no older than forty five, there was a somberness and an underlying fatigue in his gaze and in his features which betrayed the traces of past trials, nightmares and addictions. Drugs or alcohol? Perhaps both. He wore a rather weatherbeaten brown leather jacket over a plain black teashirt and blue jeans that covered the upper part of his boots.

I asked him what he wanted to drink as the waiter stopped by us. "First some water for Major, please" he said, nodding at the pitbull. "I'll have a Coors" he added as an afterthought.

I felt self-conscious about my tea and to keep him company ordered a Coors beer as well.

I could sense the lingering unease in his demeanour as he watched me guardedly. He seemed to assess whether I could possibly have something in common with him and probably decided there was not much. I knew he was right on this but I wanted to build a connection and show him I could be open to some of his ideas even though I came from a different world.

"Lowell told me you'd have a lot of interesting things to add to what he told me about this country and its history" I explained engagingly. "I am trying to learn more but I can tell you that I understood fully what he was referring to. We can make similar observations and judgments about Europe nowadays."

He seemed to warm up a bit and as the beer bottles were brought he took a swig from his and said: "The USA got a lot of its problems from you people. Most of what's wrong with our system came from England, Germany and France."

I was not surprised by that typical reflex which makes many Americans accuse the corrupt old world for the loss of their pristine innocence but I knew he had a point.

"I have heard and read that the colonization of North America and later the political system of the new country was based on Free Masonic ideas and occult protocols" I replied. "It was Queen Elizabeth's astrologer and occultist John Dee, the original 007, who first called for a British Empire in America, claiming that it had first been settled by Welsh sailors in the early Middle Ages...."

"And then Francis Bacon who advocated rule by a secret elite in his New Atlantis, the island-republic of Bensalem, like an offshoot of Jerusalem" Jerry continued. "His House of Solomon, the power centre of his ideal state was in fact controlled by Joabim the Jew and that is the model for our government."

I saw that he had gone straight for the jugular. I had some trouble connecting Dee and Bacon to Jerry's physique which, despite years of visible neglect, still bore witness to an athletic past. His voice was also curiously high pitched, out of sync with his still powerful build. By then, thankfully Boy George's androgynous lullaby had been succeeded by the inimitable sound of *The Doors*. Jim Morrison's charred voice soared in *L.A Woman*. For a second our attention was drawn to the tune and to its rather inconsistent lyrics.

> *Well I just got into town about an hour ago*
> *Took a look around, see which way the wind blow*

And further on:

> *I see your hair is burning*
> *Hills are filled with fire*

Before the haunting refrain: *L A woman c'mon.*

"His swan song" I noted.

"Raven fits him better" he said.

"As in Edgar Poe's story. How high he must have been when he wrote this"

"Morrison was another screwed up child of the US Military Complex" Jerry said with a shrug. "Mentally wounded from the cradle by his Admiral of a father."

"But destroyed by the Hippie drug culture" I qualified.

"Well, yeah, he got into it when he joined Hirschman's drama class on your fringe countryman Artaud's theories but it's poetic justice that his dad commanded the fleet in Nam when the fake Gulf of Tonkin incident was alleged to start the war escalation. That lie made so many victims and Jim was one of them. I wonder if Admiral Morrison got that when his son broke all contacts with his parents?."

"Who knows?" I said "but Morrison's interest in the Dark Side is typical of America, I think."

"Celts, Puritans and witches—What d'you expect" was his pithy response.

"You seem to read a lot" I remarked in a tone of praiseful surprise.

"I have had lots of time when I was wounded and then sick" he replied matter-of-factly. "Makes you think and ask many questions, at least to yourself."

"You were in the military?."

"Camp Lejeune, 2nd Reconnaissance Battalion and then Marine Special Operations Regiment" he stated without showing a hint of pride. "Deployed to Vietnam. Wounded there and spent long time in recovery. Then on a second tour where I got some nasty bugs in the swamps. Discharged as unfit coz I had already had a major amoebial infection during tropical survival training at Camp Lejeune. You have to drink the swamp water and forage for your food. By then I had seen many horrible things, including what our government did in Nam."

He fell silent and thoughtfully took another sip. I could see the sadness but also a dull anger in his eyes. His left hand as if by reflex reached down and patted the silent, crouching Major on the neck.

"You mean Napalm, Agent Orange and all that?" I asked.

"Yeah, and the massacres of villagers, men, women and children, the Phoenix Programme 'wet' missions and the CIA's drug dealing in the Golden Triangle. I saw and heard bits and pieces of information and later on I got the whole picture."

"I read Henryk Kruger's *The Great Heroin Coup* a couple of years ago" I said.

"More of this is becoming known now" he replied glumly.

"Are you from here?" I asked to break a heavy silence.

"Grand Junction" he said laconically. "A real red town (I knew that, contrary to the European ideological association, red means

Republican or Conservative in the USA). "So many there go into the armed forces. Patriotism and also few other opportunities."

"Yet" I said "I don't think you are a typical GOP supporter. I don't know if you voted for Reagan but it seems that you are unhappy with the political system in general. Tell me if I am wrong but, like Lowell, you probably don't trust either party."

"You bet" he replied unhesitatingly. "George Wallace had it right when he said there isn't a dime of difference between Reps and Dems. Reagan is personally a good guy and has the right instincts but no guts and no real power. He is shadowed by VP Bush, the stooge of the deep state. We are governed by a small financial elite which controls everything: the armed forces, the media, research, education…You name it. This started even before Independence but it got stronger over time as private banks took over our currency and our politicians. They were behind the Civil War. Old Abe Lincoln tried to reclaim the power of the state to print the money and he was killed for that, as was JFK a century later."

"I am a bit surprised to see you mention approvingly two presidents who are not favorites of your ideological family" I said. "Aren't you people more on the side of the Confederacy."

"Some of us are, especially the guys from Dixie" he replied. "It's a cultural thing but we are all against the Federal Reserve System and we agree that Kennedy, though his father was from the Mob, took on the deep state and paid with his life. His old man was against Jewish power but knew, after the war, that his side had lost. His son tried to change things and I acknowledge that even though he was a Catholic Liberal and surrounded himself with the usual elite cohorts handpicked by the Rockefellers."

The Federal Reserve

I found that the conversation was taking an unexpected turn. Jerry sounded more original and independent in his views that I had expected.

"So you see the real turning point in US history with the creation of the Federal Reserve in 1913?" I asked.

"It solidified what was planned for a long time by power clubs like the Committee of 13, the Committee of 300 and the Roundtable conference, all set by British imperial elites, Cecil Rhodes, Lord Milner and others, allied to some of our early billionaires" Jerry said with the confidence of someone who thoroughly masters his subject. He was clearly familiar with Professor Carroll Quigley's influential work on the Anglo-American Establishment but I wondered whether he rejected the creed of English racial superiority proclaimed by those upholders of British hegemony. "The so-called Colonel Mandel House set up a semi-official task force, the *Inquiry* and convinced President Wilson, who was his pawn to adopt the project of a Federal Reserve Bank, a private monopoly to control the currency, finance and the economy. Then the secret meeting at Jekyll Island between Rockefeller, Senator Aldrich, Morgan, Warburg and Schiff, who stood for the Rothschilds, set it up and they smuggled it through Congress while most members were on leave. That is how the world was brought together under a cartel of plutocrats. Just read the statements of Congressman Louis McFadden about the FED in the thirties. He called it one of the most corrupt institutions the world has ever known and a superstate acting to enslave the world by controlling credit. It is still sacking the United States as he pointed out."

"I know McFadden's verdict and even FDR excoriated the money lenders in his 1933 inaugural address but Colonel House was what we could call today a social-democrat" I objected. "He admired Lloyd George for his Labour reforms in the UK and in his novel *Philip Dru* he envisioned a kind of benevolent dictatorship to impose an income tax on the freewheeling companies of his time and abolish the tariffs."

"The people who want to bring the world under their financial power often like to pass for liberals" Jerry replied doggedly. "That is the case for their head honcho, David Rockefeller and it is also true for the Rothschilds. Do you know that the late Lord Victor Rothschild, a British MP helped give the atom bomb to the Soviets through his mole at Los Alamos Klaus Fuchs and that he was the hidden lynchpin of the Cambridge Five, the group of elite Soviet spies in England in the sixties? Those guys support Communism, at least in the Soviet

Union from the beginning as it enables them to keep the Cold War and other wars going and make money from it while keeping the West unified against the Red Threat. Mandel House was a smart multimillionaire deal maker and shadow man who saw there was a risk of revolution in the US. He engineered reforms to stave that off. Heck, his book starts with a quote by Mazzini about how to protect private property and prevent class war while doing something for the unwashed masses, so to speak."

"Indeed that was also the time when Teddy Roosevelt set up the "Bull Moose" Progressive Party to limit the power of the super-rich" I pointed out "and Wilson implemented many of the steps proposed in House's Book."

"Yeah and notice how Senator Aldrich, the champion of the Fed in Congress on behalf of his son-in-law Rockefeller, who had long opposed income tax changed sides and supported the 16th amendment in 1919 although it is still illegal because it was not passed by the constitutionally required number of States. By then crafty Old Rocky and his billionaire cronies had introduced the private foundation and trust legislation which enabled them to protect their assets. Meanwhile Mandel House and his friend Louis Beer got the League of Nations set which, however the US Congress, still nationalistic at the time, refused to join."

"I gather you have read Gary Allen's *Rockefeller File*. It says somewhere there that not-for-profit foundations actually are tax-exempt funds or something to that effect."

"It is par for the course in the system which is actually not capitalism but corporate fascism. I should not say that because people who think like me are called fascists by the State but what I understand about fascism is that it unites the nation around a programme of national solidarity. Here we find that too socialistic because we are individualistic or libertarian, if you want. We have no ideology, only our faith, the wish to live as we want and get rich if we can. If the USA were really capitalist, as it was in the early years after independence, we would not have a few huge family-controlled monopolies running our government."

I had to object to Jerry's reasoning which I found economical with historical facts, though I was aware that someone so familiar with the sort of literature he was quoting from could hardly be objective.

"I can't think of any time in the history of America when it was a free enterprise paradise of the kind you describe. It started as an agrarian colony resting on slave-labour with a strong feudal legacy. Right from the beginning your leaders were traders, plantation owners and bankers like Hamilton. They took slavery and removal of the Indians from the land for granted. There were elites and privileges and the average American did not participate in the making of the Constitution as there was little communication, no real popular voting system and no equality for people of colour, women or even non Anglo-Saxons. The US began as a clubby syndicate of business and political interests."

Jerry shook his head: "I realize that" he conceded "but given the means available at the time, it was the best that could be done. As you know Hamilton, who was some sort of a British Crown agent like many other Americans were and are even today, set up, against Jefferson's better judgment, a Bank of the United States which President Jackson later rightfully closed down. In our first century we had several leaders who fought financial monopolies and even the two-party system, a British elite implant. John Adams spoke against it and said it would be the death of popular sovereignty. The London City bankers made sure we were ruled like the UK, bled us through the Civil War, dragged us into European killing fields and got us into ever rising unredeemable debt."

"Now you sound like Lyndon Larouche" I quipped. "He claims that the Queen of England is the secret boss of this country."

"There is some truth about that" Jerry said doggedly. "If you look at the gang that forced the Federal Reserve System and then the Great Depression on us and later set up the United Nations and the World Bank, all interlocked and propped by the Rockefeller, Carnegie and Ford foundations and their many thinktanks, you'll find some of the same names; the powers behind the throne, Averell Harriman, Harry Hopkins, Sumner Welles, Bernard Baruch, Isaiah Bauman, Prescott

Bush, the father of our Vice-President who is a *Skulls and Bones* member like his dad. The Yale S & B secret society is like the dark Church of our top elite, along with the Bohemian Group which is their summer camp. The visible link is provided by the Council on Foreign Relations, a Rockefeller finishing school for world managers later expanded into the Trilateral Commission, set up by David Rockefeller on his estate in 1972. The goal is global control, through a combination of free enterprise, in name only and theoretical communism, used to keep some countries in check under repressive governments that depend upon our friendly oligarchs who don't really care how the system is called as long as they stay on top."

I felt understandably uncomfortable. The picture he drew was a bit too simple and all-encompassing to fit the complexity of the world. I met the eyes of Major, the pitbull but found no solace in the animal's sad stare. He was surely used to those depressing assessments.

"What is the problem with Harry Hopkins in your view for example?" I queried. "He ran a big part of the New Deal as the right hand man of FDR and then he managed the Lend-Lease programme to help win the war. That sounds fairly straightforward."

"There is more than meets the eye" was his instant response. "Hopkins, whose grandmother was an Israelite began as a protégé of the Strauss family, the owners of Macy's and Bloomingdale, through his first wife who was a Hungarian Jew. They introduced him to Roosevelt on whom they had a big hold and later Hopkins remarried with an heiress of the Macy family. The Hopkins couple lived for three years in the White House and some people called him the real president. FDR wished him to be his successor, which could have happened if Harry had not died from cancer in 1946. He was a Rockefeller asset, like Kissinger later on and a slew of other honchos. Many of us are convinced that he was a Soviet agent; he supported Stalin all the way against the Germans, even facilitating the transfer of nuclear secrets to the USSR."

"The charge of espionage against Hopkins has not been proven" I objected. "I know there were allegations that he was designated as Agent 19 in coded messages from the NKVD but so many people were suspected then."

"There is circumstantial evidence" Jerry rejoined. "Western governments were deeply penetrated by Bolshevik propaganda and willing to support Communism in order to defeat Hitler and Mussolini. In England, the Tavistock Institute was set up under the guidance of Kurt Lewin from the Frankfurt School to devise methods of controlling the masses and in this country Columbia University hosted the Frankfurt School offshoot, the Institute for Social Research while one of them, Herbert Marcuse set up shop at Brandeis in California from where he famously advocated polymorphous perversity like Wilhelm Reich also did. These people were subversive deviants and cynical nihilists. Critical Theory is the matrix of nihilism. It shows you that everything that exists is wrong and nothing right can ever be built so that the only worthwhile job is sabotage and destruction."

He paused for a second and took another gulp from the bottle before continuing:

"Of course you hear that was all meant to figure out social dynamics and understand collective psychology but the goal was to promote free and unnatural sex, drug use and social disintegration. You know, there is a racial angle to all this. The chosen people flock together to destroy the others. Since they can't rule a majority that does not believe in their prescriptions, they must break it down in order to control it. That is why they devise gay liberation and gender politics as weapons to generate tensions. I guess you must have heard of the Frankist sect of Ashkenazis? The Rothschilds are their hidden rulers."

Conspiracies Galore

I saw that he was adamant in his convictions and thought it necessary to raise the debate.

"Don't you think that there may be some merit in the process that created the League of Nations and later the UN, international institutions and facilitated Détente with the USSR, even if it was all engineered by the Rockefellers and other tycoons, irrespective of their religion or ethnic links?" I argued, fleetingly feeling that in his mind at least I was playing Devil's advocate.

"Why not if it were an honest to God attempt to keep the peace and help solve economic problems? But that is not the case. The Big Business conspiracy is connected to the Marxist racket and it has only produced more wars and greater misery for the many while multiplying the wealth of the few. As we speak, since this administration has changed the rules for Savings and Loans companies there is a huge rip off being carried out in the USA on the average Americans. Their savings are being sucked into all sorts of schemes that will benefit only the money managers, hedge fund owners and other vultures. There will be a crash soon. Mark my words. As I told ya, I have witnessed the crimes it carried out in Nam and I still can't sleep at night. You must know of General Smedley Butler's book *War is a Racket*?

"I am confused to hear you refer to that call for socialism" I said, gasping in mock disbelief. "I thought you belong to a Far Right group. Smedley Butler was surely an All American war hero and became the Major General of the Marine Corps so that you may feel a personal connection with him but he was on the left of the Democratic Party and he campaigned for the end of capitalism."

"The end of the rotten plutocracy we are living under" Jerry asserted stubbornly. "The thirties were a time of great political confusion. I have read so much on that period. Arch-conservatives like John Raskob were leaders of the Democratic Party and allied with others who were GoP stalwarts. At one time all those fat cats from the Rockefeller, Du Pont, JP Morgan and major Wall Street brokerage firms drafted the American Legion to plot a coup against Roosevelt in 1934. They wanted Butler to join it because he would lend it a patriotic popular façade. True American conservatives would not support this, anymore than they would support a Mandel House style socialist dictatorship. All those ploys are tricks of the big global capital. Their only goals are power and money and they control the supposedly opposing Parties."

I could not repress a shrug. We were back to the resilient racial theories which the Ku Klux Klan and affiliates had earnestly perpetuated. Would the US ever exorcise the ghosts of divine election, slavery, eugenics and segregation? "Raskob, the head of GM and later of Du Pont, built the Empire State Building. He was a Catholic Conservative" I said. If I remember well he was a Knight of Malta. That does not exactly qualify him as a Jewish conspirator."

"Look beyond appearances" the indomitable veteran marine shot back "John Jakob Raskob was from a German Jewish family that had converted to Catholicism and so were several of the big names behind the conspiracy, beginning with the Rockefellers who were not named although their fingerprints were all over, with their main companies, Chase Manhattan, First City, Standard Oil, Mobil, GM and others. The Congressional investigation into the plot denounced by General Butler was run by Samuel Dickstein who made sure that none of those worthies were called to testify as they were too powerful to be questioned. Dickstein was accused later of being a Soviet agent."

"So what about the report to Roosevelt at the time from Dodd, the American Ambassador to Germany that the leading American business dynasties were close to the Nazi regime? That was confirmed by many other sources since then."

For a second Jerry seemed nonplussed.

"I don't hold a brief for FDR" he said, defensive but undaunted. "He came from the Delano opium trading family on his mother's side and the New Deal was a big socialist scheme which illegally confiscated private gold but the big fish who claimed to oppose him actually bluffed. Then as now there are many connections between Communists and Capital monopolists. They have foodfights among them but they come together to protect their positions. In Germany Hitler may have won the support of large industrial corporations because he had the masses behind him and his national welfare project and they had to deal with him but the US "business plot" of 1934 was another con-game, which is why Butler spoke against it. Our cartel owners only liked Hitler as long as he allowed them to run their businesses and prevented Bolshevik nationalisation."

I had to agree that, to those who concentrate so much wealth and power, the logos used by politicians to define their policies matter little as long as they continue to pull the strings. Social welfare measures that stop short of hurting their positions are actually welcomed if they can prevent turmoil and rebellion. I did not need to be reminded that Rockefeller funds had often poured into ostensibly left-wing projects. John Rockefeller II's patronage of the revolutionary Leninist artist Diego Rivera was a symbolic instance of that tactic but it was less significant than the family's long standing support for New York's Union Theological Seminary which had advocated socialist measures, at least by US standards during the Great Depression. I pointed it out to Jerry.

"The UTS was behind the left-wing National and World Councils of Churches" he commented. "This was all meant to turn protestant folks into socialists and make them accept Communism as a decent ideology. The Council has been under Soviet influence from its origins and our CFR-Trilateral Commission crowd likes it that way since it facilitates the gradual takeover by a world government that David Rockefeller has written and talked about for so long. He fancies himself with his brothers as the dictator of the global socialist-capitalist federation but, like his dad, also sponsors and controls anti-communist icons. John Foster Dulles was a trustee of the Rockefeller Foundation and a CFR member as also John McCloy, the CEO of Chase. Dean Acheson studied and clerked under justices Frankfurter and Brandeis who pushed him into the upper spheres of government. Were those top guys true patriotic Christian Conservatives? Not in my book. They are all members of one big hegemonic tribe and they always find agreement with people like the chairman of the Aspen Institute, near where you live, Joseph Slater who was another key man behind the founding of the UN and the OECD and a prime mover at NATO, the Ford Foundation and Standard Oil."

I knew that the bugbear of a Rockefeller dominated, global tyranny exercised through the UN was commonly invoked in American "patriotic" right wing circles since the fear of a Soviet invasion by Stalin's spies and troops had receded. The comparison with the Luddite dread of technological progress crossed my mind but I could not deny that what the "liberal" billionaires on Wall Street had in mind for the future of America and for the world did not match the biblical aspirations of simple citizens such as Jerry, feeding on the ante-bellum nostalgia of an agrarian economy in which settlers lived by the Good Book and upheld the law with their guns. That belief system had shaped the country in its early days but it was now little more than an anachronistic longing. I was reminded of that damning autopsy of American oligarchy in the first part of the twentieth century by Frederick L Allen, *The Lords of Creation*. It laid out the reasons for the simmering revolt voiced by the former Marine sitting across the table.

THE VIETNAM WAR AND THE DRUG EMPIRE

I wanted to hear more about the experiences he had endured during his tours of duty. How many Americans like him had come back broken and haunted for life by the atrocities they had witnessed in Indochina! Did that predispose them to embrace all encompassing conspiracy theories?

"You mentioned Operation Phoenix in Indochina?" I reminded him. "Were you involved?"

"Not directly but some of my buddies were in the Provincial Reconnaissance Units and they were often ordered to assassinate unarmed civilians on the basis of allegations about their VietCong affiliations. I know some of them were tasked with torturing prisoners although much of that was left to the Viets. You know that is where the practice of throwing people from helicopters or bombers in flight originated, to be applied later in South America under the similar Condor program. Other servicemen, Marines, Airmen and Infantry were used as couriers for heroin to finance the illegal operations that the CIA and the special forces were tasked with. Read Fletcher Prouty's *The Secret Team*. It reveals a lot about the Military Mission to Saigon led by Colonel Lansdale which was the start for the whole thing."

"I have heard that the Vietcong were actually assisted by US Black Ops to keep the war going but that does not make sense to me."

"Unless you accept that some of the leadership in Washington wanted to pour oil on the fire and prolong a profitable conflict" Jerry retorted mercilessly, with a dark glint in his eyes. "Much of the top brass in the White House and at the State Department came out of Rockefeller stables."

"And what did President Kennedy think or do?"

"He first went along under the advice of Rostow, Acheson, Rusk and McNamara but later he tried to pull out. In 1963 he approved a National Security Memorandum which planned for all US troops to leave Vietnam within two years."

"1963 was the year he was killed" I noticed.

"What a coincidence, right? Twenty days after President Diem of Vietnam was murdered by his generals on 2 November with the approval of our Embassy. It turns that the people who plotted both killings were involved with the war racket or were working on its behalf."

I raised my hand to object: "Diem was killed because he antagonized too many people and had turned the Buddhists against him. I can believe that Harriman, Cabot Lodge and the US military attaché in Saigon John Dunn, as well as the new CIA head in the region William Colby played a role in that decision. I don't see the connection with the US President's assassination."

"Well, neither the Vietnamese strongman nor JFK danced to the tune of the powers-that-be. They went by the beat of their own drummer so they were both removed."

"And then, what ensued? Did those who commissioned the two coups get their way."

"Naturally the war went on under Johnson and Nixon for another ten years. In Vietnam, with Diem and his brother gone there was no statesmen left who could stand up to the Americans. In the US Nelson Rockefeller and his pals, Allen Dulles and Lyndon Johnson, The CIA, Israeli Intelligence, the Mafia and all had reasons to get rid of a President who was no longer listening to them. Permindex, the company that put the contract out to foreign soldiers of fortune linked with the French Connection drug ring, probably on behalf of former Stern Gang hitman, Yitzhak Shamir, was a Mossad front with strong links to Meyer Lansky's, Mickey Cohen's and Sam Giancana's *kosher Mafia*. Jack Ruby was one of their assets. That lot built and owns Las Vegas, which amounts to a huge chunk of our economy. Some of the same gang later killed Bob Kennedy as well, to stop him from going after them."

"How do you refute charges that are just tying together the names of all the people you don't like and who, I admit are not likeable to accuse them of the JFK murder without proof?"

Jerry did not flinch. "There is proof" he said. "Some of us have it and so does the government, but what is not officially declared remains fiction. That is the rule of the game. What is true for most people is not what happened but what society prefers to live with. As some of our politicos put it, the goal is to get closure so that the country can move on. If you read the Warren Commission Report, the book by Prosecutor Jim Garrison and others like it, you'll know what I mean. I have checked the background of Permindex. Its chairman was Lincoln Bloomfield and its main financial backer was Tibor Rosenbaum's BCI, a financial arm of Mossad. Rosenbaum was a Vice-Chairman of the World Jewish Congress and an old associate of the ubiquitous Victor Rothschild. There is also a connection with that French drugdealer in Venezuela, Christian David."

I nodded in tacit but crestfallen assent. "Back to Phoenix?" I asked.

A bitter smirk appeared on the former Marine's face. "What else is new?" he said. "Terror against civilians, deception, murder, drug-running, skullduggery and eventually treason; counter-insurgency techniques perfected in Algeria by David Galula and adapted by our own CIA men, Peer de Silva and Nelson Brickham. Galula's recipes that had failed the French in North Africa were gladly used by our bosses with predictable results. They never learn. In the end more than eighty thousand Vietnamese were "neutralized," out of which twenty five thousand were bumped off in various ways, a substantial part tortured to death. The PRUs often brought back ears of their victims to prove the killings. Keep in mind many were drugged to carry out their missions. The army had ways to trigger adrenaline releases in your body to make you hyper-functional, ruthless and tireless. You know why so many of our POWs have not come back? The Government in DC did not want them back. They would have revealed embarrassing facts about the conduct of the war."

A man passed by with his dog, a boxer on a leash. The latter gazed mournfully at the squatting Major and lunged forward, prodded by lust or curiosity but the pitbull did not stir. The man pulled on the leash and mumbled a command to the boxer. They went on their way.

"Major is a quiet fellow" Jerry stated. It was the first inkling of softness I noticed in him.

"Who was in charge of Phoenix?" I insisted.

"At first the same people who had Ngo Dinh Diem killed. That was the team built by Allen Dulles in Washington with Colonel Lansdale. They recruited some cowboys to do the dirty work. The coordinator was the CIA station chief in Saigon, first Peer de Silva and later Ted Shackley who now works with our VP Bush in his Special Situations Group at the White House Crisis Management Center. Those people are still in charge and the tactics have not basically changed: deception, subversion and murder for profit and power."

"That sounds like much of human history" I quipped consolingly, knowing he would not smile. "I believe Colonel Bo Gritz carried out some of those missions to deal with heroin lords in the Golden Triangle?."

"Sure, as the head of the 5th Special Forces Group, the B-36 although he is a braggard but many of us who have been involved in this business have turned against the system, like General Butler in his day or like Colonel Parker now. Trenton Parker has all the goods on the guys who killed JFK and Martin Luther King and one day it will all come out although he has been arrested over a year ago to prevent him from speaking out. The funds from the trafficking were handled and laundered by Nugan Hand bank, whose real name should read the CIA piggybank. There's a huge, worldwide network of such financial institutions which manage the black budget of our secret government."

"It has long been known, especially since the Church Congressional Investigation that the CIA also carries out drug experiments on animals and people" I added.

He replied impassively as if he were bored to repeat an evidence once more "*One Flew over the Cuckoo's Nest* is based on Kesey's and Hunter's stint as patients at the "Farm" in Menlo Park. I was there too for a short period like many others."

I did not have to ask him if he had been given psychotropics. The answer seemed obvious.

"What was the point really of all this testing?"

"Gathering knowledge on human reactions to many chemicals" he said tiredly. "Remember that's part of our government's self-imposed mission: find out anything and everything about everything and especially about people. It is the House of Solomon in Bacon's New Atlantis, got it? They picked up what the Nazis had started and they are desperate to move ahead of the Soviets. Importing drugs and spreading them around is a possible way to prevent social unrest and make politically dangerous people addicted and helpless while raising cash to fund projects that have to stay under the radar. The deep state shoots many crows and doves with the same bullet. I found out that a bigwig in pharmaceutical research, Albert Kligman injected a number of American prison inmates with Agent Orange, manufactured by Dow Chemical of course, a jewel in the crown of our economy. Others had done the same with radium and syphilis strains in the fifties. Infecting unsuspecting civilians and soldiers with toxic agents for the sake of research is a chronic habit of our masters."

The evening was gradually shrouding the glow of that radiant day. My eye caught a tall, lithe woman swaying by in a long billowy dress. The fabric was soft and translucent; one could peer through it at her curvaceous nakedness but I did not feel the habitual elation. There was too much heaviness in me in spite of the dusky gossamer atmosphere.

"You paint a depressing picture" I said in a sinking voice.

"That's what this country has become" he said with a deadpan face. "I know I have mentioned many books but I want you to read this one. It is not high brow stuff but it talks about what needs to happen." He pulled from a pocket on the inside of his leather coat a paperback book in a garish crimson cover. The cover read *The Turner Diaries*. I glanced at the author's name: Andrew Macdonald. Had I seen it in a bookstore I would have assumed it was a Maoist revolutionary volume.

"Is he one of your ideologues?" I inquired, putting the tome away in small briefcase I usually took with me.

"He is the founder of the National Alliance" Jerry explained with a perceptibly respectful expression. "Macdonald is a pen-name but in real life he is a physics professor, an aeronautical engineer and he comes from one of the big families of the Confederacy."

"Is he connected with the Aryan Nation group?"

"We have many like-like minded organizations all over the country, like the White Patriot Party. One of my buddies is setting up a new one now up in the northwest. You may see some action soon" he added elliptically.

I saw that he would say no more but what I heard was not soothing. We both got up after I paid the bill, brushing aside his attempt to share it.

"May I ask you one last thing?" I inquired.

"What's that?"

"If your enemy is the transnational oligarchy in this country. Why are most of your fellow rebels so focused on race and why do you hate the Blacks who are the most exploited of all by the current system."

His brow furrowed and his stare grew hard again: "Our main target is the ZOG, the Zionist Occupation Government" he said quietly "but Negroes and other primitive races are flooding the nation and destroying its identity. They are used by ZOG to wipe out the white Aryan Christian character of this country and turn us into another Brazil. In South Africa where the Europeans are a minority, ZOG and all its underlings are pushing hard to force them to live in constant proximity with Blacks, Arabs and Asians and under their power which will bring barbarity. Read the book. You'll see what is going to happen here."

I shook my head as I watched him purposely move away, realizing the futility of trying to argue on that. A man whose sense of pride and identity are so tied with his beliefs will not willingly abandon the latter. There was no point telling him that whites in South Africa or Brazil had no valid claim, or at least no greater claim to the land than the people who had been there for millennia. Can anyone justify occupying anyone else's lifespace because that he believes he is superior? Could he deny that African Americans had been brought to the United States unwillingly as slaves and that they were at least as much entitled to sharing in the land as their former owners? I was saddened by the prejudice which warped an otherwise intelligent mind. Whatever was true in his verdict about of his nation became irrelevant in the context of his ethnic bigotry which was rooted in the famous Doctrine of Discovery, the very basis for the USA's claim to nationhood. The racist 'Hitler syndrome' condemned his cause as surely as it had doomed the Third Reich to utter destruction despite its stupendous material achievements.

XII

A House Divided

... The eye of a scrutinizing observer might have discovered a barely perceptible fracture which extending from the roof...made its way down the wall

Edgar Poe, The Fall of the House of Usher

IT IS DARKER THAN YOU THOUGHT

On the road back to Boulder I reflected on the conversation I had just had and tried to sort out the confusing impressions it had left me with. I could not but feel that Jerry's idiosyncratic but profusely detailed account of recent history portrayed the rather incoherent ideological condition of his nation. The United States was indisputably ruled by an immensely powerful financial and technocratic class which controlled the political system and all aspects of society, beginning with the famed military industrial complex. The democratic electoral process could be viewed as an elaborate though messy ritual between two parties which prevented any other political force from participating meaningfully in policy-making. Indeed the two parties were private corporations which shared ownership of the state on behalf of the real or deep government in the middle, the head of the American eagle in control of its wings on either side. The masters of the game were federated within a cartel intended to protect their wealth and hegemony. It mattered not so much if those rulers were members of the Rockefeller and a few other families or if they were unknown persons or organizations acting behind them. Against that Leviathan, to use a term employed by Hobbes, militants, dreamers and activists such as Jerry were relegated to the periphery and as devoid of relevance as the Ku Klux Klan's political agenda. Their ideas about society, the economy religion and the homeland mattered little in the scheme of things as they were romantic, outdated and inconsistent when not criminal. Like many of those popular icons of American rugged individualism produced by Hollywood and embodied by James Cagney, John Wayne or Clint Eastwood, the remaining opponents of the system were reduced to the role of lonely cowboys or outlaws, heroes of their own imaginary movies. They fed on a smorgasbord of confederate nostalgia, racial fascism, "minuteman" patriotism, small scale capitalism and biblical archaism which locked them in a war of words with Left-wing dissidents even though they shared their hatred for the ruling social system. These self-proclaimed "Aryans" proudly latched on to their constitutional right to bear arms but decried the militarized police superstate that had come into being. They detested pacifism and anti-war protests but reviled the far-off wars waged for the profit of the big businesses at home. They pointed the finger at Du Ponts, Mellons, Rothschilds and Rockefellers but could hardly refute the view that those were after all superheroes of the private enterprise system even if they had turned it to their overwhelming advantage. The distinction the so-called "Far Right" customarily made between good white Christian monopolists like Henry Ford and evil Jewish ones highlighted the internal contradictions of its theories. Race and religious belief were the last bastions behind which it could take refuge against the current status quo.

Who could believe that an uninhibited free market protected from Jews or any other alien ethnic or religious sect would remain fair and respectful of small landowners and entrepreneurs? After all, those professed libertarians and reactionaries tended to seek guidance from Adolf Hitler who had brought industry under state control, hardly a libertarian dream.

I pulled out the book he had given me and leafed through it. It was a war manual of sorts set in a fictional format and situated in the last decade of the twentieth century, a strategic plan for violently overthrowing in the near future the US system, from "all white" enclaves to be set up first in southern California. The novel described the occupation by the rebels of the Vandenberg Air Force base and their taking control of its nuclear weapons in order to deter a full scale assault by the regular armed forces. Their target was the hated North Eastern seaboard establishment, its Zionist patrons, its banking hegemony and its liberal, multi-racial melting pot mentality which had conquered and subjugated the rest of America. The imaginary narrator and hero of the war was a character called Earl Turner and one of the first acts of the rebellion was the bombing of the FBI headquarters in reaction to the imposition of a dictatorship by the Washington oligarchic system. During the ensuing civil conflict Turner was introduced to a secret leadership called "The Order" which masterminded the nationwide insurrection. The dramatic events included multiple sabotage operations, terrorist attacks, mass hangings of racial enemies and traitors and a nuclear suicide mission against the Pentagon as well as nuclear strikes on New York and Israel, in a global context of revolutions and civil wars.

I sensed in this violent fantasy the anger and thirst for revenge of someone who hailed from "Dixie" and might be descended from the defeated soldiers of the Confederacy. I knew how ruthless and humiliating the treatment of the Southerners had been at the hands of the victorious Yankees. The unspoken verdict from Washington was *Vae Victis*. Everything below the Mason-Dixon-Mason line was fair game. Much of the post-Civil War literature in the South had been haunted by that harrowing experience and many still held grudges. The author of the book predicted or advocated a merciless military uprising to defeat the detested rulers and their minions and tools, the blacks, Latinos and other "non-whites," professing that mass killings were an inevitable part of the struggle for liberation. By comparison, *Mein Kampf* read like a polemical but even tempered treatise of political philosophy.

I sensed the bitter irony of that call for a war of liberation against the supposedly democratic government of the "land of the free" in which freedom was indeed held to be the only universally shared religion, even if, like all mass official creeds it was neither logically proven nor widely reflected upon. It was just a given: Americans are free because their nation had been founded so that they might be. The puritan pilgrim fathers had fled the old world to break the shackles from its political and religious strictures but had they not forged even more constraining ones in their new settlements? Since then their immigrant successors had been trying to flee from themselves all over the continent.

When I arrived at Higman's home I found him a merrily obstreperous mood. He had already had a drink or two and insisted on serving me some of his favourite Bourbon when we sat at the kitchen table, waiting for the dinner he was cooking to be ready.

The professor had a solid celtic temperament. His tipsiness did not dull his intellectual faculties or at least not at that early stage. His voice might have risen to a higher pitch and his speech was a tad slurred but his mind even sharper than when fully sober.

When he inquired what I had been up to all day I gave him a brief account of my meeting in Denver. Although I did not provide too many specifics I expected him to react abrasively to the ideology that Jerry personified; after all he was supposed to be on the other side of the political spectrum but I should have known better. Howard loved nothing better than an argument which normally demands an opponent.

"So young man" he told me after making a quick inspection of the simmering pots on the stove and tasting the concoctions they contained, "you have been drinking with the devil…Hope you had a long straw, Eh?"

"Actually he did not really feel like the dark lord" I reflected aloud "more like an older wounded child with a lot of readings in his head and bitterness in his gut."

"This country has got a lot of people in that class" he mused while peering at his glass. "They are the heirs of our founding ideas but they are of two kinds, lying on the opposite fringes of our society. The Nature lovers, peaceniks and luddites were inspired by Emerson, Whitman, Muir and Thoreau and they became the flower children in the sixties. They want nothing to do with government, technology, war and capitalism. They would have liked America to remain a wild garden of Eden as it was when only *Injuns* lived here."

He was interrupted by the scent of something burning and shuffled back to the stove.

"Almost too late" he grumbled jovially 'but it's OK. The pilafs' bottom should be synged anyway."

I thereby learned that he had been preparing a persian dinner.

He came back to his glass and pick up his thread: "The second kind of rebels is the old wagon migrant and cowboy variety. The guys who settled the West with their bibles and shotguns. They really believe in the law of the Colt and reject any political system beyond the merest sort of municipal management. If they can't do the police themselves they are willing to elect a sheriff but that's as far as it goes. They are against income tax and almost all other taxes which they equate with Communism. They are your lone rangers, militias, right-wingers and eventually your neo-Nazis, not because they want to live under a dictatorship but because they don't like other races and religions and believe they are the chosen people. They may hate the Jews but that's because they want to take their place as God's favourite children, got it?"

"Very clear" I said. "Have you seen this book? And I held out *The Turner Diaries*.

Higman barely glanced at it and shrugged. His eyes narrowed into slits on his lined brick-pink face and he puckered his lips into a sarcastic sneer.

"I see you are being exposed to our classics" he quipped. "The American Tolstoy... Our own professor Pierce?"

"Is that the author's real name?"

"Yessir. William Luther Pierce He got his degree in physics from our University and worked for years as a top aeronautical engineer at Pratt and Whitney. A very smart man and a well spoken, learned fanatic served by great charisma."

"Where is he now?"

"Somewhere in Washington DC or Virginia, the haven of so many of our Dr Strangeloves and would-be fuehrers. Pierce, who belongs to an old family from the elite of the Confederacy is the leader of the National Alliance, an openly neo-nazi movement. He has bought an estate where he publishes his books and magazines and inspires many young people to rise against the Republic but he is protected by the First Amendment and he even has a church. He is some sort of a prophet as well" he added chuckling.

"What sort of religion does he promote?"

"His own brand of pantheistic evolutionism, close to theosophy. It is quite acceptable in principle as he talks about the gradual rise of all life towards ultimate union with the divine All. The rub in the ointment is that he sees the Anglo-saxon race as the highest in the pecking order and declares that this crowning achievement of Nature should not be marred by mingling with inferior breeds and should thus keep them far apart or eventually slaughter them all if it comes to that. It is like the impaling punishment, it begins well and ends in a gruesome way." He emptied his glass, visibly satisfied with his ghoulish joke.

"What a character!" I said. "How did a presumably well bred Christian American come to this? His novel is incredibly violent and hateful and his visions of mass executions and of blowing up New York and the Pentagon!"

"Can you believe the *Diaries,* the Mr Hyde side of Pierce's Dr Jekyll, has sold more than a hundred thousand copies to date? Americans are a very rough lot, as you should have found out by now" the Professor stated in a booming voice. "D H Lawrence commented on our taste for mayhem and murder. We started as outlaws, most of us and we still are. On top of that we are great at invoking the Bible for justification, even for Lynch laws, cold blooded shootings or nuclear strikes. As a matter of fact the Old Testament lends itself to any interpretation if you just select the convenient passages but Pierce gave up Christianity after he read HG Wells and got to know Gayley Simpson, the author of *Whereto White Man?*

"No idea what that is!"

"Let us have dinner" he said. "Food is ready and we don't want it to get cold. Here is the butter to be dropped on the pilaf and here is the mutton.... I ask guests of the World Affairs Conference if they can cook and then I make them teach me their favourite recipes. I learnt to make this dish from an Iranian historian."

UNEARTHING ROOTS

We began to eat and he forthwith resumed his explanation with the clarity of a seasoned teacher:

"William Gayley Simpson was an American born in a devout family who grew up as a liberal Protestant with socialist leanings and ran the Civil Liberties Union for several years before eventually turning into what we would call now a white supremacist. His book, which came out only a few years ago is quite profound and well written, mind you and he does not preach violence as such but he rejects Christianity as a debilitating and utopian semitic creed unsuited to the real world and to ... Can you guess? The white race. He predicts the death of western civilization unless it recovers its original purity and in that at least he agrees with old Adolf. Simpson is a home version of Nietzsche, the Hegel of our Aryan Neo-pagans. Pierce and all the latter's followers and sympathizers owe him a great debt."

"You have opened my eyes to the hitherto unknown universe of American reactionary thought" I said "and this dish is exquisite. It brings back to life my days in Tehran, Isfahan and Shiraz." I noticed that he relished the sincere compliment.

He poured me some red wine. "Pouilly Fuissé from the Old Country," he recited. "I think it's from 1978.... Let us drink to France and the Ayatollahs and down with Fascists. Even those on the left!."

As we moved to his beloved study-cum-TV room where he served us, against my better judgment, choice Georgian cognac—"a present from a Soviet speaker at one of our conferences" he explained—I decided to elicit his reactions to some of the insights I had gleaned during the last few weeks since my arrival in the country. By now, there was enough trust for both of us to be open and I had confidence in his no-nonsense skepticism to protect him from credulity and conspiratorial fantasies.

"Tell me" I began "what do you make of all those reports that the USA is essentially ruled by a Rockefeller-guided secret government."

As I had predicted he did not show irritation or voice sarcasm.

"It is a fact that since almost a century that family and a few others have worked together to build a control system which is quite effective though not all powerful" he said carefully. "You must have heard of the Council of Foreign Relations, the Trilateral Commission and all the foundations and thinktanks."

"In Europe some of us, though not many, are aware of the Bilderberg Group which is tied up with all of them" I added.

"Yes, Bilderberg is the relay station. The official founder was a rather obscure fellow called Joseph Retiger or something like that but I am given to understand that the real mover behind it is Baron Victor Rothschild who used as his proxy a gilded royal puppet, Prince Consort Bernhard of the Netherlands."

"A former officer in the German army during World War II."

"You see how effective the US and other NATO states have been in recycling and recruiting former Nazis when they had use for them. The fact is that almost all the people who run our financial, military and foreign policy are drawn from the Rockefeller stud farm: Fed and World Bank chairmen, secretaries of state, national security advisers, treasury secretaries of state and defense: Dean Rusk, George Kennan, the Dulles brothers, McGeorge Bundy, MacNamara, Kissinger, Bzrezinsky, Alexander Haig, Brent Scowcroft, Paul Volcker, George H Walker Bush... You name them and I have not even got to the Presidents yet. Gerald Ford was widely seen as a stooge of his non-elected VP Nelson Rockefeller who wanted to build a world government while his brother David, from the top of his Chase, Morgan and First National City Banks, was busy setting up a global banking and financial presidium. Nelson, despite being a Republican, also happened to be a close pal of and a major influence on LB

Johnson, so he had his hands in both parties. The other three brothers were looking after technology and real estate investments, arts, culture and philanthropy...All fine and dandy in principle, except it was meant to increase evermore the reach and glory of the dynasty."

"I am impressed to hear you describe the situation in terms similar to the rather extremist voices on the opposite side of the political spectrum" I commented, "What about the Bohemian Grove?"

"That is an annual camping vacation for the selfsame elites and it enables them to bond with the West Coast movers and shakers, although all those who reach that level of financial might are effectively bi-coastal. Don't misquote me. I didn't say bisexual. All groups need to connect through some rituals, preferably secret and somewhat outlandish ones, in order to feel special and separate from the *hoi polloi*. That is what the Bohemian Grove provides, like so many other rather folksy or bizarre associations we have here, from the nice, middle class, innocuous Lions and Rotary Clubs all the way to the cloak-and-dagger Masonic and Maltese orders, Boners, Shriners and KKK."

"What do you make of the inborn, racially based affiliations? I am hearing so much about Jewish power."

The old professor lost a bit of his relaxed casualness. Was alcohol heating him up or was he, like all, uncomfortable with a mere allusion to that taboo topic?

"Look" he said in a raspy voice. "I won't deny that our nation is based on a biblical belief system which grants Hebrews a privileged position both theologically and culturally. During the last World War the buzz was that Jews were coming to America in much larger numbers to build the New Israel in the Near East and here as well. Some rabbis and zionists even believed that the Third Reich was fated by G-d (he spelled it aloud: G hyphen D) to rise in order to make that possible. I won't get into eschatological claptrap, not my thing but the result is here.

As you know successive Federal Reserve Chairmen have been Ashkenazis almost since the first in 1914 when the effective boss was

Deputy Chairman Delano, with few exceptions, upto the present one Paul Volcker, a protégé of Robert Roosa. Like Volcker they were connected to the Rockefeller Institutions and banks, prominently Chase Manhattan with its fifty thousand corresponding banks worldwide, and to the allied Lehmans, Solomons, Lazars, Goldman Sachs, Kuhn Loebs and Warburgs. The Fed holds the reins of our economy although it is a syndicate of top private banks, most of which are within the Rockefeller orbit. Not much the White House or Congress can do to influence it. If you check out the people in key positions in our government, the media, the arts and sciences the military and strategic research institutions, you will notice how many of them are occupied by members of that community. Now, how do I feel about it? As a sociologist I am fascinated by the permanence of human associations rooted in parentage and religious practices and I conclude that it is a fact of life. In the past in Europe and elsewhere you had, and still have to a point, aristocratic elites related by blood and history. Here, whatever little history we got has given rise to ethnic and confessional networks like the Boston Brahmins, the Virginian bluebloods, the Philly Quakers, the New York Dutch, the Mormons, the Sicilians, the Dixie planters and of course the Jews. The latter are clever, aggressive and hunt in packs although they also fight like alley cats among themselves. They know how to build coalitions and take over anything they are interested in. Hell, when Richard Wagner a vituperous anti-semite, became successful and famous, he was surrounded by fawning Israelites who ended up performing his works against his will.

Here we have the Disney Corporation, set up by Walt Disney, a guy who hated Jews and now being essentially taken over by Zionist interests, like the rest of Hollywood was long ago. They have a genius for managing money so perhaps it is right to let them do it. In your beloved India you had Brahmins running the state and business castes in control of trade and finance, so nothing new here."

"It all goes to show that human equality and equal opportunity is a pipedream."

"Calling for a return to our small town and village dwelling past is definitely like whistling Dixie" Howard responded. "When you read Tocqueville, you realize it was not so great anyway. The young nation provided an open season to crooks, con-men and charlatans since the only general ideal was making money. Those who succeeded best became our legendary robber-barons. John Rockefeller Senior was nicknamed "wreck-a-feller" by his hapless victims and his own father, the son of a German Jewish immigrant apparently was a bigamist snake oil hustler - I meant petroleum door-to-door salesman. Our first cities quickly grew to be ugly, unruly and corrupt and our "free press' was unbelievably venal and slanderous. Dickens in the eighteen fifties was appalled by what he found here. I am not sure what nostalgics of early America are harking back to, apart from open land to be taken away from the natives."

"But do you see this oligarchic regime as a deeply evil one or are you neutral?" I asked.

"It is never good when so much power is accumulated by so few. They usually make sure that nobody they don't like gets a seat at the high table or even a chance to be heard. This said, there are no absolute rules. The real world is nasty and brutish but it has the advantage and the inconvenience of being ... real. Some of our greatest dissidents have come out of the system. Think of Daniel Ellsberg, a RAND insider and his leaking the Pentagon Papers in 1971 which exposed the skullduggery and deception behind the Vietnam War. Nelson Rockefeller led the Congressional investigation into the CIA's illegal experiments and practices on prisoners and test subjects. Humans remain unpredictable and sometimes they feel the need to atone for their guilt. Anyway you can't fool all the American people, that is why we have two parties" he chuckled.

By then, Higman had regained his uproarious feistiness. I felt like lightening up the conversation but I had one more query:

"So you think there is after all some sort of a secret government or a deep state?"

"A permanent or shadow government, yes" he confirmed. "But don't most countries have one too? The difference is that this one is much bigger and has a global scope. If you put together in an interlocked virtual consortium the 'seven sisters' as we call the hegemonic oil giants, the most powerful banks and insurance companies, the major print and television media owners, the top technology corporations such as IBM, ITT, GE, Texas Instruments, Motorola, Safeway, General Foods and the richest intellectual research centers and universities, such as MIT, RAND, Harvard, Yale, Stanford and so on, what do you get? The closest thing to a global state not elected by any outside persons and benefiting from the full support of the top Intelligence agencies, beginning with the CIA, NSA and the rest of the Alphabet soup. You can see that in this set-up competition is somewhat restricted by hidden cartel practices. The people at the top of the pyramid are into monopoly, not for open and fair free-market race."

"In practice one can see the effects of that in world events" I commented. "I am told that a particular Bilderberg meeting in Sweden planned and triggered the Middle Eastern oil shock of 1973. The goal was to fill western banks with all the dollars earned by the OPEC nations and then lend them to developing countries in order to gain greater control over their economies and policies. South America was devastated when they could not repay their astronomical debts and had to give up control of many coveted natural resources."

"The Arab and other oil fields owners were given expense accounts to upgrade their lifestyles" the professor pointed out "but in fact they could merely spend the interest on their capital which was in the hands of our financiers. The latter were literally minting money from it."

Dewey's Children

"Yes, I know about fractional lending" I assured him. "Banks create multiple fictional monies out of deposits they hold and land them many times over. They thus generate revenues and take over assets out of nothing. Talk about virtual alchemy. But let me turn to education, your field. How do you evaluate the General Education

Board set up by the Rockefellers to reform the national system on the basis of John Dewey's ideas, at least from what I heard?"

"That is quite a bugaboo for conservatives" the professor answered after a moment of reflection - or insidious torpor. "I must tell you that much as I respect Dewey's towering contribution to the social sciences and education, I can't always make sense of him. Depending upon who reads him, he is seen as socialist, a closet Trotskyist, a liberal, a progressive or even a CIA-funded anti-Communist which of course fits in well with the ideas and interests of our supreme rulers and did even more so in his lifetime, when Marxist influence in the academic system was waxing strong. Dewey looked like a happy compromise between the Status Quo and the feared revolution and some have accused him of leading leftists down the garden path in the name of democracy. No wonder his pedagogical recipes were supported by the Rockefeller Funds and followed by the Education Board."

He paused to pour himself a glass of water from a decanter next to him.

"However there is something weak about the basis of Dewey's teachings" he continued. "He never really explains how democracy *per se* can solve all problems and lead civilization to its peak achievement even if that affirmation of his fills the heart of the average American with satisfaction; democracy means many things to many people but he takes the concept for granted, almost as a revealed faith despite his claim to be scientific, repeating that it is mostly about public participation, a truism.

I am also afraid that by insisting on the need for pupils to take more control of the teaching process he has lowered the academic standards and undermined school discipline. As a liberal myself, I should approve of that but I have a feeling our students are turning increasingly ignorant inasmuch as their self-confidence increases. They tend to think they only need to know what they believe can help them. Too much pragmatism can result in crassness, especially in a society which is mostly concerned about making money and where intellectuals are pigeonholed as conceited eggheads."

"I can't say that I appreciate Dewey's influence on artistic philosophy and taste" I added. "He provided a rather facile justification for modern art, including the worthless or ugly facets of it."

"All in all, for the almighty American Establishment he was a man on the right side of history" Howard concluded, getting up from his capacious armchair. "Remember" he added wagging a chubby finger "our celebrated intellectuals are heralds of our system and irregulars in the Cold War army. An officially promoted theory is an ideological weapon in the service of the State or at least the deep state. In that way we are like the Commies, except that they can only sing one tune and we have a whole repertoire, from Negro Spirituals through Rock n Roll to Civil War anthems."

XIII

The Belly of the Beast

The time's now come
The very minute bids thee open thy ear

Shakespeare, The Tempest

THE HORSEMEN OF JONES'S APOCALYPSE

On the next morning I returned to Aspen where August was drawing to an end. I frequently saw my local friends, in those lazy days of late summer. Nancy Pfister was still in Molokai but Florian Scott Halazon, Andre and Jyoti Ulrich, Mary Jean Dartmoor, Jerome Canty, Patricia Hill, Nadia Al Mamoun and Camilla Sparlin were around and we got together every now and then at one of the town's watering holes or in our respective homes.

One day I got a call from Lowell who told me he had flown in from Dallas for a week and wanted to know how I felt about my meeting in Denver.

"We should talk in person" he said, hinting perhaps that it was better not to speak on the phone. I accordingly invited him to drop in for a drink at his convenience and we agreed for the next day.

At the appointed time as I was on my wooden balcony, enjoying the late afternoon light I saw a gleaming silvery AMC Rambler station wagon enter in the Fasching Haus lot and out came Lowell, looking every bit a Texan in a checkered shirt, tawny suede jacket and tall brown leather boots. He waved at me, strode leisurely towards my door and we shook hands while he uttered a true-to-style "Howdy Sir?"

His frame towered in my rather small living room as we exchanged small talk. After he sat down I handed him a Budweiser beer according to his choice and apologized for remaining faithful to my five o'clock tea habit.

"So how did you find Jerry?" he quizzed me, half-leaning forward with an inquisitive glance.

"Possessed by his ideas" I said carefully. "He knows his stuff by heart and there is no breathing space for dissonant input. He has it all worked out in his mind."

"Most of those in his corner are like that" Lowell commented, shaking his head. "As you and I know, they have a point and it is interesting to listen to some of it as long as they are only use words but once they swing into action, we have a problem."

"You think he would do something illegal?" I asked.

"Could be. Those guys are not armchair intellectuals, even if some of their teachers are (I guessed he was referring to Pierce). They are former military or ranchers who believe in putting their guns where their minds are. I am told that Jerry has joined something called the Order, a secret group which plans to raise hell somewhere soon."

"It seems like they are trying to implement the plan outlined in the Turner Diaries. The occult leadership of the rebellion is also called the Order" I said.

Lowell frowned and stared at the can cupped in his large hand. He was clearly not surprised that I knew of the book and probably had expected Jerry to hand it to me.

"This country is not ready for a violent uprising" he said slowly. "It may come one day but not in this decade or even this century. Everybody is too busy chasing dollars on his own and Reagan has sold a lot of political Quaalude to the average American. However I worry that some hotheads may try to raise trouble and kill innocent people in the process before getting busted or creamed too. This country is so manipulated by the spooks and the underworld they work with. Take the Jonestown massacre in 1978. It sounds and looks like it was the result of a CIA experiment gone wrong, although maybe by their standards it actually succeeded."

"What do you mean by that?" I said, hardly repressing a shudder. He had referred to the slaughter and mass suicide by poison of some nine hundred followers of the self-proclaimed sect leader James Jones. That "hecatomb multiplied by nine" had taken place under mysterious circumstances in their utopian new settlement in Guyana in 1978. Jones who had died there on that day as well was famous in the USA where he had powerful friends. He reportedly bribed politicians with girls and drugs. He had been received at the White House and praised by the then president and first lady Rosalyn Carter for his social welfare work.

Lowell hunched forward and said in a lower voice: "These are experiments on human populations. Targets are usually minority sects that are ideal areas of study because they are isolated from the outside and already under tight control. If you pull the string of their leader, with or without his consent and knowledge you can get anything to happen in that group. It is even more valuable if the followers are non-white. You probably figured that our rulers want to have the blacks totally at their mercy. They put as many as they can in detention, especially young males of course and they make sure they remain uneducated, poor and violent so that they don't have a chance to enter the ruling structure. People like Jerry are racists, but they may not harm blacks as badly as our real elite does behind the scene. Lincoln, the great abolitionist wanted negroes to be sent back to Africa as he did not think they could peacefully coexist with whites in this country."

"Yes, I find that interesting but unsurprising" I noted. "One of Lincoln's coloured friends, the occultist and abolitionist Paschal Beverly Randolph professed that "negroes" would not survive in America and exhorted them to migrate to India. By the way, the future President is said to have joined about 1853 Randoph's Rosicrucian order which gave rise to the secret Brotherhood of Luxor. The gossipy aspect of all this is that Randolph taught what he called "sexual magic" which at the time was definitely a taboo."

"I dunno about that" Lowell reacted with a wicked smile "but it would not surprise me. Anything goes in our great country and Abe may have had some surprising personal hobbies. I at one time was a Shriner, believe it or not."

"I think that the Order of the Mystical Shrine of Memphis was very popular and powerful once" I said. "FDR was initiated into it but was it anything more than an exotic mock oriental fancy dress club?."

"I never heard of any secrets, political or mystical when I was a dues paying member" the Texan said "but does one ever know what goes on at the leadership level of such fellowships? I remember that it sounded like an esoteric Islamic brotherhood of sorts and I was impressed as a young guy by the severity of the punishments that were threatened if one broke the vows taken to gain admittance. It was very much like the masonic curse of Hiram Abif."

"When the Order of the Shrine was founded, Islam was very popular in the American upper classes" I remarked. "There was widespread fascination with the romance and poetry of the Arab world and I believe that the man who set up the society drew his inspiration from a lavish ceremony he had been invited to by a wealthy North African dignitary in Marseille in the late eighteen hundreds. You know, that's when newborns here were given names like Omar and Zuleikha."

"Back to Lincoln and Afro-Americans, his successors in power just make sure to break them. Jim Jones was helped and funded by various figures connected to the Intelligence community. That is how he grew so powerful. He blackmailed corrupt politicians like San Francisco Mayor Moscone and out-of-control homosexuals such as his accomplice in the city council Harvey Milk. He definitely got Moscone elected by fraud. I was told he procured young girls for the mayor and little boys for Milk. Needless to say, the latter enjoyed virtual immunity due to the protection of the queer tribe while Moscone had Mafia links."

"Many people at the top must have known about the Jonestown conspiracy if there was one" I objected.

"Well, why d'you think Moscone and Milk were shot dead a few days later by a lone 'nutter'? They both had been a big supporter of Jones and had entrusted him with government responsibilities. In fact

Moscone made him chairman of the city's housing commission. Of course, officially nobody made the connection."

"Given this background, It could be very dangerous if people like Jerry come together and rise across the country" I pointed out.

"Yeah but it won't happen any time soon. The militias blow a lot of hot air but unless they are directly attacked on their turf by the Federal Forces they won't budge. That is what Pierce's followers desire: a rash move by Uncle Sam to confiscate all individual weapons which could be resisted massively but Uncle Sam is in fact Daddy Warbucks. He is making money from all those arms sales and is not about to kill the goose that lays the golden eggs. That is the sad story about our patriotic Conservatives. They hold on to their pieces for dear life, believing that it keeps them safe from the evil ZOG but all they do is spend their savings on that arsenal while enriching the hated oppressor and it only helps them shoot each other in anger or by mistake. Russian roulette in a circle."

"However I am told that there are several major state secrets that would cause tremendous damage to the Federal Government and to the political system if they were revealed" I pointed out. "Jerry is expecting something big to break out and bring about a major crisis of legitimacy. What do you think of that scenario?"

WAITING FOR REVOLUTION

The Texan looked at me for a second, shrugged slowly and said: "Don't hold your breath. We have had many scandals, our system totters but holds up in the end. Everyone knows about Watergate which was peanuts in the larger scheme of things. It definitely destabilized the presidency and exposed this country's real game to those still dumb enough not to have seen it before. Much worse secrets are suspected by everybody. The Kennedy murders of course as well as Martin Luther King's shooting. All that believed to be the work of the shadow government or at least of somebody in the government. Yet what happened? As long as official entities deny and appoint commissions of inquiry which dutifully cover up the evidence and produce whitewashing con jobs people just roll their eyes, sigh and move on. Many are happy to believe that we—that is the people we elected—aren't so bad after all and others have jobs to keep, mortgages to pay and families to raise. Enough reasons not to look for trouble. Also, any movement that looks like it could gather strong public support to change the system is quickly penetrated and neutralized from inside."

I could see he was right but I raised the issue of Colonel Trenton Parker's *Pegasus* report on which Jerry had laid accent.

"Parker has the goods on a lot of top politicians in this country, with regard to high-profile assassinations and also manufactured conflicts like the war in Nam" Lowell responded unhesitatingly. "The Pegasus team was set up by Truman to spy on the newly founded CIA and report to him directly but as a result Parker and his men collected evidence on what was done by people at Langley, at Foggy Bottom, in the White House and elsewhere. They had wiretapped the conversations of Edgar Hoover, the FBI Czar and got access to this dossiers with which he blackmailed the US political establishment and made sure no one dared fire him so that he kept the job until his death. I've heard the information implicates people like Lyndon Johnson, Richard Nixon and Allen Dulles in the contract on the Kennedys. That is why Colonel Parker has been detained a year ago and is in solitary confinement to this day. However the Pegasus files have been given to one of our honest Congressmen Larry MacDonald and he is working on it. There could be some fireworks in due course if an investigation is launched."

"I remember that Larry McDonald is one of your heroes from what you told me at our last meeting" I said.

"A true-blue American in the Georgian tradition and a cousin of General Patton" the Texan stated appreciatingly. "As of this year he has become President of the John Birch Society and he is one of the chief opponents to the Rockefeller pro-communist, world government project. In 1980 he moved a resolution in the House to launch an investigation into the Council on Foreign Relations and the

Trilateral Commission. He also calls for dismantling the Federal Reserve and bringing back the gold standard."

"You told me McDonald co-founded the Western Goals Foundation with General Singlaub. Did he not also write the preface of Allen's *Rockefeller File?*"

"You bet he did and he is now planning to run for next year's presidential election."

"As a Democrat? He seems like a fish out of water in the Party given his extreme conservatism" I pointed out.

"He is an old-fashioned Southern Democrat. You see parties mean nothing in terms of ideology in the US now. We have already discussed that. The Democratic Party has been colonized by socialists and extreme liberals against the will of much of its base. That is why it lost a big part of the South to the GOP which was the historic enemy in Dixie since the Civil War. Otherwise decent conservative stalwarts like Wiliam Buckley lost the plot and now support the system but then he is a member of Yale's Skulls and Bones like his friends in the Bush family, so what can you expect? This is all part of the Rockefeller takeover of both main parties and McDonald is one of those who still resist."

"This all sounds like the strategy advocated in *Silent Weapons for Silent Wars*, suspected to have been produced by the Office of Naval Intelligence. It talked about distracting and confusing the population with irrelevant, contradictory information and particularly actual and potential opponents" I mused.

"You got it" he said. "It is the old Trotskyist strategy, with added technological tools for mass mind manipulation through ultrasounds and subliminal images on television. Trotsky was controlled by British Intelligence and our tycoons supported him when he fled the USSR and came to Mexico. That is why Uncle Joe Stalin had him pickaxed in order to stop the sabotage that was being carried out against his regime by his old enemy's Zionist network.

Trotskyism has remained a powerful weapon in the hands of the global overlords to take over and break down the Left with the pretense of leading it to victory. The British taught us that trick when they mentored us for setting up the OSS and then the CIA. Our Intelligence agencies are still under London's influence. Originally the bigwigs of the MI6 and the Special Branch, people like Stewart Menzies, Charles Hambro, Mountbatten and Irving Brown piloted our fledgling spook outfits from the UK and as we all know, the Brits had multiple double and triple agents, shared with the USSR, as Michel Golieniewski aka Alexis Romanov revealed in the fifties. The Cambridge Five were not isolated black sheep. They were just the exposed tip of the iceberg. In the US James Jesus Angleton was also working for Israel's Mossad and possibly for the Soviets, in touch with Victor Rothschild, Blunt and Philby. Hell, if you believe Golieniewski, Henry Kissinger is a Trotskyist soviet agent, sent by a secret Soviet network called ODRA and known by the code name of Bor… Seriously, but what a well deserved pseudonym!" he chuckled.

"Golieniewski is not exactly reliable as an informer" I objected. "After defecting and being given shelter in the US he has claimed to be Tzarevich Alexis, the martyred son of Nicholas II and Alexandra but on another topic, I am told that Reagan is now starting a new anti-Marxist semi-private organization to fight communism and spread democracy abroad."

Lowell shook his head dismissively. "That will still be run from behind the scenes by our clandestine establishment" he said. "The goal is to expand the reach of so-called market democracy, that is in fact the power of our multinationals which will fund this new foundation for promoting American values or rather their business interests as they fund the other big outfits which serve the same ends."

"Don't be so definitive" I argued. "I have talked to a few people in the know in Aspen and they tell me that they are confident of psychologically and economically defeating the USSR in the coming few years. China as we can see has taken a sharp turn towards capitalism with the "little helmsman" Deng Hsiao Ping so the death of communism is in sight."

"Defeating the USSR and turning it into a colony makes a lot of sense to our rulers" the Texan explained in his drawling bass voice. "But that is about empire, not about freeing people from

Communism. At home we now have a huge mix of economic 'tax and redistribute ... or waste' socialism, moral libertarianism and religious conservatism. We are told it all goes together somehow and we are happy to spread that toxic brew to the rest of the world which we want to unify under Wall Street control."

"Do you believe the Iron Mountain document is genuine?" I asked, wondering whether he would support my own view on that point.

"It rings true" Lowell replied after a second of silence. "Iron Mountain is indeed the site of a storage site for corporate documentation set up by a man called Herman Knaust who was very active in resettling European immigrant Jews in Hudson during and after World War Two. He promoted his facility as a secure holding place in case of nuclear attack and it's near the Headquarters of several major corporations, including Standard Oil and Manufacturers Hannover Bank, at the heart of the global imperial strategy, so that it was the right location to hold that kind of secret confabulation. Once the paper was leaked, the best way to disclaim the information was to claim that it was a hoax. Old tactics!"

"One of various things fails to convince me in the apparently seamless theories spun by the likes of Jerry" I said "is the claim that all those hidden societies and organizations are connected and work together to achieve the same objectives, whether it is the Masons, the Bonesmen, the Bohemians or even the Knights of Malta. I can see the synergy between the Council on Foreign Relations, the Trilateral Commission and the Bilderberg Group. I can also accept the link with Skulls and Bones and other campus fraternities and lodges. You can even throw the B'nai Brit and the Mormons into the pot. That is clear but what about so many cloak-and-dagger or cock-and-bull associations which exist mainly to flatter the egos of their recruits and increase the prestige and influence of their office-holders? It is rather childish to credit them with grand plans for the future of the world and even more naïve to believe that they have the power to implement them."

"I won't argue with you about that" Lowell said as he got up slowly, ready to leave. He strode towards the door, turned towards me and added: "Take the Knights of Malta. The ones from Rome are mostly supporting the Vatican's politics while tooting their own horn which makes them feel mighty proud. In this country we have another order of Malta which was implanted here by some white Russian exiles and merged with our York Rite Masonry so that Christians of all denominations, or even anyone who professes to believe in God can join. It's a bit of a joke if you ask me because it claims to be the successor to the Russian Hospitaler Order set up by a Tzar in the eighteenth century under the sway of the Orthodox Church. They also allege some connection with the Catholic Caddo Indian tribes of the Mississipi, converted by French missionaries in the sixteen hundreds, which is why our Maltese Knights are nicknamed the Natchitoches. I won't worry about them although some may be quite powerful individually and use these organizations to further the goals of the Cabal on top. Being conservative and elitist, they may dislike or accept Jews, Catholics or protestants but are part of the Status Quo Right that the Regan administration represents. That's it."

I walked him to his car. We remained silent while we shook hands. I was pondering the many sobering things that had been said and his mood had also grown somber. I watched the Rambler slowly glide away in the pale glow of dusk.

Digging Deeper

I could not but be troubled by some of my visitor's statement and although, as a former associate of the Hunts he could be forgiven for harbouring considerable suspicions against the US government, I found it hard to believe that the rise of Jim Jones's sinister People's Temple and the ensuing massacre in Guyana could be related to foul play at a very high official level. I spent the next few days doing research at the hospitable municipal library on the history of "Reverend Jones" and his South American commune and realized that various facts about that story would make anyone suspicious. The connection to the political system in California, particularly to

Mayor Moscone and some of his supporters in the militant homosexual faction in the San Francisco Bay area was irrefutable., even though Moscone was alleged to have been on Jones's posthumously discovered hitlist. There was also evidence for the sympathy or forbearance that the People's Temple was said to enjoy in certain spheres of the federal government, extending up to the White House. Various active and influential backers and funders of the ominous cult leader had links to the CIA and the Pentagon, including the father of Tim Leyton, Jones's follower and confidant who had shot Congressman Leo Ryan at Jamestown where the latter had gone to investigate the mysterious settlement and rescue those who wanted to get out of what was in effect an open air prison. The American Embassy in Guyana, after seemingly expressing opposition to Ryan's mission had been reluctant to assist it. The then-Prime Minister of Guyana, Forbes Burnham who had welcomed the construction of Jonestown on land leased by the People's Temple was identified as a CIA asset although he was a Marxist politician. Was that a reason for the choice of that jurisdiction?

Despite the high profile of Leyton's victims at Jamestown, including a sitting federal legislator and NBC reporters and press photographers, Leyton's trial was still ongoing at the time, five years after the events and he was seemingly benefitting from powerful protections. In other circumstances, I thought, his murders would have earned him the death penalty. On the day he had shot the visitors to Jonestown, on 18 November 1978, all or almost all the inhabitants of the commune, including about three hundred children had been found dead from mass cyanide poisoning, in a giant killing field. Was Jones reacting to the inevitable prospect of arrest and trial or was he eliminating all witnesses, unless other people had done it for him? It was reported that he had rehearsed the extermination on various occasions, making all the denizens of the settlement drink what they were told was a poison that would kill them in thirty minutes. It sounded as if he had carried out experiments to test the blind submission of his followers to his orders. That in itself reminded one of MK-ULTRA "scientific" techniques of mind control.

Jones was an avowed communist and claimed to admire the North Korean and Soviet regimes but that had not visible harmed his reputation in a big part of the US establishment. He had a personal death squad in his service which was called the Red Brigade and, coincidentally or not, the Italian Red Brigades which had operated around the same time were suspected of being manipulated by US clandestine agencies and allied European powers as part of the "strategy of tension" intended to prevent Marxist parties from coming to power through elections. Of course it was nearly impossible to prove the role of those who pulled the strings unless they made a confession so that only educated guesses were available.

Was Jim Jones a dupe, a puppet or a double agent whose task was to discredit the USSR as part of the Cold War disinformation agenda? Born in a poor family in a small town of Indiana he had risen early in life to a prominent and powerful position as the leader of a large organization with vast cash resources. It was easy to believe that he had been supported by some influential entities but were they American, Soviet or North Korean?

Lowell and Jerry, like many who thought like them, were convinced that the Jamestown mass murder was a "false flag." Not long before the massacre took place, Jones had invited a Soviet official who came to speak at Jonestown and expressed his sympathy for that socialist experiment which harked back to Che Guevara's guerilla wars in the rainforest of South America. In the last months of his life Jones was addicted to various drugs and warned almost continuously about the CIA's plots to kill him and his followers. He promised the latter a blissful life in another world after leaving this one. Like Hitler and other megalomaniac leaders he was headed for self-destruction and bent on taking all his sheep with him in death.

The FBI ruled Jones's death a suicide by gunshot although some concluded instead that he had been shot pointblank by someone else. He had ingested massive doses of pentobarbital which would by itself have been sufficient to kill him.

As is often the case in such dark and mysterious cases, it seemed impossible to draw definitive conclusions. Jones could indeed have been a sincere if deranged Marxist-Leninist (although he had called his only legitimate son Gandhi) and an atheist despite the fact that he continued to regard himself as a pastor, or he could have been a remote-controlled or manipulated individual, an asset of the Deep State. What would have been his task? At first perhaps gathering a number of problematic individuals, both black and white under his command and isolating them from the mainstream of society. The final mission could have been to discredit all such social utopias in the future by bringing the People's Temple to a catastrophic end.

It felt too devious and cruel to be true but by then I had come to believe that anything was possible. Most people in Jones's group were not valued members of the American society but rather poor and hapless individuals so that they could easily be dispensed with. Still, it was more logical to assume that Jones was just another fire-breathing preacher, among the many that America has produced—a handgun in the right hand and a Bible in the left - who, affected as he was with a mental disorder since childhood, had gradually gone insane. However drugs indisputably played a major role in his psychic deterioration and that particular connection with the psychedelic counter-culture could not be denied.

That a man as ominous as Jones had been allowed to operate for so long in the USA and take charge of hundreds of children for whose foster care he was financed by the American social services beggars belief. I found that throughout the existence of Jonestown, which defined itself as a Maoist commune, it had received some sixty five thousand Dollars a month from the US welfare administration which thus effectively supported it.

I had trouble absorbing the information collected by the sources I consulted on this tragic case. It revealed extraordinary callousness and irresponsibility on the part of many officials and citizens who had entrusted their offspring to Jones although the latter had a record of physical and sexual abuse on adults of both genders and had fathered children from a number of women in his flock. He exhorted them to regard him as their husband, father and god at once. How could such an obviously charismatic but sinister man win the "friendship" of

Vice-President Walter Mondale and Mrs Rosalynn Carter? Was it because, exceptionally among white preachers, he had a majority of black followers and fought racial discrimination? Was it because of the support he got from the powerful and militant homosexual community? Indeed, Harvey Milk had written to President Carter a few weeks before the final tragedy to vouch for his friend Jones whom he called "a man of the highest moral character."

KA 007

As I was absorbed in that research, I saw on CNN that a Korean Airline plane bound from New York to Seoul had crashed off the coast of Sakhalin, in Soviet territorial waters, north of the northern Japanese island of Hokkaido. Early comments alleged that Flight KA 007 had been shot down by Russian Air Defence and the tragic story almost immediately took a menacing turn as sparks of a world war flickered out of the embers of the old East-West antagonism. The hawkish Reagan administration could be expected to react fiercely to the loss of a civilian plane with all its passengers by one of its allies.

The news came on September 1st and the coverage of the tragedy became obsessive On the next day Lowell called me from Dallas. There was no perceptible emotion in his voice but he bypassed the usual opening greetings: "You heard about KAL 007?" he asked.

As I was about to tell him that the very code number of that flight evoked Fleming's thrillers, international intrigue and the "license to kill" he proceeded to say: "Congressman Larry McDonald was on that flight."

My only reaction was stunned silence.

"The plane seems to have strayed almost two hundred off course to enter prohibited USSR airspace and to have ignored repeated warnings from Soviet Aircraft and military command posts on the ground" Lowell added. "It was then either shot or forced down. We are trying to find out."

"Goodness" I finally uttered. "That could lead to a world war."

"Unless the powers-that-be here wanted the Soviets to act that way" the Texan said imperturbably. "It puts them in the doghouse of world opinion and gets rid of McDonald and his investigation. Two birds with one stone. Another thing, Trenton Parker was freed today. Any connection? McDonald's papers may be gone forever!."

I took a few seconds to process the implications of what he had told me.

"Do we know for sure the plane was shot down? Moscow denies and there are contradictory reports although the US Government has already gone ballistic."

"That figures" Lowell commented. "We'll see. According to the Federal Aviation Administration, the Boeing was forced down on a Sakhalin airfield by Ruskie fighters. It was tracked by the Japanese from Hokkaido losing altitude gradually while flying in circles for several minutes. If so the passengers might be in Soviet custody."

"Given the tension between the USSR, the US and its allies, trying to get a clear picture of what happened will be a nightmare" I remarked.

"I already checked that the Soviets were conducting missile tests in that area at the time" Lowell indicated. "They are very touchy about that sensitive border so close to the Koreas and Japan. For a jet to have strayed so far and for so long in their airspace is irresponsible at this time, after all the war noises our government has made and I am not expecting either Moscow or Washington to disclose the real facts about this. I saw the press conference of George Schultz, our Secretary of State on TV and it sounds like the government is eager to gain maximum mileage out of this. It is cold war politics wrapped in righteous outrage."

"Where was the Congressman headed?"

"To Seoul for the celebration of the thirtieth anniversary of the defence treaty with South Korea; something which neither the Chinese nor the Soviets see with great favour but the real mystery is why the airliner deviated so far from the set course. It seems to have flown over the Sakhalin island after entering forbidden Soviet airspace off Kamchatka, beyond the tolerated buffer zone."

"What do the Russians say?"

"For now they deny bringing it down and claim that it was a spy plane. Nothing would surprise me."

After he hung up I switched on television and tried to gather more facts but the information was repetitive and confusion was evident. In the following days the situation took a dangerous turn. On the 5th of September President Reagan made an angry speech, accusing the USSR government of committing a crime against humanity and promising dire retribution. By then it was becoming clear that the KAL 007 plane had crashed at sea and that there would probably be no survivors. Search and rescue missions were made very difficult by the international tension. The American navy and its Korean and Japanese allies were not allowed to enter Soviet waters and the Red armed forces conducted a parallel search in the Soya and Tartar straits, around Southern Sakhalin and the small Moneron island over which the plane had last been observed. Dozens of surface vessels and submarines from the hostile powers circled in close proximity and often almost collided while warplanes flew overhead. I spoke with Lowell on the phone on two other occasions and he pointed out to me that right from 1st September the US State Department had taken the unusual step of ordering the National Transportation Safety Board to transfer all documents pertaining to the accident to the International Civil Aviation Organisation. In his view this was meant to protect sensitive data from public exposure since the ICAO had no power to subpoena any government and could therefore not demand clarifications over and above what was volunteered by the various concerned powers. I felt that it was perhaps an act of elementary prudence, showing that despite the inflamed rhetoric, the White House did not wish to lose control over the disclosures which might have caused an irresistible wave of anger in the public, forcing it to take aggressive action against the USSR. Another telltale sign was that the records of the radar stations which had tracked the airliner on its fatal journey were destroyed within 30 hours even though they were a critical part of forensic evidence. It seemed as if the Government wanted to protect, if not the Soviets, at least itself from unwelcome scrutiny.

Partly as a result of the secretive attitude of both the superpowers, a heavy mystery continued to hang on the tragedy for several years but It was revealed within a few days that a US Boeing RC-BS spy plane was deployed off Sakhalin on that fatal night, watching the Soviet missile tests. Eventually it became known that the Boeing had been shot down with two Air-to-Air missiles by one of the three SU-15 scrambled from Sokol airbase to intercept it, after it failed to respond to warning rounds. The Reds had apparently mistaken the civilian airliner for a military target. When the Soviet navy located the debris deep under water, they recovered many items but almost none of the bodies as if the passengers had disintegrated. This gave rise to further suspicions that the people on board the plane had been captured and taken to some secret location but as time passed, those theories became increasingly improbable.

The detailed facts were only revealed by Moscow in 1991 when it finally admitted having recovered the "black boxes" and made the recording tapes available, after the demise of the Soviet Union. However given various rather peculiar and as yet unexplained circumstances, I suspect many still believe, like Lowell that Congressman McDonald was the intended target of that shootdown, even though that implies a collusion between the Kremlin leadership and certain elements in the US establishment. Since this supposition has been accepted as a fact by many dissidents in America, it would be difficult to remove their doubts about the real circumstances of the KAL 007 tragedy.

XIV

Secrets from Outer Space

*I have wandered home but newly
From this ultimate dim Thule*

Edgar Poe, Dreamland

Across the Prairie to the Garden of the Gods

The first fortnight of September was dominated by the news surrounding the Korean airliner downing and amidst those dark forebodings I was relieved to get a call from Laura Hollyfield who offered to take me with her to Colorado Springs. She was going to meet a retired military officer who had knowledge of the Bill English case she had told me about during the conversation at Richard's home. She had taken an appointment with that senior commander on the following week. My hopes were raised by the prospects of that visit and I promptly accepted. It was agreed I would go down to Denver from where she planned to drive the seventy mile distance to Colorado Springs along Highway I-25.

"You should visit Colorado Springs anyway" she added "It is one of the nerve centres of aerospace defence of the country as you know."

"And also the site for Nikola Tesla's most ambitious experimental research" I recalled.

In the following days I gathered more information about the city. I already knew about the NORAD headquarters located under Cheyenne Mountain, from where surveillance of the entire North American airspace was carried out and I had heard of the National Air Force Academy but I found out about more about the newly renamed

Aerospace Defense Command (ADCOM) located on the Peterson Air Force Base and about the North American Aerospace Defense Command (NORTHCOM), hidden in the deep bunkers beneath Cheyenne Mountain, next to the US Civil Defense Warning Center and the headquarters of the 1st Air Force, assigned the task of protecting the American mainland (CONR). There was an alphabet soup of ominous initials designating an array of organizations and systems geared to fight all threats, known or unknown, in and beyond the atmosphere and I was prepared to believe that part of that formidable multi-dimensional panoply was intended to deter and harm assailants that might not be Russian nor even from this planet. I was particularly intrigued by the fact that the Cheyenne cavern complex was built to escape the otherwise devastating effects of electromagnetic pulses (EMP), a potential weapon still little known in 1983.

The succession of 25 ton blast doors that reportedly gave or barred access to the sprawling three story warren of chambers, hangars and tunnels, excavated under 2000 feet of solid granite further demonstrated the extraordinary precautions taken to resist an attack of unprecedented magnitude and I suspected, from the apparently exhaustive but disarmingly public information that was available on the facility, that a lot more had been kept secret about it.

"Our government is in the habit of saying a lot, accurate or misleading, about what it wants to hide. It shows the proverbial tip of the iceberg for PR benefits. After all a threat must be known to the intended targets to be effective but not so much as to reveal its weaknesses or help them to counter it" Laura pointed out when we began our road journey in downtown Denver where I connected with her in the lobby of the Brown Palace Hotel on the appointed day. She wore high brown boots over tucked-in Guess jeans and a leather jacket on a poppy-red shirt. Her eyes were shaded with broad designer sunglasses and I had to tell her that she looked superb. She smiled nonchalantly, habituated as she must have been to receiving compliments on her appearance.

"I guess that some of the technologies deployed at Cheyenne far exceed the capabilities that are available on the market" I commented.

"The rule is that the Military keeps thirty years ahead of the civilian sector, at least as far as the hardware Is concerned" Linda explained. "The computer systems developed for the NORAD and associated organizations are incredibly sophisticated. I have read about the set up and interviewed some experts for my investigative work. DELTA 1 was installed in 1967 as a giant array of computers to record and monitor any object detected in the airspace by the many sensors and radars deployed around the continent. The Space Defense Operations Center (SPADOC) became operational in 1979 in order to expand and improve the reach and coverage of the surveillance. It is articulated around the CPS or Core Processing Segment which consists of massive Honeywell computers. It is all under the WIMECKS...."

"Which is?"

"A sort of acronym for the Worldwide Military Command and Control System. Picture a giant cobweb of radio and cable links connecting all of America's defense installations and bases, at home and around the planet, to the central spider under Cheyenne Mountain. The structure is so arcane that it has become unwieldy even for the CPS and is now undergoing a massive upgrade at huge cost.

Although we are not told that much about what is being done, the story is that a prototype of a new dramatically simplified but much more manageable and powerful WIMECKS Information System, WIN for short is being tested. The Air Defense Command, now serviced by a state-of-the art computerized command and control system codenamed SAFEGUARD has been put under the authority of NORAD's Space Surveillance Center which in turn reports to the Strategic Air Command, the SAC that is in control of the ICBMs, the long-range bombers and other nuclear and conventional payload delivery vehicles. Under SAC you also have the Air Defense Command for Satellite Systems and the Ballistic Missile Defense Center, the BADC All that to make sure we can blow the planet to dust many times over, an ability of which we are very proud " she concluded with a bit of sarcasm.

I congratulated her for her mastery of the subject.

"You are incredibly fluent with all those exotic systems and acronyms" I said, sincerely impressed.

"I have spent month poring over those reports and checking facts with my sources. Indeed there were days when I even had dreams about that stuff" the young woman replied "and I still feel I have barely scratched the surface of what is going on."

"Talking about classified information" I mused "why does the person you are taking me to agree to speak to you about things that are a secret?"

She took her hands off the wheel to throw them in the air. "More people than you think are willing to talk" she said. "Usually they don't want to be quoted but off-the-record they like to take those things off their chests. I guess it's too heavy to carry to the grave and when they are retired and think about it, they look for confidants. A very human desire but I have sometimes wondered if they are not tacitly allowed or even encouraged to let some of the information out, if only to raise an awareness among people who can handle it…Then it is up to the listeners to dismiss or forget the story if they prefer to. Anyhow, government-related sources talk to people who really want to know and have done their homework. They are not dropping a bomb on a clueless John Smith."

"And what about me, a foreigner? Will he speak in front of me?"

"She threw me a sideways glance and flashed a smile. "I have cleared it. He knows what you are doing and has no problem. He is a space enthusiast and was involved in some way in the establishment of the National Space Foundation this year. Remember, he will speak only as a private citizen about his beliefs and ideas…"

"And the Government will deny any knowledge of his actions and words" I recited, paraphrasing the signature line from *Mission Impossible*.

Meanwhile Laura's olive green Ford Coupé had exited Denver, gone past the Denver Technological Center and glided along the

Interstate across the Colorado plateau. The Rockies bound the distant horizon on the right. We passed the exit to Castle Rock and evoked the periodic open air concerts that are held in that natural amphitheater. Soon we reached Monument Hill which marked our entrance into the more mountainous Douglas County. Occasional horses and herds of cows could be seen in the pastures which lined the road. The Sun's paler glow and the russet tree leaves signaled the advent of fall. Linda had switched on the radio and by chance or habit tuned into a Rock and Pop station. I quickly recognized the song:

Livin' easy
Livin' free
Season ticket on a one way ride
Asking nothing
Leave me be
Goin down
Party time
My friends are gonna be there too

The hoarse voice rose louder, foreshadowing the refrain amidst the hypnotic thrumming of strings:

Hey Satan
Paying my dues
Playin a Rocker band
Hey mamma
Look at me
I am on the way to the promised land
I am on the highway to Hell
Highway to Hell…

"I would not have guessed you like AC/DC…" I said in mock disapproval.

"A few years ago I was, like everybody, a Rock fan even though I am conservative girl" she replied "but with advancing maturity I got somewhat disturbed by the lyrics. The evocation of drug use, the call for the Devil and the hint of blasphemy about the promised land being hell, that is the spirit of the Sixties and they are at the core of much of popular culture in this country." She had already switched the radio to KVOD, the classical music station and the exquisitely nostalgic melody of Mozart's 20th piano Concerto filled the vehicle and our souls.

As the last dreamy third movement came to rest, Laura spoke again, waving at the wide placid panorama that unfolded outside the windows.

"This area, like much of the west was settled by gold diggers in their rush to find the mineral and get rich fast. See how quiet it looks now. Our country bears the marks of this feeding frenzy. In the end many of us see life as a treasure hunt."

"The quest for treasures is one of the oldest pursuits of mankind, after the search for food" I commented. "It has a mystical dimension, like everything else because the treasure in the end signifies power and happiness, in whatever material or invisible form it is located. Ancient civilizations have spawned beautifully evocative hymns, poems and tales about those who seek and find the bounty. Think of the Indian, Chinese, Tibetan and Russian legends on this theme."

"And what about the Golden Fleece and the Argonauts in Greece" Linda added "or our pirate stories from more recent times."

"The myths and fables tell us that to find the treasure, one must follow certain rules, grow wise, understand cryptic messages and detect hidden traces. If he does not, he will fail or else the treasure will become a curse. Even allegedly true filibuster annals show how those 'gentlemen of fortune' were doomed by their ill gotten pelf in this world and beyond."

"I wonder if that is not our problem" Laura wondered "our ancestors got hold of immense wealth when they occupied this pristine continent but their only guiding principles were self-interest, justified in their minds by some convenient religious claims. We are paying the price for the past, a past that we are adding to everyday on the same track."

As I silently pondered her words, I saw briefly images of the many Western films I had watched in previous years; dusty deserts and waving prairies. haphazardly built precarious settlements with their clapboard saloons, brothels and banks lining unpaved streets filled with drunken gunmen, penurious cowboys and cheap women; corrupt sheriffs, bedraggled wanderers, shady money-lenders and adventurers of all ilks and, far in the distance crimson twilights shrouding empty Indian encampments, dead bodies scattered amongst the wigwams and totem poles.

I realized how fragmentary those visions were but they still conveyed an undeniable reality about the formation of the American nation, a reality that had been embraced and propagated worldwide by the country's entertainment industry. The new country had fed on the loot and destruction of its older inhabitants by some of the less appealing specimens of European humanity. The vignettes about hordes of greedy outlaws slaughtering Indian tribes and buffalo herds to seize the land were as factual as the mental frescoes showing rows of African slaves picking cotton under the ruthless watch of horse-riding, gun-carrying planters. The industrial massacre of the Civil War added one more gory chapter to a continuously violent and predatory history, although the rest of mankind, with rare exceptions did not offer a much nicer picture of its past.

Dorothy Kilgallen, Marilyn and JFK

I needed to get my mind off those grim reflections but what came to my mind was not frivolous.

"Tell me" I said "what do you know of Dorothy Kilgallen whom you mentioned in our first meeting?."

"Nothing that is not publicly available about her" Laura replied slowly. "A well known society columnist, reporter and TV show panelist who knew everybody and had high level access. She investigated the JFK assassination and some say that she interviewed Jack Ruby in his cell, although that is disputed. She was close to Marilyn Monroe and apparently talked to her hours before the latter's sudden death in August 1962. There is a theory that Marilyn told her what she had learnt from John Kennedy, in pillow talks about UFOs and Aliens but was that the damning secret that got Kilgallen killed or was it something more political? As a matter of fact she was the first to allude in an article to Monroe's affair with one of the Kennedys and that was two days before Marilyn's body was found lifeless. Kilgallen did not believe that it was a suicide and she said so in her columns."

"Yes but you must also have read her piece in the *LA Examiner* on 22 May 1955 in which she reported from London that a high ranking British official had told her about Alien bodies being in the custody of Her Majesty's government."

"That was one of the many articles by her and others I went through as part of my research more than ten years ago. However it happened a decade before Dorothy's death so that it could not be the cause of it. As you know she had a regular nationally syndicated column, *The Voice of Broadway* in the *New York Journal American*. Nobody knows the name of the official who spoke to her. Some speculated it could be Lord Mountbatten whom she had met and who was privy to top secret matters but it isn't proven. In the article she repeats what she was told about scientists having examined the wreckage of a "mysterious flying ship" and about its small, four feet tall crewmen. She added that her contact in Britain found that "frightening" and confirmed that "flying saucers" came from other planets but that it was not to be disclosed as it would alarm the public."

"Yet he told her, knowing that she would write about it?"

"That is always the paradox in those top secret leaks. It sounds to me as if some people in the inner circle don't agree with this policy of deception and want to give the public anonymous warnings for which official confirmation obviously is not available. I guess a secret always arouses rumors, no matter how well kept it is" Laura speculated.

"Unless some men can't resist the temptation of intriguing a beautiful woman by letting her in on dangerous cloak and dagger stuff. That seems to have been the case between JFK and Monroe" I ventured "and Kilgallen died in rather suspicious circumstances in her Park Avenue townhouse in November 1965 while under FBI surveillance, according to her own hints."

"Yes, there are questions about her end. She had an alcohol problem and took sleeping pills and other chemicals but she was only fifty two years old. The fact that she had exposed the obvious cover up mission of the Warren Commission made her very unpopular with President Johnson and Edgar Hoover. She had a huge following, remember. When she covered the crowning of Queen Elizabeth at Westminster, some quipped that her dress and jewelry outshone the Monarch's finery. In her last year, She was putting together a book about John Kennedy's murder and it was obvious that it would be damaging to the LBJ administration and the CIA since her articles had already pointed to shady assets of the Agency like Clay Shaw. That for most people is what got her into trouble. We don't know what Ruby in his cell told her but according to her later casual remarks, he had been very candid, perhaps because he knew he would soon die anyway."

"Let us hope your military contact is as candid" I concluded on a upbeat note even though I could not overcome skepticism.

Buried Citadels and Clandestine Memories

By then the Rampart Range which towers over Colorado Springs on the West came into full view, behind the Ackerman Rise and we soon reached the 156-B Exit. A sign read *United States Air Force Academy – North Gate.*

"We are close to the city" Linda noted. "The Academy's campus is huge, over 18 000 acres, a large part of it is wilderness."

We entered Colorado Springs at Exit 153 and, leaving behind us the road to the famed Garden of the Gods, turned East and through the Austin Bluffs Parkway connected with Pike's Peak Avenue. The famous summit of the same name could be admired in the clear sky on our right.

"We are early and so I'll make a detour. We'll drive by Knob Hill, the site of Tesla's short-lived lab" Laura indicated. "Unfortunately nothing is left of it. You'll have to imagine it from the street."

"It is a shame to think that this pioneering station where Tesla had built the largest electromagnetic coil in the world was taken apart within months of being set up in the very first days of 1900" I commented. "Yet the experiments he carried there were awe-inspiring."

"Well of course here money is everything" she noted somberly. "The fact that he could not pay bills and was not generating any profits spelt the end of the venture."

"I rather think that what he was getting to was too much of a threat to the big business houses he depended up for funding" I argued. "Neither JP Morgan nor his partners wanted free electricity for all. There was no market there and they were interested in building lucrative monopolies."

We reached Powers Boulevard and drove south. "We are going towards Peterson Air Force Base, the headquarters for the US Space Command and the COC for NORAD and NOTHCOM, in conjunction with the Cheyenne Complex" my cicerone explained. "Actually this is the peacetime HQs while Cheyenne is the wartime refuge. Peterson also shelters the Army Space and Missile Defense Command as well as the 46th Aerospace Defense Wing which has been renamed the 1st Space Wing earlier this year. There are reports of extensive underground bunkers and silos beneath, connected with Cheyenne Mountain through deep tunnels and also with Fort Carson, to the South, the HQs of the 10th Special Forces Group and of the 13th Air Support Operations Squadron. Peterson hosts technical training and simulation facilities for the more advanced and unacknowledged programs of the Air Force, including the rumored Space Force, said to be far more advanced than NASA in its exploration of the solar system. A few months ago USAF broke ground for the new Falcon Station a few miles from here. It is to be the HQs of CSOC or Consolidated Space Operations Center, which includes Missile Defence Integration and Operations; what most people know as Star Wars. As you can see we are right at the heart of the continental military system."

"It is a project for the control of space" I remarked, feeling a mixture of awe and foreboding "but they could not easily carry out 'Alien' related operations here in the sight of all the personnel and visitors" I objected.

"That is only a control and monitoring center. The actual technical research, test and launch facilities are spread around the country, in restricted areas of Nevada, California, Arizona and New Mexico. You know some of the names: Los Alamos, Groom Lake, Wright Patterson, Edwards, Holloman, Vandenberg, China Lake and Tonopah to mention only a few."

"Not to forget the various labs and research centres of the Defense and Aerospace giants" I added "Lockheed, Grumman, Northrop, McDonnell, Hughes, Douglas, Martin Marietta, Raytheon, General Dynamics and so on."

We got out of the parkway and turned west into a quiet, tree lined street in a residential neighbourhood and Linda parked the car in view of a large house built in the style of Frank Lloyd Wright, so popular in the inter-war years. An unfenced lawn fronted it and a couple of tall cottonwood trees, the endemic *alamos* of the South West framed the soberly white minimalistic structure.

We walked on a cobblestoned pathway towards the square timber door of the house. I had noticed the name J A Caswell on the mailbox planted on the edge of the lawn. Laura rang the buzzer and after a few seconds a man opened.

He was white-haired, bewhiskered, still athletic and tall. Light grey eyes rested briefly on Linda before sizing me up impassively. Nodding us in, he shook both our hands without smiling. However there was warmth in his glance, His close cropped haircut and his manners were unmistakably military.

I had expected a better protected villa within a walled enclosure but I thought that we were in Colorado Springs, a partly military community and less than half a mile from one of the highest security Air Force facilities in the country, the headquarters of Continental Defense, no less. Then I noticed a discreet but sosphisticated electronic alarm system behind the door.

"Let's move to my study" the General said in a quiet deep voice. I detected a hushed Texan accent.

He ushered us into a large, austerely furnished room. Book shelves lined with volumes occupied two of the walls. Behind the desk, above a cabinet diverse mementoes, guidons, ensigns, citations and trophies were enthroned or entombed together in a glass case with the usual assortment of silver cups and statuettes used to reward sporting exploits.

I rapidly surveyed the books from my leather upholstered seat. They were mostly on history, strategy, aeronautics, geography along with various American and European military biographies. I spotted a few physics, mathematics and psychology tomes as well. There was also Sun Tzu's *Art of War* and the classics by Clausewitz and Jomini.

Laura began by thanking our host for accepting to meet us. She had obviously described me at some length before our visit because the General did not ask any question on my position or motivation and seemed to have already placed me. I got the impression that he was familiar with Laura's work as she did not introduce herself and referred to their earlier communications.

"I wanted to have this face time to review the situation with you in the light of what you can tell me, now that retirement gives you greater freedom" she proffered earnestly with her trademark seductive smile.

Caswell nodded slightly and after a moment of silence commented: "I appreciate what you do and I agree that much evidence is already publicly available to allow interested people to find out about the truth, at least in part. As a young man you know that I listened to some talks by Major Donald Keyhoe and met him after reading his books. I became a member of NICAP and formed a friendship with his deputy, Richard Hall. Later I was in touch with various officers involved with this stuff including Colonel Hathaway, ADC for the Senate Armed Services Committee. Hathaway had been with Senator Richard Russell when travelling on a train in the USSR they sighted in daylight two flying discs in 1955. That observation was duly reported to the relevant US government agencies and both Russell and Hathaway were secretly debriefed at the Pentagon; so they could not discuss in public what they saw but Hathaway spoke to me and he even gave me the name of the USAF Colonel who conducted the debriefing on behalf of the NSA and the NRO. This was serious stuff. Me, I was never formally pledged to secrecy because I didn't work on those classified programmes but of course I heard a lot of things from people in the know."

Laura directed at me a fleeting but triumphant glance as if to say "bingo." I was paying close attention.

"When I studied your background I discovered that you were early in your career in the staff of General George Schulgen when he was in Army Air Force Intelligence" she stated "and that said a lot because Schulgen made some very revealing comments on the matter of UFOs and was in close contact with General Twining about the whole thing."

"Yes he was not too bothered with secrecy" Caswell noted, shaking his head "and he was one of the top brass as head of Requirements Intel Branch in 1947 when the Roswell incident took place. He went to Korea for the War Reparations Tour. He was a bit like MacArthur, Twining and other officers who spoke rather freely at times about what we are confronted with. On the other hand others such as Vandenberg and Curtis LeMay were quite paranoid on the subject and shut down any attempts by outsiders to find out."

"How would you define it yourself?" Linda asked point-blank.

There was another instant of suspenseful silence. Caswell almost closed his eyes and his face took on the solemn immobility of a sleeping mask.

"I'll tell you no more or less than my seniors and colleagues" he let out in an even voice: "we have discovered that we live in a very complex universe full of life of all sorts and some of those lifeforms are somehow involved with us in intricate ways. At least one is generally protective towards the earth and human beings while others are far less concerned about our welfare and can be quite dangerous, if not to our species at least to us individually if we are at the wrong place at the wrong time. It's the old story of life. There are strangers and unknowns, friends and enemies, allies and predators, angels and demons, goblins, fairies, ogres and witches. Children and so-called savages are more in tune with reality than we rationalist adults."

I caught the disarray in the general's now open eyes. Here was a man grimly aware that most of the fundamental concepts he had been taught by society were invalid.

Laura was pushing on relentlessly, hoping that our host's temporary vulnerability could lead him to say more.

"Early in your career you were exposed to some of the information filtering out of the Roswell and other cases, from what you told me earlier" she recalled. "What are the more recent reports that you have seen and which you regard as proven and true? I would like to stick to what is not open to doubt."

"We have reports coming from official sources all over the world" the General acknowledged. "Because of my personal interest and my former position, I get to see and study only some of them but I am given details not available to the public. In the last few years very interesting accounts have come from Brazil for instance and we are in touch with the armed forces of that country among others, to evaluate the potential threat although there are strict limits to what we can share. We operate on a need-to-know basis, as usual."

"Are you referring to *Operation Prato* in particular?" was Laura's immediate query.

Caswell nodded. "There are others but this was a real eye opener for Brazil. The Pentagon was consulted by COMAR on this."

I knew the background to that allusion. Operation Prato had been carried out by the 1st Regional Command of the Brazilian Air Force between October and December 1977 in response to a rash of sightings and alerts in the States of Maranhao and Para, involving several towns and hundreds of witnesses, beginning in and around the Bay of San Marcos, near San Luis, the Maranhao State capital. The most alarming reports concerned people being badly burnt by scorching beams of light shot at them by strange low flying craft which often caused power failures along their paths. Even car engines stopped when the objects hovered above them. Some communities had been gripped by panic and several witnesses claimed they had seen menacing beings who became popularly known as *chupa chupas*, due to the fact that they were said to suck blood from goats and even from some of the people who came across them. Several victims had indeed been treated for their wounds.

In view of the persistence and gravity of the alerts the Brasilian Air Force and two federal agencies, the National Information Service (SNI) and the CISA (Information Service on Aeronautical Security) launched two successive inquiries , one in late October 1977 and the second before the end of November under the leadership of Brigadier Protasio Lopes de Oliveira from the first COMAR's 2nd section. They collected a lot of evidence but could not come to any conclusion about the source of the multiple phenomena which involved flying vessels evincing extraordinary performances in speed and manoeuvrability. I heard Laura mention that she had been in touch with the second-in-command of Prato, a Colonel Ferraz de Barros. General Cantwell said he had also communicated with him despite the language barrier but did not make it clear whether it was in person, by mail or on the telephone.

The facts were obviously real but it was difficult to say more because there was no explanation other than acknowledging the "alien" character of the events.

Return to Roswell

Ms Hollyfied moved back to more familiar circumstances and asked our host: "How and what did you get to know from Roswell early in your career?"

The General shook his head and stared at his large open palms for a second.

"I heard of Roswell soon after it happened as a junior NCO" he reminisced slowly. "Nothing very precise but it had an impact because the rumors came from higher military ranks where gossip on strategic matters is usually based on facts. We all knew of the place as the cradle of the American space programme, with Robert Goddard and the JPL founding team led by Jack Parsons, so there was some odd logic to the flying saucer crash report. Even Von Braun acknowledged that Goddard's experiments were more important for rocketry research than the German projects and, to throw in a bit of trivia, Parsons, who was a real Satanist died accidentally or was murdered on the day of 1952 when the National Capitol Building was very publicly buzzed by dozens of flying saucers. But back to Roswell, in 1947 it hosted the base for the 8th Army Air Force Squadron which was tasked with the delivery of nuclear weapons, close to the Los Alamos-Alamo Gordo-Sandia complex so there was some sort of an apocalyptic aura around it. Much later as a senior officer I saw some classified reports which indirectly at least supported the ET related version of what had happened in July Of 1947."

The young woman's silent elation could be felt. I was hooked. Our host sounded as if he was not going to hold information back.

"Have you kept copies any of these documents with you" was Linda's next question. I held my breath.

"These are things you were not supposed to keep or copy. They were "eyes only" or at least not destined to me." I noticed the answer was too generic to amount to a denial.

My female friend did not waste any time before raising her next query: "Did you hear of Majestic 12 or of any related operation?"

"Not precisely of course since I would only have been briefed about it on a need-to-know basis but in the sixties I had inklings, like many others in the services, of a secret supervisory body set up by special executive order from President Truman at a meeting he held in September 1947 with Defense Secretary Forrestal and former Manhattan Project head Dr Vannevar Bush. It was meant to organize and oversee information gathering and action related to UFOs. The names of von Braun, J.Robert Oppenheimer and Edward Teller came up in this connection. A secret CounterIntelligence Corps memo from late July of that year was shown to me by a colleague in the early seventies. I think it had been prepared for G-2, the Assistant Chief of Staff."

At that point I could not resist the temptation to insert my own question and asked Caswell if he had come in contact with any colleague in any way involved with the management of the Roswell situation.

"I was too young to have access to the top brass of that generation" the General explained "but I recall chatting with a fellow from the Signals Corps in 1954 or thereabouts. We evoked various UFO stories in the news at the time, including the massive overflight of the National Capitol and he mentioned that in 1947 he had been posted at the SCEL at Fort Monmouth, New Jersey when a number of unidentified craft were tracked, zipping at fantastic speeds and suddenly stopping dead in their tracks after going through uncannily high-G turns.... The SCEL tracked the same type of vessels on several occasions during the fifties and sixties"

"What is SCEL?" I asked.

He gave me an indulgent glance, understanding that I could not be expected to be cognizant of the myriad acronyms used in his profession. "Signal Corps Engineering Labs. That guy remembered that many of the objects were tracked in late June and early July 1947."

"In your long and distinguished career, you may have met personnel who participated in the disposal of bodies and craft" Laura suggested.

Caswell lifted his eyes as if to conjure echoes from the remote past. "Well yes if I take into account the fact that one of my buddies had started his service at 4th Army Headquarters under General Thomas Handy who apparently oversaw the dispersal of what had been recovered around Roswell in various protected facilities. From what my friend said once, he had seen a paper trail regarding the shipping of bodies and equipment by air and road transport but I could not get any more information from him. He was sworn to secrecy and, as you may know there is something called McNab laws to dissuade servicemen from breaking the law of silence."

"What about the Interplanetary Phenomenon Unit?" the relentless Linda asked. "Any insights on that?."

I felt the General was enjoying the probing questions which gave him an excuse to revive half-buried memories. Everyone likes to recall episodes of the past, all the more when it revives the impression of having witnessed significant historical events. He readily shared his knowledge about the IPU which, he explained, had been set by President Franklin Roosevelt in March 1942 in response to a memorandum from General George Marshall regarding the recovery of pieces of an unknown spacecraft in California by the Armed Forces. He told us that the recovery was most probably related to the passage of a UFO over the greater LA area on February 25th of that year, an event which attracted considerable public and media attention since the anti-aircraft batteries repeatedly fired at the craft after military searchlights zeroed in on it. There were even rumors of people on the ground being killed.

The General thought that the IPU had been merged with MJ-12 ("or whatever other names that programme was given at various times") by Truman who wanted the UFO issue to be monitored by both the CIG, later to become the CIA, through the new Office of Scientific Intelligence or OSI, and the Military. His Air Force Liaison Robert Landry briefed him regularly on behalf of the Pentagon as I had been told on another occasion.

"In those years, believe it or not, we lost a number of warplanes in UFO encounters and pursuits, not because they attacked us but because we tried to intercept or shoot them down and our birds's engines and controls went dead" Caswell explained calmly.

"In November 1952 Eisenhower was elected President and given a briefing document about the current status of the UFO issue. He had however known about it at least since 1947 when he was COS of the war department and had been shown the stuff recovered from Roswell by General Hoyt Vandenberg, the army chief" he added.

"That more or less checks out with what I have garnered about the Twining-Cutler document from 1954" Laura noted excitedly "but can you throw some light on Area 51?"

"That is the elephant in the living room" the General chuckled, visibly basking in the electric atmosphere. "It was selected by the CIA to host the Headquarters of R&D on the UFO issue at the behest of Nelson Rockefeller, the President's Cold War Planning Tzar in 1955. They took land owned by the Department of Energy which has been heavily involved in certain aspects of UFO research because of the priority given to mastering the power generating technology of alien crafts. The DOE also escapes public attention better than the Military and commands virtually unlimited and unsupervised budgets. Area 51 is part of the Nevada Atomic Test Site and there are several other facilities with distinct code names in that zone and in various places in the USA. The choice of that particular location was calculated to scare people away due to the widespread fear of radiation. Nuclear research is a convenient cover for many other things. Now Area 51 is like a sovereign territory where many US laws don't apply and there are many different facilities operating above and underground. It is a virtual country half the size of Rhode Island."

"As a matter of curiosity, why is it called Dreamland?" I wondered.

"Various reasons are given but I am not sure which is the real one" Caswell remarked. "One that seems very likely is that in certain areas of research and experimentation the personnel involved operate in an altered state of consciousness in which they no longer know if they dream or are awake. That could be induced by drugs or hypnosis, unless the proximity of the Aliens or their materiel induces an ASC. It's also known as Paradise Ranch or Watertown.

I was reminded of the training dispensed at the Monroe Institute and of the rising 'focus levels' described by the founder. Many things were falling in place as the pieces of a giant puzzle gradually began to fit together.

XV
A Vault Opens

Never the mysteries are exposed
To the weak human eye unclosed

Edgar Poe, Dreamland

THE GRUDGE PAPERS

"Come on General" Laura pressed on with her most engaging tone of voice "Can you show us any document that confirms or reveals specific aspects of this matter? You told me you had done a fair bit of research on your own. There must be some tangible results of our investigations."

Caswell appeared to hesitate for a second before getting up and taking a few steps towards an unobtrusive safe placed between the cabinet and the bookshelves that hid the wall behind him.

His back was turned so that I could not see if he used a key or an access code but when he returned to his armchair he held a manila envelope which he put down solemnly on the desk.

"You may take a look at this" he said quietly "but I won't be able to let you have a copy as it was not allowed for circulation. I have to respect government decisions."

Laura and I held our breath while he opened the unsealed envelope and pulled out a ream of documents which he handed to my friend. She instantly began to read it, leaning towards me so that I could see the pages as well. The scent of her hair wafted to my nostrils. There was a hint of perfume. Gloria Vanderbilt's perhaps.

The title of the document typed was *Grudge 13 Report*. It was a carbon copy. As we went through it I was aware that I would not be able to remember the details of that extensive account, even though some of the information was familiar. What follows is based on the tape recorded account given by former Green Beret captain Bill English who read the original Grudge 13 report in 1977. The transcript was later published in the Majestic Documents collection that I perused in more recent years. English's report is faithful to the text that I read in Colorado Spring on that day of September 1983.

"I am well aware of Grudge-Blue Book Reports 1 to 12" Laura noted. "While the first one from 1950 is a rather clumsy debunking attempt, the others mostly list investigated cases which they try to explain more or less successfully and sometimes don't."

"This is a different animal" Cantwell retorted. "Just read. It was classified *Top Secret Ultra* under Code Red unlike the others which were intended mostly to keep outsiders offtrack by making them believe they were told everything that was happening in this area by a truthful government. English who reported on it is personally in the know of UFOs because he was involved in the search and recovery of a B-52 lost over Vietnam whose pilots had radioed that they were being set upon by a UFO. His team found the plane in the jungle with little damage but the crew had been mutilated, rather deliberately it seems. That background may help explain how he was able to see this document in the annotated original with its revisions and additions over ten years."

I voiced my own thought on the issue:

"It would make sense that, if the White House decided to throw a big cloak of secrecy over the UFO issue since Roswell, after passing the National Security Act they would disavow the conclusions of Project Sign that UFOs were alien vehicles and set up Grudge in 1948 to deny everything while continuing with the real clandestine research. In fact Grudge was closed down in 1951 and Bluebook took over, claiming at least to be more honest in its analyses, though it was another sham."

Here is English'account:

The document's second page was a copy of a standard USAF Disposition form entitled 'Analysis Report'.

Further down was 'Analyse enclosed report under code red measures, give abstract breakdown and report on validity. Observe all code red measures. Analysis required immediately.'

The pages measured approximately 8" by 11." They were bound, paper back style. Across the centre front It read, "Grudge/Blue Book Report No. 13." It was dated 1953-(1963).

Across the front was stamped in red ink 'Top Secret Need To Know Only Crypto Clearance 14 Required.' The third page consisted of an appendix with numerous notations made In It. Notations dealt with Inserts of what appeared to be photos-and additional notes. At bottom It read G/BV Page 1 of 624 pages. English remembers that it was enigmatically headlined: Some notes on the practical applications of the Worst Nemo equations.

From this point on I will quote verbatim the transcribed version of Bill English's version:

"Table of Contents,
- Part 1, "On the design of generators to accomplish strain free molecular translation."
- Part 2, "the generation of space time discontinuums, closed, open and folded."
- Part 3, "on the generation of temporary pseudo acceleration locas."
- Part 1, Chapter 1 "design criteria for a simple generator and control system referring to equation 17 appendix A."
- Part 2, Chapter 1 "Continuation of Einstein's Theory of Relativity to final conclusion."
- Part 3, Chapter 1 "Possible applications of Einstein theory of relativity at conclusion."
- Part 1, Chapter 2, "Reports of UFO encounters, classification 'Close Encounters of the 1st Kind' subtitle sightings and witnesses."
- Part 2, Chapter 2, 'Close Encounters of- the 2nd Kind' subtitle UFO sightings witnessed within close proximity.

- Part 3, Chapter 2, "Close Encounters of the 3rd Kind," subtitle UFO encounters and extraterrestrial life forms witnessed and personal encounters. Subtitle/colonies relocation thereof.
- Case histories.
- Chapter 3 Part 1, "Military Encounters with UFO's."
- Chapter 3 Part 2, "Military Reports Concerning Sightings on Radar and Electronic Surveillance of UFO's."
- Subsection 2, Analysis Report, J. Allen Hynek, Lt. Col. Friend.
- Appendix continued on for about 5 pages.
- Opening subject page consisted of a report of the findings as written by Lt. Col. Friend and his analysis."

At that point Laura commented that Colonel Robert Friend was a technical officer involved for many years in the clandestine military investigations of the UFO issue at Wright Field, later Wright Patterson, in the late fifties and early sixties. She had seen his name in several documents related to government operations in that sphere but recalled that he never made very definite statements, either out of ignorance or mandatory discretion.

"Friend was not privy to the highly classified stuff" the General pointed out. "He was, like his colleague Colonel Bill Coleman, more of a public relations officer whom any visitor could meet by appointment to seek or give information on UFOs and weird sightings but he was not privy to the Q or above security clearance stuff as he had no need to know. His job was to collect witnessings and purported evidence from outside and pass it on while trying to give a non-committal but reassuring impression to the public. He came to WP in 1958, more than ten years after the really sensitive R&D began and left his job at AMC in 63, the year that this report was put in its final form. The Foreign Technology Division had by then been separated from the AMC and put under the direct control of USAF Assistant Chief of Staff for Intelligence.

Friend had no access to ATIC, the Air Technology Intel Center which did the most sensitive analyses and I don't think he even knew anything about the German Paperclip scientists who had worked at Wright Field on 'foreign materiel'; people like Steinhoff and

Strughold. 1964 was the year, by the way, when RAF Air Marshall Thomas Pike, the Deputy NATO/SHAPE commander provided a classified assessment of the UFO challenge to his boss, Hyman Lemnitzer, the SACEUR following observations of large saucer armadas over Europe. That was a secret but official confirmation that the elephant was in the room."

"General Lemnitzer is notorious as a former US JCS Chairman who advised Kennedy to stage a false flag attack by shooting down on an US airliner or a decoy in the Caribbean to justify an invasion of Cuba" I chuckled, triggering sad glances from both the other persons in the room.

"Operation Northwoods" Caswell multered.

What we read in the following pages was summarized by English in his testimony as follows:

"Sections remembered very vividly are the photographs and the reports concerning captive sights of various UFOs to include Mexico, Sweden, United States. and Canada. There were also what was then classified Close Encounters of the 3rd (sic) Kind. It was made very clear that these people whom it was determined had genuine CE 3's were moved in the middle of the night by Air Force personnel and relocated to various sites in the Midwest and northwest parts of the United States. In many cases these people experienced physical ailments from exposure to various types of radiation.

One case especially noted and remembered very vividly was entitled 'Darlington Farm Case' out of Ohio. Case apparently took place in October 1953. Man, wife and 13 year old son were sitting down at dinner table. As they sat there the lights in the farm house began to dim. Dogs and animals raised ruckus outside. 13 year old boy got up from dinner table to see what was going on. Called his mother and father to come look at the funny light in the sky. Father and mother got up and as they got up the son went outside into the yard. Father and mother went out onto the porch.

When they got out on the porch one of the dogs broke loose from leash beside house and came running around front. Boy began chasing it out into the open field. As mother and father watched the light cam down from the sky. They described it as a round ball of fire and it began to, hover over field where boy and dog had run to. As they stood and watched, the mother and father heard the boy start screaming for help whereupon the father grabbed his shotgun which was right next to the door and began to run out into the field with the mother following. When the father got to the field he saw his son being carried away by what looked like little men, into this huge fiery looking object.

As it took off the father fired several rounds at the object, to no avail. They found dog, its head was crushed but no sign of boy or any other footprints of the little men who apparently carried him off. Father immediately called Darlington police and they immediately came out to investigate. The official report read that the boy had run off and was lost in the forest which bordered the farm. Within 48 hours the Air Force made the determination that the family was to be relocated and the mother and father were picked up by Air Force Intelligence and all personal belongings and possessions were loaded into U.S. Air Force trucks and moved to a northwestern relocation site.

The mother was in shock and had to go through a great deal of psychotherapy and deprogramming as did father. One Interesting aspect about this case was classification under the Air Force report which read it was a genuine CE 3 and that for the good of the national security the mother and father had been relocated to re-location zones Z21-14. Not sure whether this indicated map grid coordinates or latitude longitude.

According to the report there were at least 4 relocation sites across the United States. Depending upon which type of encounter these people had, the report Indicated that there were extensive medical facilities available at these relocation sites to deal with all medical emergencies up to an including radiation poisoning. The report mentioned a site located in the Utah-Nevada area, but no indication of Its purpose or what it was for.

Report gave clear Indication of reports of human mutilations, most notably was a case witnessed by Air Force personnel in which an Air Force Sgt. EE-6 by the name of **Jonathon P. Lovette** was observed being taken captive aboard what appeared to be a UFO at the White Sands Missile Test Range In New Mexico. This abduction took place in March of 1956 at about 0300 local and was witnessed by Major **William Cunningham** of the United States Air Force Missile Test Command near Holloman Air Force Base.

Major Cunningham and Sgt. Lovette were out in a field downrange from the launch sites looking for debris from a missile test when Sgt. Lovette went over the ridge of a small sand dune and was out of sight for a time. Major Cunningham heard Sgt. Lovette scream in what was described as terror or agony. The major, thinking the Sgt. had been bitten by a snake or something ran over the crest of the dune and saw Sgt. Lovette being dragged into what appeared to him and was described as being a silvery disk like object which hovered in the air approximately 15 to 20 feet.

Major Cunningham described what appeared to be a long snake-like object which was wrapped around the sergeants legs and was dragging him to the craft. Major Cunningham admittedly froze as the sergeant was dragged inside the disc and observed the disc going up into the sky very quickly. Major Cunningham got on the Jeep radio and reported the incident to Missile Control whereupon Missile Control confirmed a radar sighting. Search parties went out Into the field looking for Sgt. Lovette. Major Cunningham's report was taken and he was admitted to the White Sands Base Dispensary for observation.

The search for Sgt. Lovette was continued for 3 days at the end of which his nude body was found approximately 10 miles downrange. The body had been mutilated; the tongue had been removed from lower portion of the Jaw. An incision had been made Just under the tip of the chin and extended all the way back to the esophagus and larynx. He had been emasculated and his eyes had been removed. Also, his anus had been removed and there were comments in the report on the apparent surgical skill of the removal of these items including the genitalia.

The report commented that the anus and genitalia had been removed 'as though a plug' which In the case of the anus extended all the way up to the colon. There was no sign of blood within the system. The initial autopsy report confirmed that the system had been completely drained of blood and that there was no vascular collapse due to death by bleeding.

Sub comment was added that this was unusual because anybody who dies or has complete loss of blood there is vascular collapse. Also noted was that when the body was found there were a number of dead predatory type birds within the area who apparently had died after trying to partake of the sergeant body. There were a number of extremely grisly black and white photos. From all indications the body had been exposed to the elements for at least a day or two. The New Mexico sun in the desert is extremely hot and debilitating under normal circumstances."

We could hardly repress a gasp when we went through the gory details mentioned above and stole at glance at the general who nodded gravely in response to our muted revulsion.

"Take it as scientific research" he said quietly "and remember what we do daily to millions of animals for experimentation or food."

We resumed reading:

"In the same section of the report it was also indicated that there were numerous occasions in which a UFO (was) tracked alongside a fired missile and on one occasion said missile was observed being taken aboard a UFO while in flight. The speeds indicated were absolutely phenomenal.

The report also indicated that there were a number of recovery teams that were activated specifically for the purpose of recovering any and all evidence of UFO's and UFO sightings. Most notably recorded in publication was what they called Recovery Team Alpha. It was reported that Alpha had been extremely active in a number of areas and on certain occasions had traveled outside of the continental United States. Alpha was based out of Wright-Patterson Air Force Base and was on the move constantly."

ALL THE KING'S MEN AND ALL HIS HORSES

"I thought the recovery project was called *Bluefly*?" Linda asked, peering at Caswell over the document.

"Yes. There were many programs started under the Project *Saucer* which became *Sign*, to make it less obvious and then *Grudge* and was part of the overall *Blue Book* Investigation, a part of which was public for cover while the important work was being done secretly under MJ-12."

"There was also something called *Pounce*" I inserted. "I am told it was an attempt to intercept the unknown craft."

"Correct" the General confirmed. "The Air Force started it in 1952 by equipping F-94 C fighters with GSAP advanced cameras. They were based in New Mexico around the sensitive Los Alamos-Sandia-Kirtland-Holloman perimeter and were designated as UFO interceptors but their effectiveness was rather limited. It was a bit like trying to hit a stealth bomber with a bow and arrows but we got some good pictures out of that experiment."

A Vault Opens   261

"Further information in the Grudge 13 report consisted of such things as reported sightings and where air force planes had been destroyed or had combat encounters or had been attacked by UFO's. Also there were autopsy reports of various human mutilations.

About midway through the report came a section which dealt specifically with photographs. Each photo was labeled and appendixed to certain reports. A number of photos in there dealt with a recovery program of some type that took place in the southwestern part of the United States. They did not give a location name but they did give grid coordinates for that area. There is no clear indication to exactly where it was. The photos dealt with special teams that were called in to recover a crashed UFO. It also dealt with alien bodies and autopsy reports, autopsy type photographs, high quality, color, 8x10, 5x7.

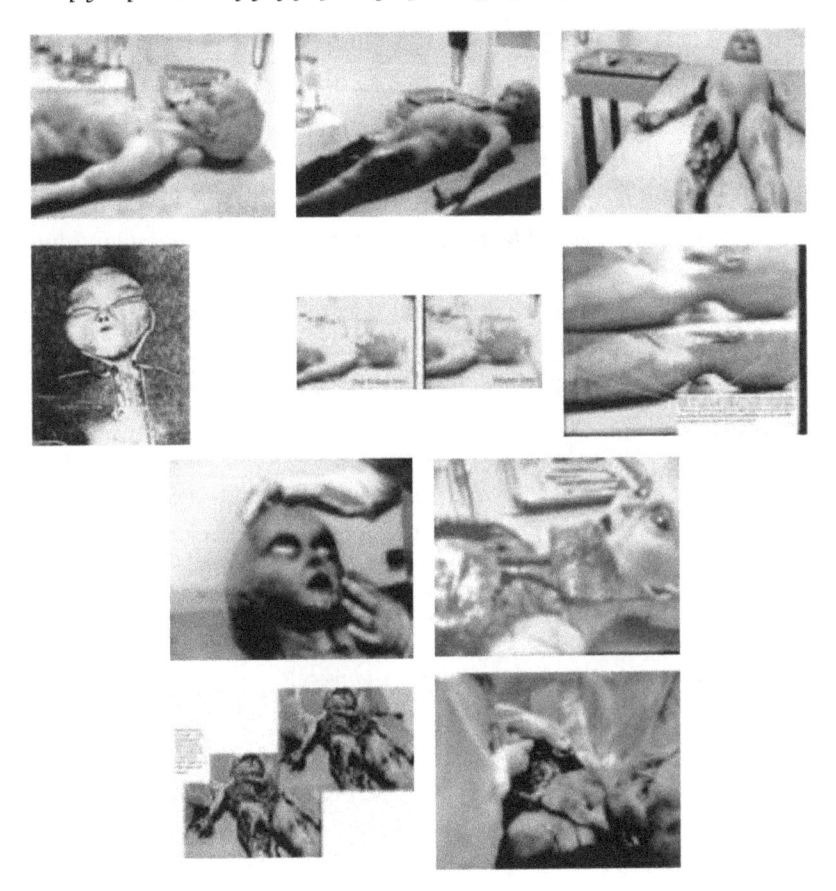

Photo number 1 showed an alien being on an autopsy table which is a metal table with runnels and traps underneath to trap fluid and feces. Body appeared to be a little short of 4 feet. Table was about 7 foot. No clothing on body, no genitalia, head was rounded cranium, slightly enlarged, eyes almond shaped, slits where nose would be, extremely small mouth, receding chin line, holes where ears would be.

Photo was taken at angle, side view, looking at body from 45° elevation, left hand was .visible, head was facing to left, body was right to left position (head on right, feet on left), eyes were closed appeared oriental-looking and almond shaped, left hand slight longer than normal, wrist coming down Just about 2 to 3 Inches above the knees. Wrists appeared to be articulated In a fashion that allowed a double Joint with 3 digit fingers. Wrist was very slender. There was no thumb. A palm was almost non-existent. The three fingers were direct extension from the wrist.

Color of the skin was bluish gray, dark bluish gray. At base of the body there was a darker color, Indicating body was dead for some time. Body fluid or blood had settled to base of body. This indicated that body had been examined before beginning autopsy.

Picture showed beginning stages of autopsy, following standard procedure, body was slit from crotch to Just under chin and green viscous liquid was in evidence. There were internal organs but these could not be identified. Photos thereafter concerned specific areas of Internal organs of what appeared as small cluster of a multi-valve heart or at least 2 hearts within the cadaver.

No accurate description of autopsy report or what was found within corpse accompanying photos. Indication that there was no stomach or digestive track per se. Later analysis showed that fluid within body was chlorophyll-based liquid which apparently dealt with photosynthesis or similar process. The report theorized that nourishment was taken in through mouth, however since there is no digestive track or anything of this nature, the waste products were excreted through skin.

One section of report did specify that cadavers were extremely odorous, but this could be accounted for by either deterioration or a number of things, but theory was that waste was excreted through pores of skin. They could only theorize in report because there was no xenobiology.

A report by Dr. **J. Allen Hynek** was included. It indicated that he had also studied the information provided by this particular case and that he felt that it was indeed a genuine UFO capture and subsequently the alien was part of UFO. Also indicated in report that he did not view bodies personally, but viewed photographs and accompanying reports from autopsies."

I then realized that Hynek had not referred to any of this in his conversation with me, nor had he in his books. He was manifestly also under some form of gag order, unless he was merely uncomfortable brining out certain aspects of the Alien enigma.

The report continued:

"Other photos dealt with a number of bodies which were vivisectioned in various ways. At one point, a head was removed from body and photographed and autopsy was performed on head. The cranium was opened and brain matter was photographed and evident. Interesting thing about photo was that there was a ridge-bone or dividing partition-type bone running directly through center of skull, from front to back, as though dividing two brains, one from the other. This seemed apparent from the picture. The skin was completely removed from cranial structure and the skull was laid bare as much as possible.

At one point the skull was cut directly in half and photo showed under developed esophagus and nasal cavities. No clear photo of eye orbs as we know them, just photos of complete vivisection of skull Itself.

Numerous photos of flesh of the being starting with cutaneous and subcutaneous micro-photographic plates. Appeared to be cellular studies done under microscope and electron microscope type photos. Extreme magnification of tissue samples."

1. Report told of sensitive military and Industrial areas at which personnel experienced missing time.

2. Report told about missing time experienced with personnel associated with North American X-15 rocket plane project.

3. Report stated that there were 17 different extraterrestrial species accounted for up to the time of the report.

4. Extraterrestrials were referred to as A.L.F.'s, Alien Life Forms in the report.

5. Report referred to one UFO that was recovered and test flown in the early fifties. The UFO blew up as the 2 Air Force pilot aboard attempted to leave the atmosphere.

6. Report refers to flying saucer program as Project 'Red Light' and that a

secret installation had been constructed in the middle of the Atomic Energy Commission testing ground in Nevada.

7. At the time of the report 11 alien cadavers were being kept at Wright-Patterson Air Force Base.

8. That additional alien cadavers were being stored at 4 to 5 other medical institutions.

9. That 2 flying saucers of extraterrestrial origin had been tested in the wind tunnel at Langley, Va.

10. That at the time of the report one disc was being stored at McDill Air Force Base in Florida.

11. That at the time of the report, 1 damaged disc was at Eglin Air Force Base in Florida.

"It was one of those which President Nixon may have been shown during his tenure" I remarked. "Jackie Gleason his friend said he had accompanied him there" Laura added.

12. That at the time of the report there had been 2 UFO incidents at Ft. Riley, Kansas.

13. That at the time of the report a detachment of the Alpha recovery team was based at Randolph Air Force Base.

14. The report discussed civilian and military personnel who had been terminated 'to eliminate potentially dangerous elements to the national security.'

15. That Gen. James Doolittle had been mentioned several times in the report with the notation that "His (Doolittle's') predictions might be correct." There was no Indication of what those predictions might have been.

16. A short segment containing the quotation, "By presidential order, certain aspects of research had been undertaken."

Even for Laura, familiar as she was with the subject matter, the information packed in this report was so overwhelming that it reduced her to stunned or perplexed silence. The General had put on spectacles and was apparently poring over some correspondence and making notes on a pad. I broke the almost eerie quietness.

"Wright Patterson is indicated as a central facility for this work" I pointed out. "It even kept some Alien bodies according to this text."

"There was and still is in the AMC or Air Materiel Command a Blue Room, a section dedicated to UFO related work there. One project was called *RedLight* and another one *WhiteHot*" Caswell explained "and it is known in certain circles that Senator Barry Goldwater was one of those who asked Curtis Le May, then chairman of the Joint Chiefs of Staff to be given access there. He says he was angrily told off and could not try again. I have heard that the most secret project of all, something called *CAUCASIAN* of which I know nothing, was supervised from there since 1952, at least administratively because I believe that now the hands on-work is conducted at S-4, under Papoose Mountain and at the so-called Ranch around Groom Lake, within Area 51 although various other research facilities such as White Sands are involved. That includes various attempts to build discs and make them fly as you gather from this report. Specific tasks are assigned to separate labs and teams on a need-to-know basis of course."

"I know for a fact that various technical programs were and probably still are carried out at Wright Patterson itself, perhaps less since Area 51 became operational. General Hap Arnold who set up the Army Air Forces Scientific Advisory Board, the AAFSAB and put Von Karman in charge of it, was a frequent visitor. The Aerobee rocket and prototypes of secret aircraft came out of there, as well as high altitude observation balloons and experimental chutes" Laura noted "but of course you must add as a major research center the Lockheed Skunkworks division at Burbank."

"Throw in Martin Marietta, Northrop, Grumman, Hughes Aerospace, Teledyne Ryan, ITT, Cray, Bell, General Dynamics, Raytheon, Honeywell, Westinghouse, General Electric, IBM and Motorola and you'll have a sample of the brains and technical means involved in this process" Caswell commented. "It is a multi-billion dollar enterprise but very few people get the whole picture. Legislative and even presidential supervision is practically inexistent and almost everything is top secret."

"It sure makes a mockery of the democratic system and of constitutional procedures" Laura noted with a bitter smile "but perhaps it is inevitable given the circumstances, even though unaccountability provides vast opportunities for corruption and misuse of power and funds."

"I have difficulties with this account of autopsies of bodies following numerous crashes" I said. "How can those beings be so easily captured given the incredible technologies they master? Here you see them dissected like frogs in a classroom, And then again there is talk of seventeen different types of creatures."

"My own conclusion is that the beings autopsied here are bio-robots" the General responded. "They are lab-created or bred and remotely controlled to carry out missions, group-think as in a pod and are apparently expandable. Some other races may be *bonafide* intelligent animals but the question remains: who sends the biorobots here?"

"Now you make me wonder if we humans are not somewhat similar to those cyborgs. We surely are expendable too. At least most of us act as if we were."

"I guess you are taking at shot at my career and community" Caswell quipped, inserting a dash of welcome humor in the midst of a grim discussion "but I have to agree that we make and use many of our greatest discoveries to kill one another."

"Let me tell you what I am coming to" Laura said gravely. "It is my impression that many of those beings come from another dimension or world.... Some call it *loka*, borrowing a word from sanskrit as in this document. Say even several parallel but connected dimensions and move either in an intermediate fringe area where our own consciousness dilutes or transits in their presence. That would explain the "missing time" experiences and the enormous, often senseless variety of impression and memories collected by abductees and contactees. They enter a dream state and as you are aware, many ancient peoples, such as the Australian aboriginals talk of the past as dream time in which the gods and heroes dwell."

"Other cultures hold that we live here in a dream and that we see the gods and otherwise invisible beings and things when we awake" I pointed out. "It is the image of Plato's cave."

"Either way, it boils down to almost the same" the General concluded. "There is another spacetime and perhaps an infinity of them which are as real as the one we mostly inhabit. A leading physicist, John Wheeler I believe, has built this into his cosmology: a superuniverse, he calls it. Can we even agree on what is real and on what real means?"

"Real from *res*: thing in latin" I said. "So anything that we can call a thing is real and etymologically, only nothingness is unreal which probably implies that it does not exist. So all is real by definition if you can only think of it."

"Universal relativity" Laura pointed out "In the Buddhist view all things exist only in relation to one another. Maya is only an illusion if you believe beings and objects are separate and solid. It may be a veil but we are parts of it and that is all there is."

"By the way" I asked "what does the reference to General Doolittle point to? Any idea of what he predicted?"

"Jim Doolittle also went to Roswell in the thirties to meet with Goddard" Caswell explained. "After the war he was the second director of NACA, NASA's predecessor"

"Where he succeeded Jerome Hunsaker, reportedly a member of Majestic 12" Laura interjected.

"So he was involved from Day One with space stuff" I commented. "Did'nt he work with Von Braun on the Special Committee on Space Science?"

"Not only that" the General explained. "He was sent to Sweden in 1946 to study the enigma of the so-called ghost rockets which were almost certainly UFOs but his conclusions have not been disclosed. There are allegations that he was flown to Spitzberg to see a crashed saucer retrieved there, so he seems to have been privy to a lot of information. That is probably what Grudge 13 refers to. The General may have made a dire assessment of the intentions and plans of the space visitors. Even after retirement Doolittle remained active in the field as chairman of TRW's Space Technology Labs."

BACK TO EARTH

As we drove back to Denver, Laura and I continued a seemingly endless debate about what we had just read and heard in the context of the larger issue that we had explored for years. I could not miss the irony of a society as new, brash, and materialistic as America's being confronted with the unfathomable metaphysical problem posed by an Alien presence. Asian and European civilizations had many centuries of intellectual and political experience they could call upon to analyse and adapt to shattering and unsuspected realities but the American nation prided itself on its self-confidence and faith in undisputed dogmas beginning with freedom, democracy and the ability of man to know everything and control his destiny. Culturally the average American had gone almost instantly from the syrupy, simple-minded lyrics of Hank Williams and the raw sentimentalism of Jazz to the bitterly incoherent and often despairing poetry of Kerouac, Guthrie and Dylan.

I had long seen the social explosion of the sixties as a release of pent up popular anguish at the nuclear threat hanging on a bleakly or unquestioningly conformistic nation. Now I was wondering if the nihilistic escapism of the beatniks was not also the subconscious raving of a generation confronted with the collapse of customary certainties in the face of a totally unfamiliar and incomprehensible reality. The glass ceiling of the judeo-christian rationalist society had been shattered by bizarre outside visitors and many hitherto dismissed or forbidden phenomena had appeared in a now unprotected and boundless space.

"As a culture without history, raised on comics and Sci Fi we are perhaps readier than others to enter the strange future that looms on the horizon" Laura mused while staring at the road ahead. "But I am also worried about how credulous and extreme in our beliefs many of my countrymen are. We are all a mix of the Bible and *Huck Finn*. Our best known writers and entertainers have a con-man side to them and our distrust of real intellectualism makes most of us believe that nonsense is tantamount to profundity as long as it is cleverly promoted."

In the following weeks some significant events filled the media. On the 20th of October, the Reagan Administration staged an invasion of Grenada in order to overthrow a Marxist regime which had toppled and killed Prime Minister Maurice Bishop a few days earlier. It instantly reminded me of exiled former leader Sir Eric Gairy who would probably be able to return to his island which was henceforth under American control.

Only three days later a massive terrorist attack killed hundreds of recently landed US Marines and French servicemen in Lebanon. It was said to be the most powerful explosive device used since the end of the second world war. Was there a causal link between the American assault on communist Grenada and the terrible blow struck at the US occupation force? The Hezbollah militia, supported by the Ayatollah's Iran claimed responsibility for the bombing of the Marine barracks, throwing a direct challenge at the Reagan administration's resolve to intrude in the Middle East in support of Israel and its Lebanese Christian allies. Again the fear of a wider conflict rose on the horizon. I was told by Lowell that the US Government was planning massive retaliation and would authorize secret operations in the Middle East beyond the pale of international law. "CIA Director William Casey has put his black Ops on the job. They are going to use terrorist methods on a wide scale" he said. "It will be ugly."

By then I was becoming familiar with the political climate and with the general American mindset which revealed itself as a strange cocktail of utilitarian day-to-day improvisations, ambitions of unlimited wealth and power and apocalyptic forebodings. After those first months of direct exposure to a variety of situations and people I was ready to go further into the maze.

Epilogue

*What the caterpillar calls the end of the world
The Master calls the butterfly.*

Richard Bach

Those first few weeks in Colorado were followed by many months and then years spent mainly in Aspen and Boulder but marked by several trips to both the East and West Coast of the country. The events narrated in the previous pages led me to revelations that lend some cogency and deeper significance to the insights I had gained hitherto.

Richard Sigismond continued to provide me with invaluable information gleaned during his ongoing research dating back many years. He made me aware of the work of Professor Meade Layne who had dedicated his life to the investigation of the UFO phenomenon after retiring from the University of Southern California and founding the Borderline Science Research Group in the watershed year of 1947 at Eureka, also in California. He had first published a journal called *Round Robin* and later brought out a periodical named *Borderlands* with the cooperation of several ufologists and researchers in the Paranormal.

Layne had many contacts in the scientific and military communities in San Diego, where he resided and across the country. He came to the conclusion that at least some of the flying craft observed all over the world were operating in another, higher dimension or a hyperspace inhabited by much subtler forms of matter-energy. He identified this usually imperceptible realm with the ether known to ancient philosopher-scientists and accordingly called the "flying saucers" ether ships and their pilots and passengers Etherics.

Epilogue

In 1950, Layne published a book entitled *The Ether Ship Mystery and its Solution* followed four years later by a sequel *The Coming of the Guardians*. It was in that same year 1954 that he received a letter from his old friend, the well known though inevitably controversial psychic Gerald Light. Light claimed to have been taken to the Edwards (then still called Muroc) Air Force Base near Palm Springs in Southern California one day in April with three other well known figures and to have been shown abundant hard material evidence of an Extraterrestrial presence. Here is the letter which was later circulated in ufological and esoteric circles and which aroused the predictable mixture of awe, disbelief, ridicule and dismissal:

GeraldLight
10545ScenarioLane
Los Angeles, California

MeadeLayne
San Diego, California

My dear Friend: I have just returned from Muroc. The report is true—devastatingly true!

I made the journey in company with Franklin Allen of the Hearst papers and Edwin Nourse of Brookings Institute (Truman's erstwhile financial advisor) and Bishop MacIntyre of L.A. (confidential names for the present, please).

When we were allowed to enter the restricted section (after about six hours in which we were checked on every possible item, event, incident and aspect of our personal and public lives), I had the distinct feeling that the world had come to an end with fantastic realism. For I have never seen so many human beings in a state of complete collapse and confusion, as they realized that their own world had indeed ended with such finality as to beggar description. The reality of the "other plane" aeroforms is now and forever removed from the realms of speculation and made a rather painful part of the consciousness of every responsible scientific and political group.

During my two days' visit I saw five separate and distinct types of aircraft being studied and handled by our Air Force officials—with the assistance and permission of the Etherians! I have no words to express my reactions.

It has finally happened. It is now a matter of history.

President Eisenhower, as you may already know, was spirited over to Muroc one night during his visit to Palm Springs recently. And it is my conviction that he will ignore the terrific conflict between the various 'authorities' and go directly to the people via radio and television—if the impasse continues much longer. From what I could gather, an official statement to the country is being prepared for delivery about the middle of May.

I will leave it to your own excellent powers of deduction to construct a fitting picture of the mental and emotional pandemonium that is now shattering the consciousness of hundreds of our scientific "authorities" and all the pundits of the various specialized knowledges that make up our current physics. In some instance I could not stifle a wave of pity that arose in my own being as I watched the pathetic bewilderment of rather brilliant brains struggling to make some sort of rational explanation which would enable them to retain their familiar theories and concepts. And I thanked my own destiny for having long ago pushed me into the metaphysical woods and compelled me to find my way out. To watch strong minds cringe before totally irreconcilable aspects of "science" is not a pleasant thing. I had forgotten how commonplace things as dematerialization of "solid" objects had become to my own mind. The coming and going of an etheric, or spirit, body has been so familiar to me these many years I had forgotten that such a manifestation could snap the mental balance of a man not so conditioned. I shall never forget those forty-eight hours at Muroc!

G.L.

The first observation that Sigismond made when giving me a transcript of the original typed letter of which he had a Xerox is that, although Light was a psychic who routinely reported travelling in his astral body and was thus not accepted as a credible voice in the scientific community, he cited three fellow visitors to Muroc who were well known and quite respected. It would have made no sense for Light to give their names, nor to announce a public disclosure from the US President within a few weeks if he was making this story up to impress his friend as the persons he named could have exposed his claim by simply saying they had not gone to Muroc with him on that day. Yet these elderly eminent men apparently never denied or confirmed publicly the statement and various other sources corroborated that something very significant and strange had indeed taken place at the Air Force Base a few weeks before the date of Light's letter. Rumors about that highly unusual event were circulated and had apparently reached people like Layne Meade since Light referred to the latter's prior awareness of the subject of his letter. Neither was he seeking publicity as the report was confidential.

Edwards which had initially been known as the Muroc Airfield struck me as a very plausible location for an "interplanetary meeting" as it was a facility of key importance for the US R&D efforts in air and space technology. It hosted the USAF Materiel Command and its Flight Test Center as well as the Armstrong Flight Research Center since 1946. It was on the Rogers dry lakebed within the base that Chuck Yeager first broke the sound barrier in a BELL X-1 plane in 1947. The 412th Test Wing and Operations Group had experimentally flown more than forty cutting edge US built military aircraft at the super-secret North Base and at the Rocket Test Station on nearby Luhrmann Ridge; Edwards was thus the cradle of the turbojet technology. Two years before my arrival in the USA the space shuttle Columbia had landed there after its maiden tour of duty and Edwards remained the home base of the shuttle fleet. It would have made sense for a meeting with Aliens to have been set up in that location.

I needed to gather some background information on the three other visitors to Edwards mentioned by Gerald Light. I knew about cardinal McIntyre, the first bishop on the US West Coast to have been elevated to the prelature, hardly more than a year before the alleged trip to the Air Base. I found it significant that he had been for years the close subordinate and Coadjutor to His Eminence Lawrence, Cardinal Spellman, the archbishop of New York who was reported to have been taken to Roswell and shown what had been retrieved from the UFO crash. It was said that the Cardinal had been asked to assess the significance of the event on the request of Secretary James Forrestal who was a devout Roman Catholic, because the Roman Church was held to possess the greatest expertise in esoteric matters involving the past and future of humanity as well as extensive documentation on occult knowledge in its renowned Vatican library.

It would be logical to assume that Spellman had confided in his Coadjutor and, on the other hand, I was reminded that the future President Eisenhower had played an important role in managing the Roswell crisis which he probably decided to cover up. The Archbishop of Los Angeles must have been aware of the secret challenge posed by Alien visitors and would have therefore been called to assess the situation, following Einsehower's meeting with the "Others", from a theological and spiritual point of view.

Edwin Nourse was a veteran expert on agricultural economics, a discipline which he had created, at the Brookings Institution of which he had been Vice-President from 1942 to 1944 before being appointed the first Chairman of President Truman's newly set up Council of Economic Advisers. He had retired in 1949 but was still regarded as one of America's foremost economists and could therefore provide an authoritative opinion on the impact and consequences of contacts with an intelligent and powerful otherworldly life form. The third witness, Withrop Allen was a retired senior journalist from the Hearst Newspapers, specialized in congressional committee reporting about which he had written a book. He too was able better than most to evaluate the political and media implications of negotiating with an Alien civilization, secretly or officially and it appeared that whoever had selected the members of this small delegation intended to gather feedback from the most relevant domains of human activity: spiritual inquiry, religious leadership, the socio-economic sphere and the press.

Previous events, proven and alleged, in Eisenhower's life were also consistent with the claim that he was quite well informed about the UFO situation. During the second world war he had necessarily been briefed on high profile but classified happenings such as the famous February 1942 "battle of Los Angeles" with hovering UFOs, on which a secret memo had been sent to President Roosevelt by General George Marshall.

In Britain Winston Churchill in about the same period had been alerted to sightings of unknown but advanced aircraft by the RAF and had communicated on this matter with the American President and with Eisenhower, then the US military CinC. Years later in early 1951, while "Ike" was the NATO Supreme Commander in Europe he received a letter from Eugenio Siragusa a Sicilian spiritualist who said he was in contact with Aliens and feared an imminent nuclear Armageddon about which they had warned him. He begged General Eisenhower to prevent that disaster and halt the nuclear race.

Rather surprisingly the SACEUR wrote warmly in response to Siragusa on March 1951. The main paragraph of his letter read: "It is my hope—and my belief also—that an enduring peace will be secured by the common efforts of the western nations. There is much to be done, involving hard work and sacrifice from the individual citizen. But the goal stands out as worthy of whatever it takes." Even more strangely it appeared that Siragusa had received three other letters from the then-NATO Commander but I did not see them.

In September of the following year, Eisenhower was aboard the aircraft carrier flagship *Franklin Delano Roosevelt*—the first vessel to carry nuclear weapons in the US Navy—commanding the massive *Operation Mainbrace* which involved scores of ships and hundreds of aircraft in the North Atlantic. He was one of several to watch from his deck a UFO that came very close to the carrier and silently hovered above it for a few minutes. He is reported to have ordered all other witnesses to keep complete silence over this incident.

One media report on what transpired reads like this:

September 14, 1952; North Atlantic, between Ireland and Iceland. Witnesses: military persons from several countries aboard ships in the NATO

"*Operation Mainbrace" exercise. Among the Sightings: one blue-green triangle was observed flying 1,500 m.p.h; three objects in a triangular formation gave off white light exhaust at 1,500 m.p.h.*

We can conclude that in 1954 President Eisenhower was no stranger to the matter of "flying saucers" which were far from being all disc-shaped.

Finally since that same year 1952 George Adamski was making stunning and well publicized statements about his meetings with "Venusians" and the photos he took of their craft were widely circulated. In such a historic and media context the claim that Ike arranged or accepted to meet with "aliens" seems less outlandish.

Researchers also pointed out that, if he had been briefed by his predecessor, Truman on any transactions carried out with Aliens, Eisenhower, obviously aware of the spectacular overflight of the National Capitol by a fleet of UFOS in 1952, must have been somewhat prepared to meet with the extra or ultra-terrestrial spacemen who landed at Edwards on a day of February 1954. It was noted for my attention that even his trip to Palm Springs for a reported holiday at the ranch of his friend Paul Helms seemed motivated by an undisclosed reason since the President had just been on a hunting vacation earlier in the month and would not usually have left work again so soon.

I had the opportunity of discussing the context of Light's testimony with Laura Hollyfield, General O'Kennan and other researchers with whom I was in contact by phone, faxmail and the old fashioned post. There was a general knowledge or belief, based on the testimony of one Earl Neff among others, that in February of 1954, on the night of the 20th to the 21st specifically President Eisenhower had unexpectedly and secretly landed at the Muroc/Edwards AFB for a meeting with certain visitors from another region of the universe, whether planetary or ultra-dimensional.

Ike had been whisked away from his vacation home at Palm Springs and his sudden disappearance had triggered concern and speculations about his health. The Associated Press even released a dispatch that the President had suddenly died from a heart attack before cancelling it when his absence was explained by his staff as being due to a dental problem which required urgent intervention. That however might have been a cover story, given the various subsequent reports that he had indeed been at Edwards on that night and that he had interacted with the crew of an alien flying craft. At least one account described the visitors as very pale skinned, white-blond haired, sky-blue eyed, human-looking beings of the kind usually designated as "the Nordics" or Tall Whites in alien lore.

Almost nothing transpired of the encounter apart from the rumor that no agreement had been reached because the "extra-terrestrials" demanded that the American Government close down the nuclear military programme and take spiritual guidance to raise the psychic level of humanity. The few political and military leaders who had been made privy to the presidential meeting were predictably opposed to such a change of course which they believed would open them to attack and conquest by the Soviet Union, not to mention the Aliens themselves since there was no way to prevent a breach of the terms of any pact on their part in view of the glaring technological inferiority of earthly powers. Yet Gerald Light stated that he was shown five different types of craft which had been made available for study and possible reverse engineering by American aerospace engineers. So some agreement must have been reached. Was the officious report about the failure to make a deal another red herring intended to throw outsiders off track?

One of the first high-profile personalities to publicize the Edwards meeting was Adamski's friend The Rt Hon. Desmond Leslie, younger brother to the Lord Leslie, a first cousin of Winston Churchill, descended from Prime Minister Lord Asquith, who wrote about it in the October 1954 issue of *Valor* Magazine.

Earlier in the year, on 15 February, a week before Eisenhower's secret appointment Dorothy Kilgallen first reported in her syndicated column about the UFO presence which she said would soon be the topic for a secret gathering of top military officers from NATO. A year later, on 22 May 1955 as I already noted , she wrote that she had been told by a cabinet level official in the United Kingdom about ongoing research on extraterrestrial craft piloted by 4 feet tall humanoids. Another British and Irish Peer, Brinsley Le Poer Trench, the eighth Lord Clancarty also spoke out on Eisenhower's Alien contacts which had been allegedly reported to him by one of the six military officers who had been with the President at the meeting. According to his informant, five craft in all, three disc-shaped and two "cigars" had descended upon Edwards although not all had landed.

Le Poer Trench wrote a number of books on UFOs and Aliens which he believed to be domiciled inside the partly hollow Earth. He was for several years the editor of the *Flying Saucer Review* and was active in a number of other study groups and publications on the subject.

In 1978 the Earl organized a debate on the UFO issue and its political ramifications in the House of Lords in which predictably the Government spokesmen claimed that they could see no evidence of any Alien contact at the official or private level. Yet there was too much smoke around the issue to deny the existence of fire.

One of many intriguing aspects of the situation was also alluded to in one of the conversations. It referred to the warning allegedly given by the 'Tall Whites' to Eisenhower regarding other Alien races or groups which had specific activities and goals not congruent with the best interests of mankind. It seemed to have come to the attention of the Nordics that certain people in the USA were involved in a pact of some kind with those other visitors. There was no clarity as to whether the latter were the "small greys" retrieved at one of the Roswell crash sites and described by Bill English from the autopsy report in the Grudge/Bluebook 13 briefing quoted in the last chapter of this book. If so it would appear that the Greys were intruders who were coming to our planet for their own ends but willing to make agreements with certain governments in order to facilitate the achievement of their objectives. The implication was that they had offered a *quid pro quo* in the form of technology transfer to the US Government in exchange for non interference or even official cooperation and there was a suspicion that under Harry Truman's watch the US Government had entered into some contract or understanding.

Epilogue

The Nordics seemingly saw that as a matter of concern, either because the Greys were not to be trusted or because they did not see humans as being morally capable of using the new technologies responsibly and feared disastrous consequences from this rapid empowerment of the demonstrably violent and selfish *homo sapiens* species.

As the weeks passed more pieces of the puzzle caught my eye. I was assured that President Eisenhower had met one or two more times with Aliens, although not with the same ones. One of those dialogues had taken place in 1955, one year after the Edwards rendez vous at Holloman Air Force Base, within the perimeter of the Alamo Gordo Bombing and Gunnery Range in New Mexico, another critical node of the American defence and advanced research infrastructure.

In 1955 Holloman was already home to the 49th Air Combat Command and of the 96th Test Group. The 60000 acres restricted area of high altitude desert also housed the Air Development Center and the New Mexico Joint Guided Missile Test Range. It was and remains a highly secure perimeter where advanced military, space related R&D was carried out. If the visitors intended to support some of those exotic programmes or at least wished to show they could access the most protected facilities of the American defense complex, Holloman was logically a venue to make an appearance.

There also it was alleged that the key topic of discussion was nuclear weapons and the increasingly powerful and dangerous tests that the superpowers were conducting at the time. It was reported that the US President actually went aboard a disc-shaped craft that landed on the base while a companion UFO hovered above, probably to ensure the security of the alien delegation. One detail that stood out among the sparse facts was that before the discs arrived the radars were turned off and, as had been the case at Muroc/Edwards, the electrical supply was shut down during the meeting. My informers told me that since high power radars interfered with electromagnetic propulsion systems the visitors had required their de-activation in order presumably to prevent accidents of the type that had occurred around Roswell in the previous decade. It could not escape anyone that for the President to have actually boarded a UFO there must have been a high level of trust between the visitors and the US side unless the White House had no choice in the matter.

The picture that was emerging was one of top level collusion, voluntary or forced, between the US Government and at least one officially unreported form of humanoid life. Yet there was also circumstantial evidence of an earlier connection from the days of the Truman presidency with another type of beings with whom the "Nordic" visitors at Edwards seemed to have bad relations or about whom they harboured deep misgivings. It could be inferred in that context that Eisenhower had not been willing or able to take the advice of the Nordics partly because his government was already involved in some cooperation with others, nicknamed the Greys although one of their codenames was the Zetas as they were held to originate from a planetary system around the star Zeta Reticuli.

If Truman had indeed entered into a agreement with the latter before, during or after the year 1947, it is likely that the implementation of that protocol had fallen under the aegis of one or several Military Intelligence agencies—headed by the Office of Naval Intelligence, was I told—and private defense contractors on which the Presidency had limited effective control, especially because of the paramount requirement to keep secrecy. Eisenhower's hands may therefore have been tied, even if he had wished to implement the disarmament and peace making measures prescribed by the Nordics despite the predictable opposition of his own armed forces and national security professionals.

Someone in a position to know confided to me that the Nordics had nevertheless received official assent to occupy a base on the territory of Nellis Dreamland, in the Indian Springs Valley near the test firing range where they built a large underground facility and stationed a permanent colony. The secrecy of their presence was protected by the restricted status and remote location of the area but it was significant that they had selected to be rather close to the Nevada nuclear test site as if to monitor the ongoing operations there.

Epilogue

I was not alone in finding absurdly unbelievable the claim that such highly advanced beings sought government permission to settle down anywhere they wished. It seemed clear that no earthly power could prevent them from having their way but my military contacts explained that the Nordics's desire to transfer certain technologies to their human hosts had made it convenient for them to establish their representatives within the territory of the premier aerospace research facility in the country.

On the other hand there was some confusion among my informants as to whether the Greys had likewise been given permission to build bases on the planet but that seemed to be a logical implication of the treaties allegedly concluded even though the American side in that deal may have had no choice, whether duress or greed was the major motivation of the US administration or rather of the specialized clandestine entity,—the rumored Majestic 12—which it had been entrusted with that top-secret relationship.

I insistently queried my contacts about the nature of the Greys whose reported hive-like behaviour and strangely insect-like slenderness evoked a sophisticated mechanical organization. Could they also be described as Etherians, according to the definition adopted by Gerald Light? The perception in expert circles was that those beings were at least partly genetically engineered either by themselves of by some other form of life. Their evolution might have been dictated by many centuries or millennia of existence in space or in artificial environments. In the early eighties the awareness and understanding of artificial intelligence, cyber-organics and bio-electronics were far less advanced than they are in this second decade of the twenty first century and the word 'android' was rarely heard but the data collected since the late forties about the Greys helped biologists and neuro-physiologists to make major advances towards the prospect of creating synthetic life or at least of modifying living organisms by artificial means.

Were then selected scientists, military commanders and policy makers interacting with sophisticated biological machines and were those machines making independent (even if collective) decisions, or were they rather remote controlled by a higher intelligence which used them for its own ends? The question appeared surrealistic but the answer might not change much about the situation. It was more important to determine whether the US Government had done a trade off with a relatively benign outside power for the strategic benefit of the country and the western alliance or whether it had unwittingly fallen under the influence of what was already called in some circles the unknown and potentially ominous Alien Agenda.

The warning allegedly issued by the Nordics to President Eisenhower at Edwards drove me to the latter induction. It appeared that for whatever reasons the Zetas had promised to transfer some of their sensitive technologies to their human counterparts and were, at least in part operating according to that protocol. What were they getting in return? They did not interfere openly with terrestrial affairs and seemed to have no desire to prevent or stop military buildups or wars on the planet, given that many of the technologies they made available could be used for bellicose purposes. Were they carrying out an experiment with mankind? An experiment that might have been ongoing for untold centuries or millennia. Did they have, as some sources alleged, a tacit or explicit understanding with the American Deep State that some humans might be captured, taken away in their craft and used for research, biological 'spare parts', hybridization or resettlement in other environments?

Too little was known to draw definitive conclusions either about the level of their scientific abilities, which was obviously far higher than ours, or about their intentions but whether they were living beings or machines, howbeit intelligent, they could not be relied upon to be more ethical in their dealings with our species than the latter has usually been towards its own and the other lifeforms. Had an American clandestine agency in the US government sold its soul and handed over the destiny of the planet to a higher power whose nature and intentions remain inscrutable to this day? Did it have a choice?

On the other hand the Nordics had given at least a sign of ethical concern even though their warnings about the nuclear menace had been received with suspicion by the American official representatives.

One possible reason for those misgivings might have been the apparent connection between those pale blond quasi-humans and the image of the Aryan supermen promoted in Nazi mythology.

Were the visitors at Edwards related to the superior beings from the Aldebaran star system whose messages were channeled by Maria Orsic and her fellow *Vrillerinnen* to the members of the secret *Vrill Gesellschaft* in Munich during the inter-war years? Some of the esotericists in the inner circle of the National Socialist hierarchy had hoped for the support of those 'Aryan' guides until Germany's final defeat. Did the US presidential team find it impossible to establish regular relations with those who had at least inspired the leaders of the reviled Third Reich? Yet the Nordics had established themselves on Area 51 with or without official American consent. What was their objective? Did they monitor US military activities? Did they provide non-military technical guidance as the message from Gerald Light indicated? There were so many questions that could not be possibly answered but could not be dismissed as insane or preposterous either.

At this stage in my investigations I felt I had no choice but to try to garner further insights about this enigma. I had to gather some of the knowledge that was apparently being acquired by certain entities in the American power structure while being withheld from the public and even from the formally supreme civilian and military authorities. My quest would take me to many places in the USA and abroad and will be narrated another volume.

About the Author

Côme Carpentier de Gourdon, born in the Canary Islands (Spain) of French parents, studied in Europe, India and the USA and has lived, traveled and taught in more than 50 countries on four continents (including several universities and academic institutions in France, India, the USA, Switzerland, Peru, Russia, Italy, China, Belgium, Kazakhstan, Lebanon and Greece). He is currently the convener of the Editorial Advisory Board of *World Affairs, the Journal of International Issues* (New Delhi, India), and a member of advisory boards of various scholarly publications.

Areas of his research, writings and teachings include international systems and world order models (geoplitics), India's culture and civilization, the frontiers of science, the impact of new technologies and the philosophy of history and religions. He has authored more than 80 published papers and monographs in English, French, Spanish and Italian and has contributed to various collective volumes on history, comparative philosophy, ex-politics and international relations (including *Raimundo Panikkar—A Pilgrim Across Worlds* and *The Relevance of Traditional Cultures for the Present and Future)*; two of his previous book is entitled *From India to Infinity* (2012) and *Memories of A Hundred Moons—An Indian Odyssey* (2015).

He currently lives between India and Europe.

www.comecarpentier.com

Lightning Source UK Ltd.
Milton Keynes UK
UKHW020704051022
409964UK00019B/1531